Social and Religious Reform

Oxford in India Readings
DEBATES IN INDIAN HISTORY AND SOCIETY

Series Editors: SABYASACHI BHATTACHARYA, B.D. CHATTOPADHYAYA, RICHARD M. EATON

RAZIUDDIN AQUIL (*Editor*)	*Sufism and Society in Medieval India*
FINBARR BARRY FLOOD (*Editor*)	*Piety and Politics in the Early Indian Mosque*
BISWAMOY PATI (*Editor*)	*The 1857 Rebellion*
SCOTT C. LEVI (*Editor*)	*India and Central Asia* Commerce and Culture, 1500–1800
BHAIRABI PRASAD SAHU (*Editor*)	*Iron and Social Change in Early India*
SEEMA ALAVI (*Editor*)	*The Eighteenth Century in India* (OIP)
THOMAS R. TRAUTMANN (*Editor*)	*The Aryan Debate* (OIP)
DAVID N. LORENZEN (*Editor*)	*Religious Movements in South Asia 600–1800* (OIP)
G. BALACHANDRAN (*Editor*)	*India and the World Economy 1850–1950* (OIP)
BIDYUT CHAKRABARTY (*Editor*)	*Communal Identity in India* Its Construction and Articulation in the Twentieth Century (OIP)

Social and Religious Reform

The Hindus of British India

Edited by
Amiya P. Sen

OXFORD
UNIVERSITY PRESS

Oxford University Press is a department of the University of Oxford. It furthers the University's objective of excellence in research, scholarship, and education by publishing worldwide. Oxford is a registered trademark of Oxford University Press in the UK and in certain other countries

Published in India by
Oxford University Press
22 workspace, 2nd Floor, 1/22 Asaf Ali Road, New Delhi 110002

First Edition published in 2003
Oxford India Paperbacks 2005

ISBN-13: 978-0-19-567702-7
ISBN-10: 0-19-567702-1

Typeset in PalmSprings 10/12
by Le Studio Graphique, New Delhi 110017
Printed in India by Repro India Limited

For Parijat and Sujat,
a book to remember me by

Contents

General Editors' Preface xii
Volume Editor's Preface to the Paperback Edition xiv
Volume Editor's Preface and Acknowledgements xvi

PART ONE

1. Introduction 3
   A. Social and Religious Reform: Conceptual Nuances *3*
   B. The Debate over Strategies *19*
   C. The Typologies of Reform and Revival *33*
   D. Imperatives within Reform *36*
   E. Debates in History, Debates on History: Situating 'Renaissance', 'Reform', and Social Change in Modern India *46*

PART TWO

2. The Conceptual Nuances of Reform 67

The Inadequacy of Reform

Growth, not Reform *67*
Swami Vivekananda

Social Reform or Social Revolution? *69*
E.V. Ramasami Periyar

Religion as the Basis of Social Reform

Social Reformation in India *72*

Keshab Chandra Sen

Religion as a Social Mission *75*

Lajpat Rai

The Past as a Cultural Resource and Reformist Demands of the Present

Reform Civil and Social *78*

Krishna Mohan Banerjea

The Essentials of Hinduism *82*

Bankim Chandra Chattopadhyay

3. The Debate over Strategies 85

The Road to Reform: Individual Moral Courage vs Cautious Deference to Tradition

Social Reform with Picnics and Tea-parties! *85*

Pandit Bishan Narain Dar

Social Reform: The Virtues of Discretion *88*

India Gazette

Reform from Within *90*

N.G. Chandravarkar

The Problem of Social as Against Political Reform

The Line of Least Resistance *93*

K.T. Telang

Does Social Reformation Require Political Moderation? *97*

Aurobindo Ghosh

The State and the Question of Social Legislation

A Legislator for Hindus *98*

William Bentinck

Reservations on the Propriety of State Interference *101*

H.H. Wilson

A Note from Sir Steuart Bayley *104*
A Note from A.P. McDonell *104*
Sir Andrew Scoble's Speech
before the Legislative Council *105*
Ranade on State Legislation in Social Matters *109*
M.G. Ranade
The State as Executor of Popular Will *111*
M.K. Gandhi
Hindu Shastras and Social Reform
The Shastras as a Guide to Reform *112*
N.G. Chandravarkar
The Inner Ambivalence of Hindu Shastras *114*
Hindu Intelligencer
The Tactical Unity of the Orthodox *117*
Jawaharlal Nehru
Objections to Hindu Code Bills *120*
Sanat Kumar Raychaudhuri

4. The Typologies of Reform and Revival 123
Revival as Reform *123*
Lajpat Rai
Revival as Reaction *132*
B.C. Pal
The Underlying Unity of Reform and Revival *134*
Sister Nivedita

5. Imperatives within Social Reform 138
The Social Agitation on the Woman Question
The Pressing Need for Emancipation *138*
Mahesh Chandra Deb
A Crusader's Testament *142*
B.M. Malabari
Mr Malabari Finds a Radical Supporter *144*
Jotirao Phule

A Critique of Mr Malabari's Proposals *148*
K.T. Telang
Men Simply Have Not Done Enough *151*
Sarojini Naidu
Misguided Men and
the Ideals of Hindu Womanhood *153*
Pandit Bishan Narain Dar

The Debate on the Nature of Hindu Marriages
Tagore Answers an Orthodox Critic *156*
Rabindranath Tagore

The Nature of Women's Emancipation:
Historiographical Debates
The Controlled Emancipation of Wives *162*
Sumit Sarkar
Nationalism Resolves the Critical Question *169*
Partha Chatterjee

The Debate on Caste and Social Reconstruction in India
A Radical Critique of Caste *189*
B.R. Ambedkar
A Rejoinder from M.K. Gandhi *199*
M.K. Gandhi

6. Debates in History, Debates on History 202
Situating 'Renaissance', 'Reform' and
Social Change in Modern India
The Alien Roots of Indian Awakening *202*
J.N. Farquhar
Renascent Hinduism *205*
D.S. Sarma
The 'Renaissance' as Understood
in Modern Historiography *207*
Barun De

Appendix A 212

List of Hindu Local Associations Concerned with Social Reform in India for the Period 1891–9

Appendix B 219

Social Legislation in Representative Indian States, 1901–39

Index 222

General Editors' Preface

The DEBATES IN INDIAN HISTORY AND SOCIETY series is an exploration in the discourse of history to focus upon the diversity of interpretations. The series is intended to address widely debated issues in South Asian history (including contemporary history) through volumes edited by experts in the concerned area of study. The editor of each such volume is asked by the General Editors to select writings focusing upon a debated theme and to write an introductory essay. The approach encourages the interrogation of history, as distinct from the common tendency to present history as a collection of 'given' facts. It brings to the reader the research base upon which scholars have founded their interpretative framework. And it opens up to the students bridge-heads into the terrain of research.

This volume, the fourth in this series, follows volumes focusing upon the historiographic debates on continuity and change in eighteenth-century India, the world economy and India between 1850 and 1950, and the construction of communal identities in twentieth-century India. In the present volume, Amiya P. Sen examines contestations around the theme of reform in Hindu society in the nineteenth- and twentieth-centuries. In what manner was the perception of self-identity moulded by the widely debated ideas of the 'reformers' in the nineteenth century? How does one account for the shifts in the battle lines between sections of the Hindu intelligentsia who supported 'reformism' and those who opposed it? How was the past used as a cultural resource in working out the social and cultural agenda of the reformists and their opponents? What were the factors that shaped the attitude of the colonial state towards social interventionism through legislation? What is the validity and empirical utility of dyadic sets of concepts we commonly use, for example, reform/revivalism, modernity/tradition, in this area of intellectual history? These and other related questions have been addressed in the design and organization of this volume. Sen presents the leading issues in the discourse of socio-religious reform through selected extracts from contemporary speeches and writings. In an insightful introductory essay he provides an overview of the vast and ever-growing literature on the subject. Aiming at an 'intermeshing of the historical and the historiographical', representative examples of historical writings have also been included.

Volume Editor's Preface to the Paperback Edition

I am naturally delighted to see this work go into a paperback edition. This gives me an occasion to thank my several reviewers and critics, who have made some valuable points of criticism. First, there has been disappointment at my not including representative pieces from well-known public figures like Rammohan, Vidyasagar or Tilak. Some others have felt that I do not problematize enough, terms like 'Hindu' and 'Hinduism'. Allegedly, I have also resorted to uncritical generalizations, for instance, through my claim that social legislation enjoyed a less stormy passage in Indian states when compared to British India.

Let me begin by addressing the last point of criticism first. Admittedly, this argument may have been more nuanced, for, the record of social reform obviously varies even within Indian states. On the other hand, I feel that in a work of this kind, there is some virtue in not getting carried away by historical relativism. On the question of using the terms 'Hindu' and 'Hinduism', my stand has been that idioms of convergence and a conceptual unity among Hindus may well have coexisted with complex differentiation in social and religious praxis. I must say that this belief has been further strengthened by Axel Michael's very thoughtful formulation of an 'identificatory habitus' with respect to Hindus (*Hinduism: Past and Present*, 2005). Constraints of space combined with practical difficulties of translating passages from various Indian languages forced me to eliminate or under-represent many prominent Hindu polemicists of the day. More importantly, this book was situated within the larger framework of conceptual and strategic debate, not public controversy over specific social reform issues.

I do fervently hope that with all its limitations, this work will continue to be of some use to graduate students, and to interested general readers for whom it was originally intended.

AMIYA P. SEN

Volume Editor's Preface and Acknowledgements

Ideally, a work of this kind should have incorporated the historical experiences of the three major communities of British India—Hindus, Muslims, and Sikhs. That effectively it does not go beyond the Hindus is only another way of admitting my limited knowledge of other Indian communities and traditions. While dealing with the Hindus, I have had to largely go by my own linguistic abilities and familiarity with source material from various regions of India. In this respect, the south has obviously suffered in comparison, as also have many parts of north and north-east India. On the other hand, this was not an attempt at re-narrating the history of socio-religious reform in modern times. My focus, on the contrary, has been on identifying major issues within that history that grew into passionate, public debates, and in turn became its critical determinants. The pace at which these debates were set, as also their polemical content, were usually determined only at select places in British India—Calcutta, Bombay, Poona, and to a lesser extent Madras and Lahore. This work, too, has had to closely follow developments occurring only within these select cities.

The history of social and religious reform among the Hindus of British India was undoubtedly more complex than would appear from this work. Many a promising theme has had to be left out either for the want of adequate source material, the practical difficulties of rendering available material into English, or simply the need to limit this work to a manageable length. I have, however, deliberately avoided taking up more than once, debates occurring around the same themes and using more or less the same arguments, even if they were to be manifest at different points of time. The controversy over determining a reasonable age of marriage for Hindus in the 1920s or 1930s is not fundamentally different in character compared to what it was in the 1880s, and to pursue the history of this controversy over a length of time, I felt, would not have enriched this work in any way. Hence, my attempt throughout this work has been to focus only on representative examples. Arguably, this has contributed to make it somewhat partial to the nineteenth century. However, in this case too, I have derived some consolation from the fact that within the chronological framework as well as the polemical, the nineteenth century was indeed the starting point of every major debate concerning Hindu social and religious reform, whether in respect of issues or strategy. It is also broadly true that debates of this kind became infrequent and less intense the further we advanced into the twentieth century.

In putting together this volume I have consciously attempted an intermeshing of the historical and the historiographical. This has been quite useful in analysing the ideological structures within both reformism and oppositional attitudes. Especially in the case of woman-related issues, recent historiography, with its use of subaltern and gender perspectives, has helped re-problematize older debates. In my choice of readings, I have preferred to include, wherever possible, contemporary writings or speeches. Some of these are from books that are not very likely to be reprinted and newspaper files that are ordinarily not easy to trace. I would, therefore, hope that their inclusion in this volume will not only give them a new lease of life but save the average reader the trouble of looking them up individually. The two appendices were inserted more as an afterthought. Nevertheless, I trust that the information that they offer will be useful in some ways.

As with all other books that I have been able to produce so far, various individuals and institutions have helped me in more ways than they realize. I am grateful to the general editors of this series for persisting with their confidence in me and particularly to Prof. Richard M. Eaton, who painstakingly went through an earlier draft with the finest academic comb that I have seen in all these years. But for him, this would have been more an ambitious work than analytical or useful. I have been immensely lucky inasmuch as the final stages of writing this book coincided with my tenure as Fellow of the Nehru Memorial Museum and Library, and I should really like to take this opportunity to thank the Director, Librarian and staff of the NMML for helping me in locating and relocating obscure sources. I have reason to thank Mrs Sushila Ambike who ungrudgingly provided me with prompt translations of certain Marathi pieces by G.G. Agarkar. Thanks are also due to several friends and well-wishers who have shown an interest in this work, especially Mrs Veena Sachdeva of the Devahuti Damodar Library, New Delhi, and to my colleagues, Dr Anirudh Deshpande and Dr Pralay Kanungo, on whom I have often inflicted my untiring passion for the cultural and intellectual history of modern Hindus. I might as well admit though that it is this passion that has also rescued me from intellectual exhaustion and professional obscurity.

A good part of the material reproduced in this book, is, to the best of my knowledge, no longer under copyright. For material that remains protected by copyright, the Editor gratefully acknowledges permission granted by concerned authors, institutions and publishing houses listed below to reproduce either wholly or in part, essays or articles indicated against each. Any error or omission, if pointed out, will be duly rectified in subsequent printings of this book.

Krishna Mohan Banerjea (1965). 'Reform Civil and Social' in Goutam Chattopadhyay (ed.), *Awakening in Bengal in Early Nineteenth Century: Selected Documents*, Vol. I, Progressive Publishers, Calcutta, pp. 128–98.

Mahesh Chandra Deb (1965). 'A Sketch of the Condition of the Hindoo Woman' in Goutam Chattopadhyay (ed.), *Awakening in Bengal in Early Nineteenth Century: Selected Documents*, Vol. I, Progressive Publishers, Calcutta, pp. 89–105.

Bankimchandra Chattopadhyay (1969). 'Letters on Hinduism' in J.C. Bagal (ed.), *Bankim Rachanabali*, Sahitya Samsad, Calcutta, pp. 229–36.

Lajpat Rai (1966). 'Reform or Revival' and 'The Mission of the Arya Samaj' in V.C. Joshi (ed.), *Lajpat Rai: Writings and Speeches*, Servants of the People Society, Delhi, pp. 45–54 and 185–98.

Aurobindo Ghosh (1973). 'The Reformer on Moderation' in *Bande Mataram: Early Political Writings*, Sri Aurobindo Ashram, Pondicherry, pp. 312–13.

M.K. Gandhi (1969). 'Speech at Trivandrum' in *The Collected Works of Mahatma Gandhi*, Vol. 35, Navajivan Trust, Ahmedabad, pp. 102–5 and 'Remarriage of Hindu Widows': Hindu Intelligencer of 12 February 1855. Reproduced in Benoy Ghosh (ed.), *Selections from English Periodicals of the Nineteenth Century*, Vol. III, Papyrus, Calcutta, 1985, pp. 111–14.

Sister Nivedita (1975). 'Revival or Reform' in *Sister Nivedita's Lectures and Writings*, Advaita Ashram and Sister Nivedita Girls' School, Calcutta, pp. 82–8.

Sumit Sarkar (1985). 'The Women's Question in Nineteenth Century Bengal' in Sumit Sarkar, *A Critique of Colonial India*, Papyrus, Calcutta, pp. 71–6, 168–70.

Partha Chatterjee (1989). 'The Nationalist Resolution of the Woman's Question' in Kumkum Sangari and Sudesh Vaid (ed.), *Recasting Women: Essays in Colonial History*, Author and Kali for Women, New Delhi, pp. 233–53.

J.N. Farquhar (1967). *Modern Religious Movements in India*, Munshiram Manoharlal, New Delhi, pp. 4–5, 431–43.

D.S. Sarma (1998). *Renascent India*. (2nd edn), Bharatiya Vidya Bhavan, Bombay, pp. 3–9.

Barun De (1977). 'A Historiographical Critique of Renaissance Analogues for Nineteenth Century India' in Barun Dey (ed.), *Perspectives in Social Sciences*, Vol. I, Oxford University Press and Centre for Studies in Social Sciences, Calcutta, pp. 192–210.

Swami Vivekananada (1973). 'The Mission of the Vedanta' and 'My Plan of Campaign' in *The Complete Works of Swami Vivekananda*, Mayavati Memorial Edition, Vol. III, Advaita Ashram, Calcutta, pp. 194–6, 212–20.

Despite persistent efforts no response was received from the following publishers at the time this book went to press.

E.V. Ramasamy Periyar (1965). 'Social Reform or Social Revolution?', trans. from E.V. Ramasami's Arvib Ellai by A.M. Dharmalingam, Viduthalai Publications, Madras, pp. 1–9.

J.G . Phule (1991), 'Opinion from Joteerao Govindrao Phule on Notes no. 1 and 2 by Mr Behramji Malabari on Infant Marriage in India', Reproduced from *Collected Works of Jotirao Phule*, Vol. II, trans. by Prof. P.G. Patil, Education Department, Government of Maharashtra, Bombay, pp. 115–18.

B.R. Ambedkar (1989). 'Annihilation of Caste With a Reply to Mahatma Gandhi', Reproduced from *Dr. Babasaheb Ambedkar: Writings and Speeches*, compiled by Vasant Moon, Education Department, Government of Maharashtra, Bombay, pp. 37–80 and Appendix A.

However, the Editor and the Oxford University Press would only be too happy to formally gratefully acknowledge permission granted by the above in subsequent printings of this work.

AMIYA P. SEN

Part One

1

Introduction

A. Social and Religious Reform: Conceptual Nuances

The Paradigm of Reform

[i]

In British India the Hindus were numerically the largest community, and numbers, as we know, can prove to be an important determinant in the modalities of change. Whether rightly or wrongly, the Hindus could also boast of a long and rich cultural history—a claim considerably reinforced by the Orientalist researches of the late eighteenth and early nineteenth centuries. Especially in the latter half of the nineteenth century this new self-awareness was widely disseminated by the print media, pioneered by the Europeans, but no less utilized by the Hindus. The Hindus were spatially distributed almost throughout the subcontinent and, allowing for regional variations, were also the first to successfully adopt modern education and adapt to new ways of life. Paradoxically enough, this made them the greatest admirers of British rule as also its sharpest critics.

In nineteenth-century India, the Hindus were quick to realize that 'reform' was not just about altering beliefs or practices, but invariably touched upon deeper questions of self-identity. Their growing familiarity with modern disciplines like history, anthropology, politics, and the natural sciences enabled Hindus not only to compare the state of their own society and civilization with that of the West but also to develop a deep self-reflexivity about their own tradition. Over time, they began to perceive themselves as a distinct community with its own history and trajectories of social and cultural development. Modern

Hindus also acknowledged the fact that the operative side to reform work was intertwined with the cognitive. Thus, attempts to bring about change went beyond the selection of issues or appropriate strategies. Above all, it needed a social subject. Hence, 'What is Hindu?' became inextricably linked to 'Who is a Hindu?' or 'What does it mean to be a Hindu?'. Hence, nineteenth-century Hindu reformers, even when targeting select groups such as upper-caste widows, Dalits, or purely local communities indulging in specific malpractices, tried to project their work as something touching upon the life of every Hindu. For exactly the same reasons, Hindu religious thinkers of modern India, rather than abide by the highly pluralistic nature of traditional Hinduism, promoted the idea of a single, nationalized religion for all Hindus. Uniquely, an amorphous collectivity of people, who were not particularly aware of exactly what elements of religious belief or practice had brought them together and who, hitherto, may not even have seriously pondered over such questions, were now being defined as a homogenous and unified religious community. In the 1930s Hindu agitators of British India opposed the codification of Hindu law on the ground that similar legislation was unlikely to be introduced in the Indian states, thus driving a wedge within the Hindu community (see objections from an ex-Mayor of Calcutta, included in Part II). Prima facie, this sounds misleading and somewhat ironical since, compared to developments elsewhere, social reform appears to have come about faster and more consistently in some major Indian states (see Appendix II).

In any case, practical reform work did create fissures beneath this imagined unity. Hindu reformers and publicists disagreed with each other on the constituents of reformed Hinduism. Major reformist bodies, it would appear, based their programmes on perceptibly different traditions or scriptural authorities. The Aryas took reformed Hinduism to be rooted in the Vedas, the Brahmos in the Upanishads, and a host of early twentieth-century thinkers in innovative interpretations of the *Bhagavad Gita*. But even those who claimed to follow a single text were not always entirely in agreement. In the 1880s Swami Dayanand Saraswati (1825–83) was drawn into some controversy with orthodox *pandit*s at Kashi and Calcutta over which components within the Vedas, namely, *Samhita*s, *Aranyaka*s, or *Brahmana*s were 'authentic' and acceptable for the modern Hindu. The problem of an universal scripture for Hindus became all the more critical with the emergence of new and radical viewpoints, as, say, from the leaders of depressed castes or communities. In the 1930s there was sharp difference of opinion between Mohandas Karamchand Gandhi (1864–1948) and Bhimrao Ambedkar (1891–1956) over 'representative' texts for Hinduism.

Also interesting is the varied terminology used to describe the reformer community. This could be 'Arya' as in the Arya Samaj, 'Brahman' as in the Brahmo Samaj, or 'Sanatan' as in the Sanatan Dharma Sabha. Here, the term 'Arya' has ethnic-ethical connotations, 'Hindu' socio-cultural, 'Brahman' metaphysical, and 'Sanatan' of that which is timeless and trans-historical. That each of these terms should imply a specific meaning and yet be accommodated within the omnibus category of Hinduism is a development that has had profound consequences for modern India.

The world of reform as one can imagine, was far from homogeneous or united in its objectives. Thus, both Raja Rammohan Roy (1772–1833) and Keshab Chandra Sen (1838–84) singled out idolatry and the worship of multiple gods and goddesses as issues which deserved top priority in any reformist agenda. Pandit Iswar Chunder Vidyasagar (1820–91) and Behramji M. Malabari (1853–1912) committed their lives and personal fortunes to the emancipation of women. Jotirao Phule (1827–90), E.V. Ramasami Periyar (1879–1973), and Bhimrao Ambedkar identified caste as the major stumbling block on the road to social progress. Up to a point, such differences were certainly determined by local histories and the traditional social arrangements at any given place. At least in the nineteenth century caste was never as sensitive a question in Bengal as it was in parts of western and southern India. However, people also switched from one area of activity to another, mostly under the pressure of altered circumstances. In Maharashtra Rao Saheb V.N. Mandlik (1833–89) turned to the subject of woman's emancipation when his attempt to bring about relaxation in caste rules failed owing to opposition from orthodox *pandits* and *shastris*. In Bengal, Keshab Chandra Sen increasingly leaned towards religious experimentation after controversial attempts at marriage reform. Vidyasagar, who had solicited state intervention during the widow marriage campaign, opposed it in 1891, when the government was forced to amend its own laws so as to further safeguard the interests of young women. For reasons not fully understandable, the conservative opposition to the amended age of consent (1891) in the Punjab was never as rabid as it was in Bengal and Maharashtra.

However, such differences notwithstanding, social and religious reform movements in the nineteenth and early twentieth centuries had a few things in common. For one, they were very largely led by the new, Western-educated, middle classes and hence failed to notice the very different nature of lower-class problems. Their class character would explain why, barring a few exceptions, they were more on the side of structural adjustments than structural reorganization. These reform movements, irrespective of their ideology or interests, also adopted similar work methods. Interestingly enough, even those opposing reform itself were quick to seize upon these. In British India the orthodox Dharma Sabha of Bengal, which opposed the move to abolish *sati*, was the first to use the method of petitioning and counter-petitioning higher authorities.

The act of defining and redefining the self under altered circumstances and in respect to new challenges was, on the whole, a more critical problem for modern Hindus than their immediate predecessors. Even as they participated in change or at least acknowledged its need, Hindus of, say, the early medieval era, were not as self-conscious about them. It is probable that the Hindu élite shrugged off the critical reflections about itself in Al Beruni's *Al Hind* out of sheer self-righteousness and condescension. That this did not recur in modern India is a fair indication of the different nature of the challenge as also of the manner in which it was met and negotiated.

Among Indian Muslims and Sikhs community boundaries and definitions of the self were partly redrawn through a series of excisions and exclusions vis-à-vis the majority community of Hindus. The modern Sikh and Muslim intelligentsia found Hinduism to be a corrupting influence at the levels of both élite and mass culture. This evidently has to do with the fact that a large percentage of people belonging to these communities were either converted from Hinduism or else continued to share syncretic religious beliefs or cultural lifestyles. Hindus, by comparison, were relatively less troubled by such problems. At least during the nineteenth century their excisions or exclusions were directed more at themselves; these were employed not so much to define the Hindu in relation to the Muslim or Sikh as to relocate the sources of 'purity' or 'authenticity' within the Hindu tradition. This made reform a useful but intensely debated category within the Hindu tradition. Especially in the case of Hindu social and religious reform, we have to allow for multiple levels of awareness, objectives, and participation.

In conclusion, we must ask ourselves the question if, conceptually, reform was a static or an evolving category for Hindus. The answer to this question, regrettably, can neither be very precise nor definitive.

There is an inner unity to modern reform inasmuch as it was always seen as a self-conscious act of mediation. It was also widely believed that reform would bring about not simply change, but qualitative 'improvement'. On the other hand, reform work often followed the trajectories of individual lives. The nineteenth-century reformer from coastal Andhra, Kandukuri Viresalingam (1848–1919), altered his perceptions about reform in keeping with the changing nature of social opposition. In Maharashtra, Mahadev Govind Ranade (1842–1901) tried to reform the ideological momentum behind reform by a characteristic reverence for the Hindu tradition and thus ended up by defining reform differently at different points of time.

A list of organizations of the late nineteenth century officially involved in social reform work among the Hindus is appended to this introduction. But, presumably, changes of one kind or another were occurring at the level of ordinary individuals and unnamed families for which, however, there is no reliable documentation. Such small but heroic sagas, regrettably, will remain unsung. At the same time, in a book concerning debates on Hindu reform, our attention must focus on matters as they unfolded in the public domain. A brief analysis of the same is produced in the pages to follow.

[ii]

Cultures across the world have had to grapple with the twin problems of conservation and change, but the way these were perceived and sought to be resolved naturally differed with time and social context. In the context of Indian civilization and culture, the use of the term 'reform' to indicate changes in religious belief or social practices goes back only as far as the nineteenth century, coinciding with the consolidation of British power and the advent of what has been generally described as 'modernity'. Surely, changes in Hindu religion and society, some of them quite meaningful, can be located at several points in our premodern history. And yet, interestingly, neither in official chronicles nor in popular idioms of the time were these known as acts of 'reform' or the labours of 'reformers'. If today we are able to locate elements of reform in the teachings of the Bhakti saints in medieval India, this follows from present-day perceptions about our historical past, not from suggestions made by the historical actors themselves.

There is further reason why in our own historical experiences the terms 'reform' and 'change' do not always intersect. In British India not every matter that required modification or change gained the status of a social reform issue. Conversely, some issues that did gain this status were not necessarily long-standing, universal social problems. The evil of female infanticide, though noticed at least as early as 1800, did not attract the serious attention of the Hindu intelligentsia and demands for its abolition remained, at best, lukewarm. On the other hand, the question of widow marriages, which generated bitter controversy throughout the nineteenth century, affected only a small minority of upper-caste women. Within the widow marriage question itself, reformers favoured child-widows, thereby eliminating women widowed in adulthood whose needs could be no less important and where, one imagines, the decision whether to remarry called for the woman's considered choice. The militant politician and member of the Brahmo Samaj, Bipin Chandra Pal (1858–1932), once made the point that even in trying to discourage infant marriages and the sexual exploitation of child-brides, reformers tried to concentrate more on the several inconveniences arising out of such practices than the very insensitivity and injustice inherent in them.[1]

In British India, 'reform' represented a specific reading of the need for change, a conscious choice of subject matter, and careful deliberations over appropriate strategy. As a paradigm, it remained an extremely influential and one which appreciably altered perceptions about the contemporary state of society as well as of the past. Arguably, Indians differed not so much over the relevance or usefulness of this category itself as the spheres to which this could be profitably extended and the manner in which this work might be best carried out. However, as the task of social amelioration became a more self-conscious one, there was a growing concern not merely in respect of ends but also processes. In other words, the attempt to bring about changes in belief and practice were palpably related to some moral and philosophical rethinking on the very necessity of change itself.

An important public figure from nineteenth-century Maharashtra, Sir Narayan G. Chandravarkar (1858–1923), once made the interesting remark that the Parsi soda-water seller at Bombay Railway Station was effectively the greatest institution for dismantling the institution of caste since he served his customers irrespective of their caste standing.[2] What Chandravarkar seems to have overlooked is that the soda-water seller was not particularly conscious of the transformative role he was playing and that his intervention was, at best, passive and involuntary. It is true that many Hindus of the time, particularly those leaning towards conservatism, shared this gradualist approach to social change. Mandlik, who generally remained on the side of the orthodox party in Maharashtra, believed that 'half a dozen Railways would settle a hundred social questions more quickly than five hundred lectures'.[3] It is just as possible, however, that there was some hidden sarcasm in Chandravarkar's remarks and in citing the instance of the Parsi soda-water seller he was only hinting at the ostentatious yet ineffective efforts of many a public reformer.

Over time reform work was increasingly identified, sometimes even by its outspoken supporters, with critiques and corrective measures produced from the 'inside', rather than initiatives taken by external agents and 'outsiders'. Especially in the latter half of the nineteenth century there was opposition to mediations by a Christian government and a non-Hindu reformer like Malabari—to cite two apt examples.[4] There were certain tactical advantages to be gained from this. As the century progressed, more dissenting groups and alternative visions of reform appeared on the horizon. For the upper castes and classes, however, it made more sense to project reform as changes born out of introspective self-reflection and periodic structural adjustments rather than concessions forced by growing defiance or dissent. We could illustrate this argument by citing the various ways in which the life and work of the Buddha has been understood in recent times. The Buddha would no doubt appear to be a reformer to those who see his message as an internal critique of Brahmanism. On the contrary, those more attracted by his heterodoxy—his dissenting metaphysics and the creation of a new religious order—would not necessarily take this position. With very few exceptions, Hindu social and religious reform in modern India identified itself with the first of the two alternatives.

The Inadequacy of 'Reform'

In the course of extended debates over reform, people changed sides with alacrity and quite often, this followed from sheer opportunism rather than a genuine change of heart. In a few other instances reformers themselves could not implement in their personal lives, models of behaviour they expected others to follow. When his first wife died in 1873, Ranade, the champion of widow marriages, was himself forced to marry a virgin. His contemporary and co-worker from Maharashtra,

Gopal Hari Deshmukh 'Lokahitawadi' (1832–92) had to undergo *prayaschitta* (expiation) for having personally attended a widow marriage. In Bengal, the Brahmo Samaj split a second time over Keshab Chandra's marrying his daughter into the royal family of Cooch-Behar at a time she had not attained the proper age.[5] Outside such inconsistencies or tactical changes, there also remained serious reservations about the sheer utility of reform itself. Excerpts from the speeches and writings of Swami Vivekananda (1863–1902) and Periyar included in Part II of this work reveal this dissatisfaction, though for palpably different reasons. Vivekananda's critique of reformism as being more 'destructionist' than creative or constructive to an extent reflects the generally reactionary mood in late-nineteenth-century India. The reaction in this case was to programmes or work methods, which, allegedly, were far too imitative of the West to be realistically accepted by the Hindus. In the 1890s, it was quite unlikely that even radicals would dare to dismantle caste by the public consumption of beef steak and champagne as Vivekananda alleged. But the Swami nevertheless made the valuable point that reform work, as carried out in India over the last hundred years or so, had no real roots in the people. Especially in a period when Hindus were politically powerless and lacked law-making bodies of their own, changes in social and religious life would endure only if founded in popular will or support.[6] Vivekananda's arguments implicitly uphold the gradualist view of social transformation—a view that was reluctant to unduly antagonize the orthodox or unleash any violent class war. The Swami never went back on reform per se, but he distrusted the intentions of an alien state and unsympathetic reformers.

Interestingly enough, Periyar explicitly mentions Swami Vivekananda as a man whose views on social reform were quite opposed to his own. Whereas Vivekananda recommended restraint and caution, Periyar consciously identified himself with the 'destructionist' method, which called for sweeping changes. In this he was guided by the belief that reform was but a manipulative game that the upper classes played to keep themselves in power. 'Reform' blinded the lower classes to the reality that the oppressors of the past had themselves re-emerged as present-day reformers and hence could not be expected to carry out any meaningful changes. Periyar also appears to have differed from Vivekananda on two more counts. First, he took social malpractices within Hindu society to be deeply rooted in Hindu religious belief, which in effect meant that social reform could not be effectively carried out without making suitable changes in religion itself. Later in this essay we shall see how exactly the same argument was also made by some orthodox Hindus, albeit from an entirely different perspective. Rather than rely on society to gradually overcome its blemishes through sustained efforts at mass education, Periyar also recommended the dramatic and radical intervention by the state in addressing social problems.[7] Excerpts from an essay written by Jawaharlal Nehru while interned at the Almora District jail (included in Part II) throw light on another interesting side to this problem. In the first place, Nehru, like Periyar, appears to have been appalled at the crass insensitivity of Indians towards pressing social problems and an inexplicable engagement with the metaphysical. Equally importantly, however, his essay reveals how orthodoxy may actually cut across community boundaries. Thus, when it came to opposing raising the minimum age for the marriage of girls, the orthodox *pandit* could be seen marching together with the *maulavi,* from whom he claimed to be religiously separated.

The palpable differences in time and social contexts within which they worked would no doubt explain the divergent views held by Vivekananda and Periyar. In terms of the social questions raised, late-nineteenth-century Bengal and twentieth-century Tamil-speaking areas were indeed incomparable. What is nonetheless of some interest here is the subtle but significant differences in the understanding of just what meaningful change might constitute. Swami Vivekananda, too, talked of an impending 'Sudra revolution' and was sharply critical of excesses perpetrated by brahmans in the name of custom or religion. All the same, it was in upper-caste, brahmanical culture that he located new sources of legitimacy and well-being for a powerless people. Unlike Periyar, therefore, his cry for 'root and branch reform' envisaged some kind of political equality, not social. It aimed at dethroning the brahman, not brahmanism.

In some ways the life and labours of Kandkuri Viresalingam, himself a brahman, reflect the points of criticism made by both Periyar and Vivekananda. Long years of handling social reform taught him to distrust upper-caste supporters, most of whom turned out to be inherently conservative and deserted the reform movement under the slightest pressure. When some of these men joined traditional authorities like the Shankaracharya in declaring Viresalingam an outcaste, the latter's attention began to focus not so much on reform as the education and the general awakening of the masses.

In their pioneering essay on Viresalingam, John and Karen Leonard claim to have found in his life and activities an alternative model of change and reform. In their view, this arises in the reformer's explicit adoption of a regional and 'vernacular' culture as against the Sanskritic and pan-Indian. The effective power behind Viresalingam's activities was no doubt his innovative and influential use of Telugu, which enabled him to work for a bigger social constituency comprising women and low castes. By comparison, neighbouring Tamil-speaking areas, which had not witnessed similar changes, remained far more conservative in social and political matters. It is equally true that the modern Telegu prose which Viresalingam used in his journalistic and other writings laid the foundation of a secular and scientific education in Andhra.[8] At the same time, such accomplishments do not appear to be unique to either Viresalingam or Telugu-speaking areas of coastal Andhra. As early as 1838, the Derozian Uday Chandra Adya, certainly more Westernized in his thinking if not more radical, had championed the cause of Bengali as the medium of public instruction.[9] Some years later Bankim Chandra Chattopadhyay (1838–94) evolved a new Bengali prose in the hope that new ideas could be best disseminated only through new linguistic forms. A closer look at Viresalingam's ideas would also reveal that, notwithstanding his courageous defiance of the Hindu orthodox, there are certain ideas or beliefs that he also shared with them. For one, his privileging the Vedas over the *Itihasas* or *Puranas* brings him disconcertingly close to the orthodox thinking on the subject. Other explanations apart, Viresalingam also seems to have understood the alleged degeneration of Hindu society and religion in the light of the traditionally popular *yuga* theory.[10] The outstanding quality of Viresalingam was the ability to scoff at his own class and to use the vernacular to mobilize the masses. Neither of these, apparently, were as effectively performed in contemporary Bengal.

Religion as the Basis of Social Reform

There has been a considerable difference of opinion and, at times, even confusion over whether or not for modern Hindus, society and religion were separate spheres of activity. Charles H. Heimsath, the noted authority on Hindu reform, contradicts himself when he argues, practically in the same breath, that whereas Vivekananda was displeased with the excessive emphasis on religion among fellow-Hindus, his own thoughts coincide with the 'culmination of nineteenth century social revolt ... suitably ... expressed in religious terms'.[11] Heimsath also seems to have misread certain important developments of the period when he claims that the 1880s and 1890s represent the peak of secularist discourse or that the political goals of nationalism 'provided a secular basis for social reform which eliminated the need to relate social to religious reformation'.[12] The 1880s and 1890s, on the contrary, represent precisely that period in our history when a secularist bent of mind began to be overshadowed by a conscious joining of religion to politics, or else articulating a political rhetoric through religious idioms. In Bengal Bankim Chandra's *Krishnacharitra* (1886), *Dharmatattwa* (1888), and the posthumously published *Srimadbhagavatgita* (1902) belong to the latter category. Around the same period Bal Gangadhar Tilak (1856–1920) launched the Shivaji and Ganapati Utsavs in Maharashtra with a view to mobilize the masses. In contemporary Punjab, too, thanks to the activities of the Arya Samaj, there were discernible links between the cultural nostalgia for Vedic religion and burgeoning Punjabi nationalism. Late-nineteenth-century Hindu discourse was, in fact, quite remarkable in its rejection of secular culture.

The interface of society and religion was a problematic even for early-nineteenth-century reformers like Rammohan Roy. In a letter that he wrote to his friend John Digby (dated 18 January 1828) the Raja had expressed a desire to introduce changes in religion for the sake of 'political advantage and social comfort'.[13] This is sometimes cited by scholars keen to underscore the secular and pragmatic underpinnings of nineteenth-century Hindu reform.[14] It does nevertheless appear significant that Rammohan should seek to derive such civic and secular benefits through a religious reformation, not social. Was he, too, suggesting, in keeping with the raging Orientalist rhetoric, that the key to comprehending Hindu society was religion? And is it not just possible that through his persistent effort at weaning away the 'authentic' from the 'inauthentic' within his religious tradition and thereafter projecting a reformed religion as the resolution of all social problems, Rammohan and like-minded Hindu reformers circumvented the very need for a secular culture? It is not fortuitous that the Raja's most persistent differences were with religious thinkers and interpreters of Hindu religion, not social reformers or social theorists. At a rough estimate, less than 10 per cent of Rammohan's Bengali and English writings were on purely social-secular questions, of which about 50 per cent was taken up by the debate on *sati*. It is also somewhat odd that he should hope to derive political advantages and social comfort by publicizing (through Bengali and English translations) Upanishadic texts, highly speculative in their content. That he himself considered these of no practical relevance is borne out by a letter he wrote to the governor-general, Lord Amherst, on 11 December 1823.[15] If Rammohan believed that there were other ways of effecting changes in Hindu religion, he did not somehow say so.

It was Mahadev Gobind Ranade's feeling that Bengal was much too preoccupied with the religious question, at the expense of the social.[16] Broadly speaking, this seems to be borne out by later developments. In the 1860s, Keshab Chandra Sen pronounced what Rammohan might have been happy to support himself. For Rammohan[17] as well as for Keshab, caste was a *religious* institution (emphasis mine) and the mitigation of caste oppression therefore required inroads into established religion. In some ways, Keshab only reinforced Rammohan's position when he argued that a spiritual emancipation had to precede an intellectual and material reformation, and that caste hierarchies would go once the Hindus ceased to be idolatrous and discontinued worshipping multiple gods and goddesses. 'The Fatherhood of God', as he put it, was the only enduring basis for 'the Brotherhood of Man'. In an 1863 lecture, excerpts from which are reproduced in Part II, Keshab explicitly rejected any thoughts of dismantling caste through a 'secular movement'.[18] Seeking legitimacy for social reform in religion was also known in nineteenth-century Maharashtra. Ramakrishna Vithal Pareskar (better known as Dr Bhau Daji, [1824–74]), a medical practitioner and twice Sheriff of Bombay, based his appeal against female infanticide on the ground that such practices had no sanction in God and religion.[19]

While Ranade expressed unhappiness at making social reform contingent upon the religious, a stronger critique of this position came from the Arya Samaj leader, Lala Lajpat Rai (1865–1928). Speaking before a gathering of the youth wing of the Arya Samaj, Lajpat Rai found the religious training of young minds quite contrary to the nature of their future responsibilities. The brahmanical emphasis on 'self-realization' he condemned as mere selfishness. Whether rightly or wrongly, Lajpat Rai associated the Upanishadic basis of brahmanical philosophy with escapist, other-worldly attitudes. These he wanted to replace by an active engagement with the world and ideals of social service.[20]

Understandably enough, the most effective challenge to the 'spiritual emancipation first' thesis came not from within upper-caste culture but from outside it. Men like Periyar and Ambedkar accepted the acclaimed connections between religious reform and social, but turned the dominant thesis on its head. Whereas mainstream reform movements had argued that social reformation had to await religious reformation, or at best that social reform ought not to suffer at the hands of the religious, these men claimed that but for the deep inequities built into the Hindu religious system, Hindu society would have witnessed far greater progress. Ambedkar insisted that the institution of caste drew its greatest support from the Shastras and that the traditional Hindu faith in Shastras had itself to be uprooted before caste ceased to be the basis of Hindu social organization.[21] Prima facie it might seem as though in embracing Buddhism Ambedkar, too, fell back on the primacy of a religious identity, even when in protest. However, his reading of Buddhism apparently gravitated more towards the socially dissenting message of the Buddha than his metaphysics. On the whole, it might be fair to say that Ambedkar did not make renunciation of religion the *sine qua non* of alternative social identities. His intentions were really to persuade the Hindus of his day to judge their religion above all by its survival value. Effectively, this meant giving Hinduism a new doctrinal basis in keeping with the momentous social changes occurring all around it.

In modern India, it is possible to locate a few men who appear to combine in themselves an uneasy mix of both these viewpoints. Altruism and the social responsibilities of religion are ideas that are strongly underlined in the life and activities of Swami Vivekananda. On the other hand, the Swami also reinforced the thesis that religion could not be judged by the purely rational or utilitarian needs of society. Vivekananda saw society and social developments to be by their very nature unstable and transitory. Religion, on the other hand, was the repository of eternal, unchanging 'truths'. 'We are asked "what good is your religion to your society?"', he complains at one place. 'Society is made the test of truth. Now this is very illogical. Society is only a stage in the growth through which we are passing ... Society is good at a certain stage but it cannot be an ideal; it is in constant flux.'[22]

In a sense, the preoccupation with religion reflects the deepening identity crisis within late-nineteenth-century Hinduism. An 'authentic' religion of proven antiquity was, in the eyes of the colonized Hindu, a cultural artefact that could stand up to every test of reasonableness and utility. The same, incidentally, could not be said about Hindu society. Modern Hindus seem to have uncritically accepted Occidental theories about the static, grossly underdeveloped state of their society. The bifurcation of the social realm from the religions originated in European cultural assumptions of the time, but this also gave patriotic Hindus a cultural peg from which to hang their specious theories about a spiritually superior India countering the inroads of a materially advanced West.

The Past as a Cultural Resource and the Reformist Demands of the Present

In his well-known study of Hindu social and religious reform, the American scholar C.H. Heimsath defined a social reformer as an 'advocate of alterations in social customs which would involve a break with the past' and an individual who had convinced himself that 'the altered ways of thinking and behaving were positive values'.[23] Broadly speaking, this is an acceptable and useful definition. At the same time, some confusion is bound to have prevailed then, as it does even now, over just how much one might deviate from the past and, more importantly, what the past itself may be understood as. In his well-known work, *Satyarth Prakash* (1877), Swami Dayanand Saraswati accused the Brahmo Samaj of incorporating in their sacred books, 'the names of Christ, Moses, Mohammed, Nanak and Chaitanya ... but not a single [name] from among the sages and seers of the past.'[24] Evidently the 'past' in this case was not synonymous with all that was premodern, but with chronologically specific and culturally determined components. Dayanand was obviously unhappy over the inclusion of the names of medieval Bhakti saints like Nanak and Chaitanya, not to speak of non-Indians like Moses or Christ. His point of reference, as with several others, was the 'golden age' of Vedic antiquity, deliberately glossing over the 'dark' interlude of Indo-Muslim rule. Of course, not everybody went by such preferences, especially in areas where, traditionally, Vedic scholarship was relatively weak. The novels of Bankim Chandra are set not amid days of 'Hindu glory' but its very opposite—powerless states and morally bankrupt rulers. Bankim explicitly rejected Dayanand's cry for a return to the Vedic ways as not just impractical but positively unhistorical. So far as he could see, Hindu religion and society, rather than be frozen in time, was constantly evolving. Hence, for any realistic assessment of the state of Hindu civilization, one had really to scrutinize the present rather than turn back to the past.[25]

Using the past as a cultural resource, therefore, was fraught with several practical difficulties. So long as there was no social consensus on precisely which elements of the past would be relevant or useful, people were bound to disagree on what needed excision or alteration. But did alteration itself mean creating new modes of belief and social behaviour or revising and revitalizing older ones in the light of modern requirements? Was it a mere change of spirit rather than form or was the opposite true? The history of social and religious reform in modern Hinduism would seem to indicate that more often than not people worked with both these alternatives in mind, quite oblivious of the inherent contradiction between them.

We have earlier noted how, despite internal disagreement or differences, reform continued to be a pressing and powerful social agenda in the nineteenth century. Here, it would be important to remember that up to a point, strategic differences were increasingly overridden by certain cultural theories, which were shared across a wide cross-section of society. Perhaps the most popular of these was the claim that from a high state of civilized existence in antiquity, the Hindus had steadily declined to a state of utter decadence or degeneration. An early example of this thesis occurs in the lecture by the Derozian-turned-Christian, Krishna Mohan Banerjea (1813–85). Krishna Mohan strongly supported the view that irrational accretions ('rubbish', as he called them) that had accumulated over time had to be vigorously uprooted from contemporary Hinduism in order to get at its ideal condition. More importantly, however, he made the point that reform could not possibly originate in the very abuses it was meant to destroy.[26] This, it has to be said, at once separates modern notions of change from those known to traditional Hinduism. The latter had devised its own methods of negotiating with the exigencies of change. This was usually performed not by allowing difference or dissidence any autonomous space for itself, but by projecting it as a part of orthodox self-reflexivity. Such methods, evidently, had two tactical advantages. First, they projected orthodoxy as a dynamic force, inherently capable of self-betterment. Further, by suggesting that it was capable of generating self-criticism and then effectively acting upon them, the orthodoxy was also successful in retaining social initiatives with itself. Not surprisingly, barring a few exceptions, reform movements concerning Hindus were either initiated or led by brahmans. In some regions the practical enactment of new reform measures also went to the credit of brahmans. In Bengal, the first man to marry a widow under the Widow Marriage Act was a brahman. It has been aptly remarked that dissidence or difference cannot flourish in a culture which usually rendered dissenting voices socially powerless through assimilation and accommodation.[27] An essay appearing as early as 1919 made the point that the medieval Bhakti movement had assimilated more than it had discarded, and that this had effectively disarmed any radical opposition.[28] Krishna Mohan's argument assumes that much more importance because, rather than rely on traditional ways of negotiating change, it speaks in a very modern language, of the 'natural' right of individuals to think and act for themselves. Hereafter, private judgement and the moral responsibility of individuals became important and inalienable weapons in the armoury of many a reformer.

In the nineteenth century, situating oneself in relation with some past became extremely important for both moral and polemical reasons. At one level, bridges between the past and present, whether mythical or historical, had to be built for the sake of cultural continuities. At a time when the power and sanctity of a literary text or an artefact was usually measured in direct proportion to its known antiquity, this constituted a part of one's credibility and cultural self-defence. Alternatively, the past could also be useful as a symbolic reminder of the shape of things to come; the promise of a new life would have to arise out of the ashes of the old. This, apparently, is the overwhelming message in Bankim's historical novels, set as they are in the twilight era of the seventeenth and eighteenth centuries. The two visions outlined above broadly represent the two views of the Hindu past. The first, which we can easily identify with Dayanand and a variety of neo-Hindu thinkers, erred in believing that contemporary Hinduism could be randomly associated with a civilization going as far back as the Vedas. But there is also a problem in the other view entertained by men like Bankim Chandra. Even if the ills of contemporary Hinduism could somehow be attributed to the rule of the Mughals, Turks, and Pathans, just where was one to locate the Good Society? Bankim, as we know, was averse to the idea of Hinduism being rooted in Vedic antiquity, and he therefore tried to wriggle out of this situation by positing the familiar theory of there being an 'essential' Hinduism as distinct from the inessential and inconsequential. In suggesting this he went against his own historical view of Hinduism.[29]

A progressive outlook upon society when combined with recurring references to the cultural resources of the past produced a powerful dichotomy from which no reformer in British India was really free. A recent study of the writings and speeches of Ranade has rightly drawn our attention to how, by reform, this great crusader from nineteenth-century Maharashtra meant different things at different times. Here, again, an individual reformer was caught between the dictates of reason and ideology, between intellectually attractive goals and cultural nostalgia. Speaking before the Ninth Social Conference, Ranade contradicted himself by first drawing attention to the compelling and forward-moving forces of social evolution, but thereafter by reminding his audience of how they could ill-afford to 'kick the old ladder' from under their feet. Roughly two years earlier (the Seventh Social Conference) he had similarly committed a *faux pas* by trying to understand social progress both in terms of human intervention and 'God's hand in history'. Here, perhaps unknown to himself, Ranade ran up against a difficulty, the implications of which might have worried many a reformer. If social progress could be attributed to some divine intervention, was the palpable degeneration of Hindus also to be explained in the light of the same theory?[30]

B. The Debate over Strategies

In many ways, successful reform work depended on a realistic assessment of reigning public moods. The government, evidently, was a key player in this respect since certain changes in existing social practices narrowed down to legal reviews and appropriate changes in existing law. Alternatively, legal sanctions had to be sometimes provided to a socially coveted issue so as to effectively protect certain citizens from social persecution. The Age of Consent Act (1891) clearly belongs to the first category. By the time this act was passed, the government had clearly realized that under the existing criminal law, it was not possible to prosecute a certain class of sexual offenders. Husbands, for example, could escape unscathed despite their brutalizing treatment of child-wives and, thus, existing criminal laws had to be suitably amended so as to make sexual cohabitation even between married partners a cognizable crime below a legally defined age. The important point here is that no indigenous agency could have possibly brought about such changes. During the Consent Bill controversy this is precisely the argument that lent moral strength to an otherwise reluctant government and somewhat weakened the oppositionists. The Widow Marriage Act of 1856, by comparison, belongs to the second category, where the government felt that rather than legally enforce unpopular changes in Hindu social custom, it was merely providing legal protection to marrying partners.

Not surprisingly, many a reformer felt that debates could be quickly and more amicably settled once the government made up its mind. Controversies lingered on mainly because people either did not have the courage to accept realities or else because they expected to derive some popularity from extended debates.[31]

At least down to the 1880s, when no notable reformist organization of national standing existed, successful reform work largely depended on the courage and moral heroism of individuals. Admittedly, there were many who failed the test. In some cases, however, such weaknesses were partly offset by the consistent support given to the case of reform, often in the teeth of opposition. Ranade, for instance, was one of few reformers in Maharashtra who took kindly to the activities of Pandita Ramabai (1858–1922),[32] infamous for her support to widow marriages, the social rehabilitation of widows, as well as for daring to turn Christian.

The fact that there were such bitter differences of opinion on appropriate strategies would suggest that in many cases, a reform issue per se was not being contested but the pace at which this was to be conducted. After all, differences could arise as much between like-minded people as those who had little to share between themselves. Very few among the Hindu orthodox were in principle opposed to the idea of female emancipation. The opponents of Rammohan were among the pioneers of woman's education in Bengal and one of them in particular, Pandit Mritunjoy Vidyalankar (1762–1811), had even anticipated the arguments against *sati*. It is also quite probable that differences over strategies reflected not differences in ideology but factional loyalties as has been interestingly demonstrated in the case of early-nineteenth-century Calcutta.[33] Finally, one must allow for subtle shades of opinion even within oppositionist camps. It would be important to distinguish reactionary conservatism or the pathological resistance to change from even faltering support to the cause of reform. Particularly in the context of Hindu reform, the term 'orthodox' need not always be interchangeable with the term 'conservatism'. Swami Dayanand could be perceived as an orthodox figure inasmuch as he adhered to the long-standing valorization of the Vedas. But this, as we know, did not take away from his reformism. Generally speaking, the conservative approach to reform was either in favour of the status quo or else willing to allow changes at a pace which rendered reform quite meaningless. The latter would not simply see that changes occurring over a great length of time did not meet the exigency of every situation or that conscious acts of mediation from to time were not necessarily inconsistent with long-term projects of public education.

At times, the progress of reform was arrested by the tendency on the part of both reformers and their opponents to fall back on the authoritative voice of tradition. The recourse to the Shastras as a reliable guide to reform eventually proved to be an embarrassment to both parties since it progressively emerged that the Shastras did not always speak with the same voice and hence lent themselves to conflicting interpretations. There was, as we shall presently see, the intriguing choice of an appropriate text. However, but for a few short, reactionary spells when allegiance to the Shastras became the war cry of the conservatives, people from various walks of life had begun to accept the fact that modern problems could not be satisfactorily resolved in the light of older prescriptions. An orthodox Sanskrit scholar of Maharashtra once admitted to Chandravarkar that, left to themselves, members of his class would never be able to procure from the Shastras support for the kind of changes being contemplated, for, frankly, these simply did not exist. Significantly enough, he also went on to add that men such as him were in any case beginning to accept the changes occurring around them.[34]

By the third quarter of the nineteenth century, the fate of socio-religious reform became tied to that of the political. For some, the needs of greater political mobilization required temporarily glossing over, if not altogether denying, the crying need for social reform. In the political sphere, educated Indians could speak of common agendas for they had but one adversary. In social matters, on the contrary, consensus was hard to come by. Loyalties were horizontally divided in one case and vertically in another. There were, of course, those who took such theories to be quite dubious, for in their view, the social progress of the nation was inextricably linked to its political successes. In any case, those who began their lives as social reformers often ended up as active politicians. N.G. Chandravarkar, who succeeded Ranade to the leadership of the Indian Social Conference, was himself elected president of the Congress in 1900. On the other hand, after long years of political work, men also realized that for a nation deeply divided along lines of caste, class, or gender, freedom was but an empty boast.

The Road to Reform: Moral Courage vs Cautious Deference to Tradition

In nineteenth-century Maharashtra there was a popularly accepted distinction between *bolte sudharak* and *karte sudharak*—reformers who merely paid lip service to reform and those who withstood great social pressure only so they might achieve their desired social objectives.[35] Such distinctions, of course, might have been applied to most places in British India, but would be especially true where traditional mechanisms of social control were still in force. In Maharashtra and in parts of southern India, the fear of being declared an outcaste was a realistic one and presumably dampened the early enthusiasm of many a prospective reformer. On the other hand, the relative weakness of such mechanisms did not necessarily ensure more courageous reformers or a far more congenial environment for reform. Nineteenth-century Calcutta, which had seen a fair degree of Westernization and some of the earliest attempts at reform, lagged behind in practical results. Coastal Andhra, where reformers lived in fear of persecution by traditional authorities like the Shankaracharya, hosted many more widow marriages than 'liberal' Bengal.

A closer look at contemporary developments, however, would reveal that a note of caution always ran alongside the commitment to reform. In October 1831 a correspondent of the *India Gazette* (excerpts reproduced in Part II), while firmly supporting Derozian 'radicalism', also felt that their methods were far too cocky and likely to unduly antagonize people. Traditions and traditional people, it was pointed out, had to be handled with greater empathy. Moreover, tradition was changing of its own volition and did not have to be goaded into change.[36] This, indeed, seems to be a cautious view of the contemporary situation as also a realistic one. A reforming zeal itself could not produce much unless it also had at least the grudging support of some people. The moral heroism of individuals would be wasted if it did not also take a serious note of social constraints or practical compulsions.

However the argument that the success of reform ultimately depended on personal commitments continued to be also made throughout the greater part of the nineteenth century. In an 1865 lecture, appropriately called 'An Appeal to Young India', Keshab Chandra Sen showed reform work to be purely objective and impersonal wherein individual happiness or personal convenience had to be left behind for the sake of a larger cause. But there was also the question of setting public examples through private efforts. The success of reform, in other words, could not always be measured in terms of its apparent popularity, but the strength and perseverance of a few individuals. Reformers, Keshab also cautioned, had to first reform themselves.[37] According to some, it was this faltering courage, the weakening of personal charisma and public involvement that accounted for the perceptible decline in reformist successes by the close of the nineteenth century. This, incidentally, is a point quite forcefully made in the essay (reproduced in Part II) by a prominent activist of the North West Provinces (NWP), Pandit Bishan Narain Dar (1864–1916). The mediation of organized, all-India bodies was important, Dar points out, but they were given to much pomposity and public display which made them ill-equipped to handle genuine, grassroots problems.

Such were also the thoughts of Mahadev Govind Ranade, who seems to have been greatly influenced by the philosopher-educationist, Joseph Butler. Butler's views emphasized the individual's moral responsibility to his society.[38] Both Keshab and Ranade thus pinned their hopes on the strength of individual examples and assumed that the individual was able to most effectively discharge his obligations when he also enjoyed a degree of moral autonomy in society.

It is not difficult to see that such arguments went against the traditionalist position, which expected the individual to be not only selfless but also self-effacing, and made the community the sole arbiter of change. It is misleading to suggest that in British India, the only protagonists of this position were the orthodox *pandit*s, Sanskritists, and *shastri*s. In truth, one of its best spokespersons was an English-educated professional and high-ranking public servant, Bhudev Mukhopadhyay (1827–94). In a series of three essays that he wrote between 1882 and 1895, Bhudev expounded in some detail, the unsuitability of Western ideas and institutions for Hindus. The more critical point that he made was that so far as the Hindus were concerned, the power or authority to effect social changes lay not with the state but society.[39] It would have been redundant to add that the powers of a non-Hindu state were bound to be all the more questionable.

The 1880s may be said to mark a watershed in the history of Hindu social reform inasmuch as after this point of time, individual interventions began to be gradually replaced by organized efforts. The birth of the National Social Conference and various provincial reformist bodies were an important step in this direction. Such changes can be broadly attributed to two developments. In the first place, more and more people began to be involved in the task of social amelioration just as reform began to affect the lives of a larger percentage of people. More importantly, however, such changes also reflected new intellectual trends in Europe and India. By the late nineteenth century, liberal social theories based on the inviolable sanctity of private rights was giving way to organic views of society in which people began to see a complex network of human interdependence and relationships. It is thus that efforts at reform in the twentieth century became more institutionalized and even adopted time-tested methods of political mobilization.

The Problem of Social as against Political Reform

In 1886, within only a year of the founding of the Indian National Congress, Kashinath Trembak Telang (1850–93), judge and, later, the first Indian Vice-Chancellor of Bombay University, stirred up some controversy with an address he delivered before the Bombay Students' Literary and Scientific Society. The address, which was given the title, 'Must Social Reform Precede Political Reform?', was meant to counter the views of Sir Auckland Colvin, Finance Member of the Viceroy's council and later Lieutenant-Governor of the NWP.

Colvin had first caused some resentment among Indians when, in responding to Malabari's reform proposals of 1884, he had made the point that societies which were reluctant to remove their own shortcomings ought not to be trusted with political concessions. Colvin also doubted if Western political ideas or institutions would actually suit Indians in the long run. 'The vast mass of the people', he wrote, 'live in the traditions of the government of their forefathers', and were bound to be 'as much out of harmony with the political atmosphere breathed by us of English birth or desired by their own countrymen of English education, as an elephant would be out of his element in Scotch mists or a banyan tree in Parliament Street.'[40]

For Hindu nationalists like Telang, such official attitudes clearly represented diversionary tactics. By encouraging social reform at the expense of the political, the government simply wanted to create further rifts within Hindu society and thereby also frustrate Indian aspirations for greater self-representation. In a letter that he subsequently wrote to the then Viceroy, Lord Lansdowne, A.O. Hume, co-founder of the Congress, alleged that even district-level officers tried to discredit this newly born body by claiming its deep involvement with social legislation.[41] Such fears may have been slightly exaggerated but they nevertheless show how difficult it must have been for educated Hindus to go one way or the other.

Telang's rejoinder of 1886 itself reflects a curious blend of caution and measured aggression. By this time, thanks to the efforts of Malabari, the campaign for marriage reform had picked up some momentum, forcing the government itself to reconsider its avowed neutrality on social and religious matters concerning the Hindu. Hence, even when disputing the claims of Colvin, Telang could ill-afford to brush aside the growing sentiment in favour of reform. This two-pronged stance also explains why, in later years, his position vis-à-vis Colvin was often critiqued but never fundamentally contested. On the whole, Telang adopted two lines of argument. First, he countered the claims of Colvin by citing the case of Britain itself, where substantial progress had been achieved despite persistent social evils. But the argument that was to make him popular in the coming years was that which suggested that changes in status quo would best advance along 'the line of least resistance'. Effectively, this made the important point that compared to the purely political, social reform would always be more divisive and hence needed to be handled with that much more caution. Whereas political campaigns could elicit certain common interests, the movement for social reform had to depend far more on ideological commitments—an unstable base in itself.[42]

Within a couple of years of his delivering the address, Telang was criticized by his compatriot from Maharashtra, Gopal Ganesh Agarkar (1806–95). Contrary to Telang's feelings, Agarkar found the 1880s to be the most propitious time for launching social reform. Apparently under some influence from men like Malabari, he bemoaned the fact that political ambitions had made fellow-Indians lose sight of their pressing social problems.[43] Dissenting voices were also heard from Bengali Brahmos such as Bipin Chandra Pal (see the excerpt reproduced in Part II). In coastal Andhra, Viresalingam carried a deep distrust for agendas promoting political reform at the expense of the social.[44] Some political workers themselves could see the regressive underside to Telang's arguments. No less a person than the militant, Bipin Chandra Pal was pained at the prospects of people fighting for political enfranchisement, yet defending social slavery.[45] Still others, like the Brahmo theologian, Sitanath Tattwabhushan, took the 'line of least resistance theory' to be cowardly and oblivious of the great recuperative powers of Hindu society.[46]

In hindsight, it may be said that with the passage of time the debate over whether or not social reform should precede the political, lost some of its relevance and intensity. This followed not so much from Indians backtracking on social reform as the fact that towards the closing years of the nineteenth century, the political atmosphere in India became far more intense and charged. Racial discrimination, bureaucratic excesses, and the reluctance to grant Indians greater self-representation in political forums eventually led to a kind of reactionary nationalism which found it difficult to accommodate the struggle for social reform. 'A certain amount of pronounced antipathy to social reform and reformers,' as Srinivasa Row was to observe in 1902, 'was becoming a passport to popularity for the Congress politician.'[47]

An implicit revival of the Telang thesis may be found in the excerpt from Aurobindo Ghosh (1872–1950) reproduced in this book. This militant nationalist, and otherwise a supporter of Bipin Pal, did not think that the removal of social malpractices would necessarily make people ready for political freedom. In this particular essay Aurobindo contested the *Indian Social Reformer*, the reformist journal started by Kamakshi Natarajan in 1889, which maintained that Indians had to be moderate with their political demands so long as they remained affected by critical social problems. Aurobindo alleged that in the eyes of the *Reformer*, political moderation and giving priority to social questions amounted to a tacit acceptance of British rule, at least in the short run.[48] This, one has to say, was never the intention of men like Ranade, Chandravarkar or Agarkar, who served as a bridge between a sensitivity to India's staggering social problems and an uphill political struggle for gaining greater civic and political rights. To an extent, Aurobindo's quarrel with the *Reformer* grew out of his discomfiture with state intervention in social matters and it is to this question that we shall now turn.

The State and the Question of Social Legislation

The attitude of the British Indian state, as we have earlier noted, was always a critical factor in determining the practical progress of reform. But such attitudes themselves were dependent on several factors—ideological-political configurations in Britain, the general situation in India, and varying perceptions of individual members of the ruling class. Thus, while the government often paraded its desire to effect the moral and social 'improvements', its preparedness for reform was invariably guided by practical exigencies in any given situation, the most important component of which was the safety and security of the Indian empire. Bentinck's Minute of 8 November 1829 reveals that the government's decision to push through with the law abolishing *sati* followed from its understanding that at the time, it was under no serious threat of either external aggression or internal rebellion. Bentinck appears to have especially considered the sentiments of Indian sepoys and, in a remarkable display of political foresight, came to the conclusion that in the unlikely event of disaffection spreading among soldiers and the civilian population, British rule would be ably defended by the class of loyal landlords created by the Permanent Settlement.[49]

Generally speaking, the government did try to play true to its paternalism and self-proclaimed responsibilities towards its Indian subjects so long as there were no overwhelming reasons against it. The events of 1857, as we know, forced it to retreat to the position of passive neutrality. On the other hand, in less than 20 years, it also went on to pass a separate marriage act for Brahmos and for those who willingly dissociated themselves from the established marriage rites of the Hindus, Muslims, or Christians (Act III of 1872)—in the face of opposition from both Hindus and Brahmos. On the whole, the government found it easier to intervene in matters where its role was limited to providing an enabling act. Thus, whereas it might lay down a minimum age for the consummation of marriage so as to protect child-wives from sexual exploitation, it could not force Hindus to get their children married at a slightly advanced age, which amounted to a direct attempt at changing customary practices. To an extent, the state's blending courage and caution also grew from realistic assessments of prevalent conditions. While it would not take the policy of neutrality too far, it also saw the foolhardiness of launching a policy which it had not the power to practically implement. Here, it would be important to remember that in the 1880s, the government's hands were forced by certain sensational cases coming to light, namely, those of Bhikaji-Rukmabai (1887) and Hari Maiti-Phulmoni (1889). In the first instance an educated woman, offended by the oppressive side to Hindu domesticity, refused to rejoin her husband in conjugal life. In the second, an adult male caused the death of his child-wife through forced sexual intercourse. The worry, however, was that many more such cases might have come to public knowledge only if the local police and district officials had the power to force offenders to admit their guilt. As matters stood, the government law enforcement agencies were not equipped to handle such responsibilities and, in any case, male members of a family often colluded with the local authorities in preventing sordid tales from coming to light.

The most bitter and extended public controversy on the propriety of state intervention in social and religious matters occurred over the age of consent question (1886–91). Hindu opinion on the question, as can be imagined, was sharply divided, but broadly speaking we may discern three major trends within it. The first, to all appearances the minority view, supported the idea of social legislation on various grounds. Malabari himself was the first to point out that ultimately the proposed legislation was only an effort to remove lacunae in existing law and as the agency that created the law, the government alone, had the moral authority to amend it. For Ranade, the state collectively represented the power, wisdom, mercy, and charity of is citizens, and was obliged to speak for such underprivileged groups as women and low castes who could not speak for themselves.[50] Around the same time, there also developed a second view that not only supported the idea of state intervention but also alleged that it was not going for enough. Jotirao Phule recommended that the government actually enforce deterrent measures like a tax or a fine on social and sexual offenders.[51] Some women themselves were disappointed at the role of the State. In a letter (dated 18 March 1887) that she wrote to her friend Pandita Ramabai, the defendant Rukmabai (who lost the case at the Bombay High Court) observed how the very nature of British rule forced it to uphold patriarchal, brahmanical laws. In reply, Ramabai said very much the same thing[52] and such allegations should persuade us to examine afresh, the complex interrelationship between Westernization, colonial rule, and the possibilities of progressive social reform. Notwithstanding its great contribution to the cultural self-discovery of Indians, Orientalism itself is guilty of unwittingly strengthening orthodox brahmanical norms. In Part II of his book we have excerpts from a letter written by the well-known scholar H.H. Wilson (1786–1860), which uphold the sanctity of *sati*.

In comparison to such attitudes, the opposition to state intervention was not only continuous and consistent but also socially more widely dispersed. During the Age of Consent Bill controversy in Bengal cries of 'Save our Religion' or 'Religion in Danger' were heard from male graduates, orthodox *pandits*, schoolboys, and housewives, thus indicating multiple levels of awareness and participation.[53] The opposition to social legislation also came far closer to acquiring an all-India character.

Such sentiments had been expressed by the Hindu residents of Madras in 1872.[54] In Bengal, this may be located in the lecture by Krishna Mohan Banerjea, which, as we have seen, was otherwise firmly committed to the cause of reform.[55] We also have it in Bentinck's testimony that Rammohan Roy actually exercised a restraining influence upon him in respect to the *sati* legislation.[56] In Bombay and Poona, Rao Sahib Mandlik and Tilak were firm in their opposition and obtained indirect support form men like Telang, who remained suspicious about official schemes for social reform. Even in the Punjab and other adjoining areas in north India, where people were not as agitated over this question, there nonetheless remained a sense of discomfiture and disquiet.

The overwhelming opposition to state interference in social matters was undoubtedly fuelled by the growing xenophobia and anti-colonial sentiments that especially emerged during the closing years of the nineteenth century. Further down this essay, we shall have occasion to see how, in the perception of some scholars, there could have been an inverse relationship between the advancing Hindu nationalism and attempts at social reform. Prima facie this would tend to be supported by the fact that in states administered by Indian rulers where citizens were relatively less politicized, success with social legislation was evidently greater. Several Indian states introduced meaningful changes in marriage laws much before they could even be seriously debated in British India.[57]

While many Hindu oppositionists were moved by genuine fears and seriously resented the idea of a Christian government interfering with existing social practices, in many other cases, such opposition also rested on rather specious grounds. If the conservatives accused the government of going back on their declared policy of neutrality, they themselves were sometimes guilty of double standards. The Calcutta-based *Samachar Chandrika*, which opposed the government's move to abolish *sati*, sought its intervention in curbing the alleged 'atheism' among Hindu College students.[58] In the Rukmabai case, many conservative Hindus, who were on the side of the plaintiff Bhikaji, urged the government to use existing laws relating to conjugal rights to decide the case in his favour.[59] Unfortunately, reformers themselves were sometimes guilty of weakening their cause through indecision and moral weakness. Thus, Ranade, who was on the side of state intervention, somewhat diluted his case by suggesting that what was sought through such interventionist acts was only the restoration of some forgotten ideal.[60] Strangely, Malabari himself placated the conservatives far too much when he claimed that reformers and their opponents were united in opposing state intervention in matters specifically concerning the Hindus.[61]

In his essay referred to earlier, Nehru refurbishes the point that tactical considerations and political self-interest was always an important determinant of state policy on social reform. In the wake of intensifying political agitation in the 1920s or 1930s, the government, he alleges, deliberately placated the social reactionaries (as for instance on the Draft Bill moved by Har Bilas Sarda of the Arya Samaj) so as to neutralize some of its political opponents. While this is indeed a valid argument, we must, on the other hand, admit that even during the period under consideration, not every political worker was on the side of social reform. In 1942 an ex-mayor of Calcutta opposed codification of Hindu law on the ground that this violated the sanctity of Smritis (see Part II).

Hindu Shastra*s and Social Reform*

To settle social and religious matters with reference to some authoritative scripture was an established practice in traditional Hinduism, and this continued well into the nineteenth century. There were, of course, some who rejected this method altogether, but such radical dissent came mostly from low-caste groups who also tried to subvert brahmanism. Our concern, however, is with those individuals or groups who preferred to remain within brahmanical culture and yet questioned the traditional recourse to shastric authority.

On 14 July 1821, the Bengali journal *Samachar Darpan* proudly claimed that considering the many learned men who took up their quarters in the city. Calcutta was the place where all shastric disputes could be satisfactorily settled.[62] This, in fact, may be symptomatic of the changes produced by the consolidation of British power, of the growth of new colonial cities and urban lifestyles, and of the way indigenous tradition was being reinterpreted by Hindus themselves. In north India, such work would have been traditionally carried out at Benares or Prayag, and within Bengal itself at Bhatpara or Nadia, Brahman-dominated settlements patronized by erstwhile Hindu landlords and local rulers. Around 1850, when the veteran Brahmo leader Debendranath Tagore developed doubts about the 'revealed' nature of Vedic texts, he promptly sent a team of local *pandit*s all the way to Benares for seeking expert opinion. But such habits were also gradually changing. In 1881, it was Calcutta that hosted a meeting between Swami Dayanand and the orthodox Council of *Pandit*s to settle the rather complex question of what exactly constituted authoritative sources of Hindu tradition.[63] By the mid-nineteenth century, Calcutta could also boast of the fact that it had amassed a vast treasury of traditional Hindu literature, some of which was already available in English translation. Rammohan Roy once made the point that, thanks to Orientalist efforts, people were no longer at the mercy of Brahman *pandit*s for the interpretation of Hindu law or doctrine. Rammohan himself consulted Sir William Jones' (1746–94) translation of the *Manusmriti*, which, apparently, he found more reliable than Sanskrit originals.[64] Prima facie, this does appear intriguing for the Raja knew his Sanskrit. On the other hand, he had always suspected unscrupulous brahman scholars of interpolation and text-torturing, and he remained unhappy with traditional exegetical methods.[65] Incidentally, in the debate over *sati*, such differences in perspectives proved to be significant for, whereas Rammohan found no support for the practice in the canons of Manu, his opponents of the Dharma Sabha attributed this omission not to Manu himself but to problems peculiar to Bengali rescensions of the work.[66]

It is equally true, however, that the orthodox party raised certain objections, which drew no convincing answers from Rammohan. The Dharma Sabha as well as the English Orientalist H.H. Wilson, who were in opposition, wondered why Manu alone among the *Smriti* writers had to be the final point of determination.[67] To this, Rammohan, contrary to all his rationality, had replied that this was indeed the intention of the Vedas.[68] If the validity of Hindu doctrine or practices were to be determined in the light of the *Manusmriti* alone, the opposition further asked, what was one to make of popular religious festivals like Dol (Holi) or Durga Puja, which had no basis whatsoever in that work?[69]

The unfolding of the debate of *sati* brings to light the two critical questions related to the use of *Shastra*s. First, just how was one to make the choice of the appropriate *Shastra*s and, further, were these authorities to be applied universally and for all contingencies or were they also to change with changes in time and social subjects? The brahmanical tradition, as Vidyasagar was to later demonstrate, was flexible enough to allow alternative points of reference, which is to say that some *Smriti* writers (presumably later figures) had drawn up contingency plans for exceptional circumstances. Thus, the laws attributed to the sage Parashar, allowed Hindus to perform widow marriages in *Kaliyuga* whereas, ordinarily, this had been taken to be *Kalivarjya*—practices to be shunned in *Kali*.[70]

With reference to the *Shastras*, there were also other pressing problems. The *Shastras* actually spoke with many voices and, as scholars like Sir William Jones had suspected all along, practically anything could be interpolated within a text to lend credibility to some argument.[71] The counter-petition on *sati* presented by the orthodox Dharma Sabha to Bentinck claims to have found some support for the practice in a *sloka* going back to the *Rigveda*.[72] The reality, however, is that very few *pandits*, especially in Bengal, would have been reasonably proficient in Vedic Sanskrit. No less a scholar than Pandita Ramabai was to argue that such claims actually betrayed an utter ignorance of the archaic, non-functional language of the Vedas.[73] The fact that the *Shastras* were open to such conflicting interpretations meant that people ranged on ideologically opposite sides could both find support for their arguments in one text or another. The Arya Samaj leader, Mahatma Hans Raj (1864–1938), contested Annie Besant's (1847–1933) objections to widow marriage and, ironically enough, both claimed to have drawn their premise from the *Shastras*.[74] Tragically, differences could arise even if the choice was somehow narrowed down to a single text or a comparable corpus of texts. In the 1850s, the opponents of Vidyasagar accused him of a double arbitration—first in privileging the canons of Parashar over those of Manu and thereafter using Parashar himself selectively. Whereas the laws of Parashar permitted a Hindu wife to remarry under several contingencies, such as when her husband was dead, missing for a long time, impotent, or apostate, Vidyasagar allegedly, had chosen to go by only one of these possibilities. If the *pandit* had employed Parashar to legitimize the marriage of widows, would he be prepared to allow the second marriage of a woman under other contingencies as well, a contemporary journal tauntingly asked.[75]

In our period, the practice of resolving disputes through a reference to some traditional textual authority was also critiqued in some quarters, though not necessarily for identical reasons. Derozians like Krishna Mohan Banerjea felt that reformers need not unduly worry over violating traditional prescriptions because many practices approved by the anti-reformist camp had themselves no basis in the *Shastras*.[76] But there was also a more rational critique coming from people like Bankim Chandra, which quite forcefully made the point that such methods were outdated and unlikely to yield any desirable results. This, in fact, was one cause of Bankim's unhappiness with reform campaigns conducted by

Vidyasagar.[77] Speaking before the Madras Hindu Social Reform Association (1896), Chandravarkar argued how ancient lawgivers could not have anticipated the future problems of Hindu society.[78] The veteran Brahmo leader, Sibnath Sastri (1847–1919), rightly observed that Shastric sanction was in itself no guarantee for reformist success for people were known to have backed out despite it.[79]

So far as the recourse to Shastric authority could be identified with the discursive need to define one's tradition, the nineteenth century reveals certain contradictory pulls and pressures. On the one hand, since the days of Rammohan, there was a serious search for not only a 'rational' but 'national' scripture. This, it would seem, was the tactical move to bring Hinduism closer to a 'Religion of the Book' comparable to Judaism, Christianity, or Islam. On the other hand, modern Hinduism also upheld the idea of religion as a plural experience, which implicitly called for an eclectic attitude towards texts. The latter—represented by modern mystics like Sri Ramakrishna Paramhamsa (1836–86),[80] Keshab Chandra Sen, and, still later, Gandhi—was never entirely obliterated. However, the passion for a single identity or the fetishization of what was seen as a homogenized tradition considerably undermined the pluralist thesis. The beginnings, as was often the case, were made in the nineteenth century itself, by excising the 'inessential' from the 'essential'—in itself a highly subjective (and, one may add, a dubious) exercise. Such subjectivities, however, were for a long time subsumed within the neo-Hindu discourse and enjoyed the support across a wide social and ideological spectrum. Thus, Vivekananda's argument that there were indeed two classes of 'truths'—the eternal as represented by the Vedas and the transitory as represented by Smritis or Puranas is also echoed by the Brahmo theologian Sitanath Tattwabhushan and a landed aristocrat from Oudh, the Raja of Bhinga.[81]

C. The Typologies of Reform and Revival

A long-standing controversy surrounds the interrelationship between reform and revival. Over time, the term 'revival', as also 'reform', has been invested with perceptibly different shades of meaning. At one level, it seems to have been used as a corrective to reformist excesses and the 'mischievous temperament' of professional reformers. This kind of thinking is commonly associated with the relatively more conservative elements within upper-class Hindu society who were not averse to change itself, but wary of bringing this about much too quickly or under the shadow of alien ideals. More commonly, however, it is seen to represent a reactionary spirit, aiming to undermine the very logic of social change through a thoughtless attachment to old and obsolete ideals. In the nineteenth century, there was clearly a polemical side to this criticism; people with any kind of reservations against ongoing reform work were much too easily classified as revivalists. In March 1896, for example, the Brahmo missionary, Gour Govinda Roy, delivered a series of lectures on 'Hindu revival' in which he made the rather dubious distinction of reviving 'higher' and 'lower' forms of Hinduism. The former he associated with Brahmos, the latter with orthodox Hindus.[82] It is interesting that Roy's objections were not so much to the term 'revival' as to what, in his perception, was being revived. In truth, his categories of 'higher' and 'lower' forms of revival were not only dubious but far from original. Such distinctions, one may recall, were also widely used by many highly educated but orthodox Hindus.

It is not very clear at what point of time and under what circumstances, the term 'revival' began to acquire a distinctly pejorative meaning. It may be reasonably assumed, however, that apologists of British rule and those who attributed every progressive change to the Western intellectual impact on India, were among the earliest converts to this position. The evangelist J.N. Farquhar, for example, found Indian reform work to be grossly tainted by backward-looking revival, analogous to the return of paganism in the early years of the Christian era.[83] Severe condemnation also came from some Indians themselves. Narayan G. Chandravakar dismissed revivalist claims as mere 'moonshine'[84] and Ranade, in his address before the 11th Social Conference (Amraoti, 1897), was uncharacteristically sarcastic in his rebuttal of revivalism.[85] Around the same time apprehensions were also expressed about a possible connection between revivalism and reactionary, strongly anti-British politics. Ironically, among those who made such allegations was the militant leader Bipin Chandra Pal.[86] Closer to our time, revivalism has been identified with sentimental anti-intellectualism,[87] a misleading concept that 'effects closures and disallows change'.[88] Some scholars have found 'traditionalist' to be, on the whole, a better term.[89] While others have called the very term a misnomer since Hinduism, being far from dead, could not have been revived.[90]

Such criticism obviously rests on a near-literal rendering of the term 'revival'. Happily, its pejorative undertones have been countered since a long time. Ranade's sarcasm was effectively rebutted by Lala Lajpat Rai.[91] In any case, it still remains pertinent to ask why the term was so widely used, straddling both reformist and anti-reformist camps, when its apparently pejorative undertones could not have been concealed from public view. A closer look at this problem will in fact reveal multiple uses of this term, in keeping with changing preferences and social contexts. Bipin Chandra Pal, once so ill at ease with revivalist postures, performed a volte-face by calling Rammohan himself a revivalist, apparently under the influence of nationalist revisionism.[92] Logically, it is not the revivalist who could have been opposed to changes per se, for even judging by the commonplace definition of the term he, too, would have sought changes, albeit with reference to some past. The most dogged opposition to reform and change in fact came from those who sought to understand their religion and social practices not so much with reference to what it might have been in the past but the sum total of what it was in the present. The revivalist, one has to say, must be separated from the reactionary.

That 'Hindu revivalism' is an inept expression because Hinduism itself was never really dead is an argument that may be critiqued from two positions. First, even going by its literal meaning, revival would suggest not so much the return of the dead as the revitalization of that which was seen to be dying. In his rejoinder to Ranade's Amraoti address, Lajpat Rai had made the point that the entire revivalist movement was based on the belief that many rational and useful aspects of past Hindu civilizations, if brought back, would be potentially useful. He also took care to add that far from attempting to replicate the past in toto, revivalist programmes called for the rejection of its regressive elements, unfit for modern life.[93] In summary, Lajpat Rai's arguments also explain why, despite facing recurring internal crises, Hinduism has managed to survive and even grow.

It was, however, also Lajpat Rai's belief that operatively, what separated the revivalist from the reformer was a greater reliance on *Shastras*.[94] This, as we have earlier seen, can be a problematic definition. Bankim Chandra, usually taken to be a revivalist, was averse to their use.[95] On the other hand, it is also not clear if, as is sometimes suggested, appeals to an older authority *ipso facto* reduced the reformist possibilities within revivalist ideology.[96] This does not seem to be the case with the Arya Samaj which situated itself within an extremely old tradition, yet adopted a strongly reformist stance. This brings us to the critical point in the entire debate. It is not the appeal to the past that by itself could render all reformist agendas inoperative or ineffectual. What ultimately mattered was how this past was interpreted and put to use. Rammohan's revival of highly speculative Upanishadic thought might, at first glance, appear to be incompatible with his pragmatism. In these texts, however, the Raja also found adequate support for a rational, monotheistic religion, with which he wished to reacquaint the modern Hindu. Here, it would be relevant to cite the fact that in his 1818 tract (*Translation of a Conference between an Advocate for and an opponent of the practice of burning widows alive from the original Bangla*), Rammohan drew upon the Bhagavad Gita to argue against sati. That an appeal to the past would eliminate any scope for reform is an argument that seems to run counter to the typical revivalist thesis that present-day malpractices were in fact absent in the past. We may fault the revivalist for his excessive cultural nostalgia and perhaps even for a tendentious reading of history, but not some inexplicable tendency of defeating his own agenda.

Over time, polemical exchanges between reformers and revivalists tended to be less frequent and increasingly marginalized by advancing nationalism. A fair idea of such developments can be gathered from the essay by Vivekananda's foremost disciple, Sister Nivedita (1867–1911).[97] In recent years, new historical insights have also enabled us to look afresh at the whole problem, not so much any ideological differences between the two camps as common social and intellectual milieu in which they were born. We are now more aware than ever of the common class origins of reformers and revivalists and of how, under conditions peculiar to colonialism, rosy reformist moods could soon change into sombre revival. 'Both Brahmo Reformation and Hindu revival', as one scholar aptly reminds us, were 'reflexes of a middle class, first of hopes at its birth and then, moratorium at its adolescence'.[98] For colonized Indians it would be also important to remember that upholding the vitality of traditional culture was not cultural revivalism but cultural self-defence.[99]

D. Imperatives within Reform

The allegedly 'despicable' condition of Hindu women and the 'oppressive', 'inequitable' institution of caste were two issues that were most commonly written and spoken about in the nineteenth and twentieth centuries. Most authors or speakers would also attribute the social decadence of India to these. The subjects of caste and the status of women came up for heated debates and discussions in national forums like the National Social Conference, regional reform institutions, and, of course, between individuals. Philanthropic bodies threw incentives to educated young men by organizing essay competitions with lucrative rewards, in colleges and universities European and Anglo-Indian teachers in particular, egged on their students to bring about reform along these lines, beginning with their own families.

By the closing years of the nineteenth century, these issues also became historically joined to each other. Most radical, anti-brahmanical movements started agitations for the social upliftment of both low castes as well as women. In this, they were guided by the belief that these two groups had suffered the most at the hands of upper-caste males. Over time, the upper classes, too, felt the need to improve the condition of women and the common people, but, to a considerable extent, this followed from the logic of greater political enfranchisement. In the long run, however, elite efforts at mass mobilization produced somewhat paradoxical results. On the one hand, most nationalist thinkers and activists admitted that caste inequities and the social backwardness among women were positive hindrances in the path of Indian modernization and erecting a collective front against the British. On the other hand, such political exigencies also led men to deliberately gloss over the essentially social content of these problems and here, evidently, we see the surreptitious return of the older Telang thesis. Some scholars suspect that rather than more seriously address the twin problem of caste and the inequality between sexes, nationalism put these on hold. In his study of Bengali women in the latter half of the nineteenth century, the well-known Bangladeshi scholar, Ghulam Murshid, offers precisely the same argument.[100] In a more roundabout way, this also appears to have been suggested by some women themselves. In two extracts (reproduced in Part II), the gifted poetess and activist, Sarojini Naidu (1879–1949) not only contests the commonplace view that there was universal male consensus on educating the woman but positively accuses men of simply not doing enough on woman-related issues. That such allegations were made in 1906, closely following upon the partition of Bengal and the growth of political extremism would seem to generally uphold the Murshid thesis. Of course, not everybody agrees with this position. Partha Chatterjee, for instance, has argued (see his essay reproduced in Part II) that nationalism did indeed resolve the Woman Question, though strictly in its own terms.

Attacks on caste inequities assumed many forms and occurred in many regions of India. In Bengal some Brahmos of brahman descent publicly discarded their sacred thread; the Brahmo Samaj itself encouraged inter-caste marriages (albeit only within upper-bracket castes) and appointed non-brahmans as ministers. In Maharashtra, even orthodox leaders were prepared to somewhat relax rules regarding purity and pollution, and this region, as we know, also witnessed powerful low-caste movements such as the one begun by Phule and the Mahars. In UP, organizations like the Kayastha Conference tried to use the social power of caste itself to bring about certain positive changes such as the reduction of marriage expenses or marginally raising the marriageable age for boys and girls. In southern India, there was growing criticism of the discriminatory treatment of untouchables and lower castes. However, such intervention rarely produced critical public debates; the upper-caste leaders of Bombay and Poona, for example, do not seem to have promptly reacted to the challenge thrown by Phule. More importantly, these agitations did not try to situate the caste question within the broader perspective of the Hindu social and cultural system. The debate between Ambedkar and Gandhi (included in Part II of this book) assumes that much more importance since it does not try to examine caste in isolation but in relation to the larger and more critical question concerning the modernization of Hindu society.

The Woman Question

'It is somewhat singular', observed the well-known historian R.C. Majumdar in 1965, 'that almost all the important social reforms of the nineteenth century should centre around women.'[101] Many others after him have similarly noted the centrality of what is now commonly known as the Woman Question, and an enormous literature has since been built upon the subject by men and women speaking with different voices.

In the nineteenth century, the entire social reform campaign virtually began with Rammohan's efforts at abolishing *sati* and, thereafter, no single issue agitated the Hindu mind as much as that concerning man–woman relationship. To an extent, this came as a response to European critiques who persistently alleged the mistreatment of women in Indian society and showed Indian women in a rather poor light when compared to their European counterparts. Official historians of India like James Mill (1773–1836) were inclined to judge the respective strength and sophistication of cultures on the basis of the social position occupied by women. For Mill, therefore, the gross neglect of their womenfolk by Indians proved the intrinsic superiority of European cultures and served as further justification for the continuance of an 'enlightened' British rule in India.[102] In the early and mid-nineteenth centuries, young graduates in upper-class families apparently took to educating their wives and other female members in the family in the belief that this would indeed reduce the cultural or educational differences between the two sexes and contribute to harmonious domestic life. This, indeed, is the major argument in the presentation by the Derozian Mahesh Chandra Deb, more recently echoed by the historian Sumit Sarkar.[103] Presumably, the problem of marital incompatibility between an educated adult (the husband) and the usually illiterate, juvenile wife cut across ideological and social divides, and, over time, even conservatives were forced to acknowledge the greater need for female education. Some members of the Dharma Sabha, which opposed Rammohan over the abolition of *sati*, were quite enthusiastic about educating their women However, there might nevertheless be a distinction between the public adherents of change and those who, for a variety of reasons, preferred to remain passive supporters. In some cases, differences in age or status would themselves account for such differences in attitudes. In practical terms, there were bound to be different responses from say the young graduates of a college and educated but middle-aged individuals. The latter were not averse to change, but somehow lost the urge to push on with reform or to respond heroically when called upon to make personal sacrifices. While there was wide agreement on the need to educate the woman, most men in fact appear to have taken education as a means to reinforce traditional, patriarchal values. The nineteenth-century Hindi poet and dramatist, Bharatendu Harishchandra (1850–85), insisted that Hindu women be educated on 'national' lines which upheld allegiance to the family and respectful obedience of the husband.[104] In late-nineteenth-century Bengal, the 'reformed' woman who allegedly read romantic novels much to the detriment of her household work (archetypically, the *Brhamika,* female member of the Brahmo Samaj) became the subject of powerful satire, turning mediocre writers into extremely popular novelists.[105]

In some cases, regrettably, women themselves tacitly upheld patriarchal values and only further damaged their own cause. The early-nineteenth-century reformer from Bombay, Bhau Daji, drew public attention to the complicity of women themselves in perpetuating the practice of female infanticide.[106] Pandita Ramabai who rendered great service to the social emancipation of women, was also the author of *Stri Dharma Niti* (1882), which instructed wives to readily conform to their husband's wishes and to please them through hard work.[107a] Many women, as one can reasonably assume, were themselves uncomfortable with the idea of relinquishing their traditional roles as mothers, sisters, or wives. Sarojini Naidu herself dwells at length on the duties before the (Hindu) sati,—'the prompt and willing renunciation of (the woman's) most dear and pressing desires.' Bonding between women, she notes elsewhere, was quite easily effected, since they all shared 'the common divine equality of motherhood.'[107b] For much of the nineteenth century, there were indeed few women who stepped out to perform public work. Women delegates to the Social Conference were first noticed at Lahore in 1893 and there, predictably, they were vastly outnumbered by men.[108] Such facts push us to the conclusion that on the whole, women lacked the power or autonomy to fashion their lives the way they liked and operated within the traditional boundaries of marriage and domesticity.

To an extent, educated Hindu men liked the idea of educated women advocating their own cause. This seemed to fit in with claims repeatedly made at the time, that women in pre-Muslim India enjoyed the benefits of education and public freedom. Further, such initiatives when taken by women themselves, could be seen to reflect man's noble intentions for the woman and used to silence European critics like Mill. Thus, the *Kesari* of 1 August 1882 expressed happiness at the fact that a highly accomplished lady like Pandita Ramabai was speaking and writing on woman-related issues—a work hitherto carried out only by men.[109] In the 1890s, Swami Vivekananda cautioned his followers against excessive meddling with woman's issues.[110] It is tempting to conclude from this that men were beginning to grant the woman, even if grudgingly, autonomous space and agency. In hindsight, however, this does not appear to have been the intention. Only a week after it applauded the efforts of Ramabai (8 August 1882), the *Kesari* categorically denied the woman's right to intervene in the work of reform, which, as it wished to remind its readers, was the man's prerogative.[111] Similarly, Vivekananda's warning to men to keep their hands off woman related issues may not so much mean allowing the woman to make the critical choices as the tendency to let matters drift until such time when she herself was fully capable of working out her own emancipation. This, as one can see, comes far too close to the gradualist argument.

In the paper by Mahesh Chandra Deb, we also find an early example of the crusader's zeal, trying to shake off old habits and create new impulses. On the whole, Deb's arguments seems to be inspired by liberal-rational notions about a more equitable man–woman relationship being a practical basis of social progress. There are two significant features in this presentation that may be said to be also generally true of modern Hindu discourse on women. First, Deb nowhere suggests alternative paths to reform outside that which must appear to men as the most appropriate. It is male-sponsored and male-determined reform, and from a radical feminist position, might even appear quite patronizing. Second, Deb seems to address not so much the problems of the woman as of the wife. The uppermost consideration in his mind is how the Hindu wife might be groomed to suitably contribute to the new intellectual and cultural demands placed upon the domestic economy of the Hindus. By comparison, there is very little on the several inequities that the woman faces at several stages in her life.[112]

Significantly, this appears to be more or less the framework even in the 1880s. Malabari's celebrated *Notes on Infant Marriage and Enforced Widowhood* (1884) also concerns the woman in the capacity of wife. There is no talk of the woman's social or sexual freedom but of how men might be made more kindly and responsible in their treatment of their women. Nonetheless, Malabari differed from the likes of Deb and Vivekananda in two important respects. For one, he did not see marital problems purely from the point of view of intellectual compatibility but as also vitally connected with the physical and moral well-being of the wife and woman. Second, he had the good sense to realize that female education by itself was not going to solve the problem of the sexual exploitation of women and mitigate in any way the sordid tales of brutalized child-wives. It was imperative for men to act and to act decisively in favour of supporting legal deterrents. The proposals of 1884 tried to employ both moral browbeating and officially-sponsored incentives to get men to refuse early betrothals. Above all, they assumed that rather than wait for matters to change of their own volition, a positive intervention by the state and other reformist agencies was a prerequisite for any success in reforming the condition of the female.[113]

Predictably, the proposals of 1884 found more opponents than supporters. But one of its supporters, Jotirao Phule, came up with more radical demands on behalf of women than had Malabari himself. Phule's replies were also written in far more polemical language and it is indeed somewhat surprising that the opponents of Malabari completely ignored him.[114] A more reasoned critique of the 1884 proposals appears in a letter (dated 16 September 1884 and appended in Part II of this book) from Telang to Malabari. Telang, unlike Rao Saheb Mandlik, did not take any exception to the fact that the author of the proposals was a Parsi and his critique more truthfully mirrors the reaction of the average middle-class Hindu on the subject. For one, Telang was quite right in identifying the Hindu family, and neither *Shastra* nor caste, as the most effective obstacle to meaningful changes in social lifestyles or domestic life between couples. Telang had also reason to believe that Malabari's intentions were noble, but the methods themselves impracticable and unjust. If a young man was to be denied a government employment or an educational stipend simply because he was married, this amounted to sparing the actual offender (parents or family) and punishing the innocent.

Another question to be critically debated in the third quarter of the nineteenth century concerned conjugality and man–woman relationships in day-to-day life. This touched on sensitive matters like the social and sexual fidelity of wife or the husband's conjugal rights over his wife. Such questions, we may recall, had surfaced during the Rukmabai case (1886) and was decided, much to the disappointment of some, in the husband's favour. Other issues, vitally related to the conjugal life of the Hindu, were also agitated from time to time. A long-standing issue of this kind was '*satitwa*' (female chastity). Rammohan's campaign for the abolition of *sati* had itself glorified ascetic denial of the self and chaste widowhood. Men of a reformist disposition themselves took a serious view of sexual promiscuity developing in women and among widows in particular. Chandicharan Sen, a Brahmo *munsef* serving at Krishnanagar (West Bengal), once remarked that in his opinion, 99 per cent of all Hindu widows were unchaste! To this, Bankim Chandra reacted with characteristic sarcasm.[115] *Satitwa* was sometimes also used to define and demarcate the Hindu woman as against her self-willed 'libertine' European counterpart. It was a virtue that more than compensated for her alleged lack of formal education or cultural finesse.[116] By the 1880s, this had grown into a larger discourse on the needs underlying Hindu marriages. It is worth noting that this discourse was also drawn into the debate over determining a proper age of marriage, but its main focus was on underscoring the social and spiritual grooming of the wife in the hands of the husband for which, understandably, a greater difference of age between married partners was highly desirable. At the time Malabari was trying to persuade men to positively change their attitude towards marriage and expectations thereof, a conservative Bengali essayist by the name of Chandranath Basu (1844–1910) wrote copiously on the essentially 'spiritual' nature of Hindu marriages.[117] The rebuttal of Basu's views appear in a lecture delivered in 1887 by Rabindranath Tagore (1861–1941). Tagore rejected the view that Hindu marriages were solemnized only in order to fulfil certain spiritual needs or that they relied exclusively on the spiritual bonding between married partners. He also refused to accept the argument, much to the consternation of the orthodox, that the responsibilities for the smooth running of conjugal life devolved primarily upon the wife. However, there was also a surprisingly conservative side to Tagore's own presentation. For Tagore, marriage was essentially a social institution and fulfilled the needs of men and women in society. At the same time, he does not appear to judge them by the same social yardstick. Thus, second marriages among men were more justifiable than second marriages among women, for, allegedly, the latter was socially more disruptive, involving a transference of name, lineage, loyalties, and property.[118]

Such conservatism, besides being concealed within reformist attitudes, sometimes also resulted from certain misguided cultural perceptions. It has been rarely argued for instance, as Pandit Bishan Narain does (in the second of the two passages by him excerpted in Part II) that Hindu prejudices against European women were born of sheer prejudice and ignorance. Rather than conform to the popular belief that Hindu women were more chaste when compared to the English, Dar argues that the ideals of English womanhood as reflected in the works of Scott or Tennyson, were morally superior to those evident in Urdu lyrics or popular Indian fiction.

Various theories have been put forward to explain this growing conservatism and the palpable weakening of the reforming zeal. Critics like Sumit Sarkar, whom we have cited above, have implicitly questioned the very premise on which this question is based, for to explain why women-related issues failed to go beyond a point one would have to assume that under conditions peculiar to colonialism this point could have been effectively transgressed. In a significant critique of the position adopted by Murshid, Partha Chatterjee has argued that rather than abandon the Woman Question altogether, Hindu Nationalism 'resolved' it in terms of 'preferred goals'. This he explains, was performed through the creation of a synthetic dichotomy between the public and the private, outward activity, and inner repose, material and spiritual. The Woman Question, Chatterjee tells us, was relegated to an area where the colonized and not the colonizer was sovereign and supreme. It was a question on which Indians simply refused to negotiate.[119]

Interesting as this thesis appears, it still leaves us puzzling over certain questions. Prima facie, Chatterjee's arguments would tend to be supported by the trajectories that the conservative Hindu rhetoric of the 1880s or 1890s took, but what he calls 'resolution' may well be an euphemism for regression. Methodologically at least, one would have to distinguish a tendentious theory born of political resistance from a deep-rooted pathological fear of change, which may not have been political even at the edges. The state, moreover, continued to be implicated in reformist intervention concerning the woman, even if reluctantly and sometimes against its will. In his autobiography Jawaharlal Nehru noted how the British government as well as the Congress were reluctant to popularize the Sarada Act (1929), aiming to legally prohibit premature marriages among Hindus. More importantly, however, he attributed the reluctance on the part of the Congress to the 'disease of nationalism', apprehending that matters would not really change even after the transfer of power to Indians.[120]

In any case, the 'resolution' of the Woman Question does not seem to have considered how women themselves might have wanted this resolved. This is a criticism that would equally apply to Ghulam Murshid, who examines not the modernization of women per se, but how, in the perception of men, women may be suitably modernized.

Caste and the Social Reconstruction of India

The fascinating quality about Ambedkar's treatment of the Caste question in his *Annihilation of Caste* is the way he examines it in relation to many other issues of social significance. It also reveals a certain balance and objectivity in its critique of the various ideological positions on the question. Thus, Ambedkar seems to have been equally unhappy with those who had neglected social questions in favour of the political, as also with the crude determinism within contemporary socialism, which took man to be a creature guided solely by economic compulsions. The first of these positions he found self-defeatist and short-sighted, the second grossly unfamiliar with Indian conditions. The former erred in believing that political freedom would *ipso facto* prepare men better for the reorganization of society, the latter nurtured the false belief that economic reform alone could bring about social transformation. The most effective method of handling social questions in India, he argued, was to get to know the ideological wells from which they sprang, and here Ambedkar underlined the need to reform Hinduism before attempting to reform Hindu society. For Ambedkar, the institution of caste clearly drew its strength and legitimacy from the traditional brahmanism and evidently, this drew him closer to the view of Periyar than with those of Vivekananda or Gandhi. Nevertheless, his views on the place of religion in Indian culture are not as radical as those of Periyar. Whereas Periyar would happily abolish religion from society,[121] Ambedkar's intentions were really to give Hinduism a new doctrinal basis and to establish the dynamic principle of change rather than fixed practices or dogma. Somewhat like Rammohan, Ambedkar also acknowledged the functional uses of religion. In his *Annihilation of Caste,* he draws upon the British conservative spokesperson, Edmund Burke, to underline the value of religion to a stable social order. Prima facie it would appear as though some of his recommendations, such as the one advocating the use of a common scripture for all Hindus, might have been quite acceptable to the upper-caste elite. In truth, however, this was quite unlikely, for even when supporting a common scripture, Ambedkar's critical position vis-à-vis Hinduism would not have entertained the choice of some traditional brahmanical text. On the other hand, his suggestion that every Hindu should be considered eligible for the office of the priest—something which has a superficial resemblance to Luther's doctrine of the priesthood of all believers—no doubt sent down shock-waves as far as the orthodox were concerned.[122]

Gandhi took Ambedkar's indictment of *savarna* Hindus (Hindus situated within the traditional four-fold *varna* system) quite seriously. His quarrel with Ambedkar was not so much over whether or not Hinduism was in need of reform as over the question of representative texts in Hinduism. Gandhi's counter-thesis employed two major arguments. First, it alleged that Ambedkar had based his entire critique of Hinduism on a wrong choice of texts (the *Smritis*), which were traditionally subordinated to the *Shruti.* From this Gandhi went on to argue that a people and their culture could not be judged by their worst specimens. In hindsight, however, one has to say that the Mahatma was defeated by his own logic. Gandhi was indeed respectful of *Shruti* (the *Vedas* or *Upanishads*), but the one text that he valued the most and on which he also chose to personally comment, the *Bhagavadgita,* was itself traditionally deemed to be a *Smriti.* This is yet another instance, as one can see, of dispute and disagreement on the vexed question of determining an acceptable textual base for Hinduism. It would also be important to remember that notwithstanding Ambedkar's criticism, Gandhi continued to uphold the *varna* structure as the basis of Hindu social organization even though he committed his life to the social emancipation of untouchables, and depressed castes and communities.[123]

E. Debates in History, Debates on History: Situating 'Renaissance', 'Reform' and Social Change in Modern India

[i]

Before we conclude it might be useful to relate explanatory theories to past behaviour, actions, and events—to join, as it were, historiography to history. The use of historiography offers us perspectives, which, for a variety of reasons, could not emerge during the period under study. After all, no nineteenth-century reformer seems to have asked himself if meaningful social reform or change was at all possible under conditions of colonial rule. Similarly, warring parties did not see as clearly as we do now that certain assumptions born of those conditions created false dichotomies of 'tradition' and 'modernity', 'liberal' and 'conservative', 'reform' and 'revival'. It is only in hindsight and using sophisticated tools of analysis evolved in recent years that we can better examine whether the impact of the West indeed created a mental revolution in modern India. At the same time, we must also be prepared to guard against the uncritical use of historiography, for these too can be swayed by ideological assumptions. Many a scholar situated on Left-Progressive historiography has conflated the revivalist with the reactionary and, somewhat naively, assumed that a rational-pragmatic view of religion dismantled religion itself and established the secularist paradigm. Theories of social change, therefore, have to be scrutinized in the light of historical experiences. In the pages to follow I have attempted to recount the historical and conceptual content of reform in the light of past and present theories.

In nineteenth-century India, reform came to be accepted as an idiom of improvement, the components of which were believed to be both unique and foreseeable. The correlation between reform and human progress was well established by the European Enlightenment of the eighteenth century and since that time has constituted the paradigm of modernity. Here, it is important not to conflate a positive outlook on the future with a positivist one. The Enlightenment had coincided with a great outward movement of the European people. There were important technological breakthroughs, economic recovery and expansion, the birth of new social classes, and new mental attitudes. Within the next hundred years or so this had grown into forms of social and cultural arrogance. Nineteenth-century Europeans not only claimed to understand and mould phenomena the way they liked, but also took this to be a kind of a certitude. The Enlightenment had carried within itself a certain universality and an intellectual curiosity towards non-European cultures. However, these were progressively overshadowed by tendentious theories about European moral and cultural superiority. Post Enlightenment Culture fast fell into the habit of categorizing peoples and cultures in a hierarchical arrangement. Eighteenth-century constructs of the 'Orient' and the 'Occident' could be useful up to a point, but these were now used as self-contained, self-explanatory categories. Thus, as against the allegedly mystical, indeterminate, sensual, and sentimental character of the Orient, the Occident represented a world-view that was 'clear, precise, instrumental, scientific, effective and true'.[124] From this the European modernist concluded that Oriental societies were not only inferior to the Occidental, but stood to gain from any historical encounter between the two.

In British India such ideas were firmly established by virtue of the victory of the so-called Anglicist school over the Orientalist. The latter had displayed a genuine sense of wonder and admiration at the more lasting achievements of Indian civilization—its religions, classical languages and literature, art, architecture, and other cultural artefacts. The Orientalist, though also influenced by certain European cultural assumptions of the time, was rarely condescending about India. On the other hand, after the spread of English-medium schools and colleges, and the opening up of India to Christian missionary activity, an empathy and appreciation for indigenous culture was increasingly replaced by impatient criticism. Colonial officials, merchants and missionaries now laid the claim that European modernism and the religious and ethical principles of Christianity (also shown to be associated exclusively with Western civilization) could be used to stir up an immobilized Orient and redeem the souls of the heathen. Historians of India like James Mill argued that the British had rescued the country from a state of utter despondency and anarchy, and that there was something providential about these developments. Ironically enough, such perceptions were shared by many Indians at the time. Until recently Indian historiography itself lay deeply anchored in such notions of historical change.

The critique of what one historian calls the 'impact-response schema'[125] constitutes an important contribution of the new historiography. The 'impact-response schema' understood social and religious reform as a series of reflexes produced by the unique intellectual challenges posed by the West. Implicitly, this assumes two things. In the first place it assumes that a rational-utilitarian critique of indigenous society and religion was either not possible or actually absent in premodern India. Second, it assumes that the historical experiences of Europe—which simultaneously witnessed a literary and philosophical Renaissance, the material transformation of the economy, and polity and the birth of new social classes —could be replicated in colonial India. Predictably, such assumptions surface very clearly in the writings of European officials and missionaries. J.N. Farquhar, for instance, found the very category of reform to have been born in the intellectual stimulus provided by the West.[126] However, such sentiments had been earlier expressed by Indian themselves. Educated Hindus of the nineteenth century believed that they were witnessing a Western-style Renaissance and actually tried to draw historical parallelisms between their own experiences and those of the Europeans. Thus, the *Hindu Patriot,* a Calcutta-based daily, compared the activities of the Brahmo Samaj to the European Reformation.[127] Closer to our time, R.C. Majumdar has reminded us how only forty years of English education 'had brought about greater changes in fellow-Bengalis than had been possible in the preceding thousand years'.[128] It is indeed quite probable that to an extent, the Anglo-American thesis about reform being entirely Western in inspiration or British benevolence reproducing a Western-type Renaissance in India drew support from admissions made by Indians themselves. Farquhar's claims about Hindu reform being modelled upon the Christian may well have found some vindication in

Brahmo Protap Chandra Mozumdar's (1840–1905)observation that the Brahmo Samaj itself was the 'legitimate offspring of the wedlock of Christianity with the faith of Hindu Aryans'.[129] Chandravarkar likewise, anticipates some of Farquhar's arguments about how Christian missionaries created some sort of a literary efflorescence in India through the active promotion of Indian vernaculars.[130]

However, if educated Hindus of the nineteenth century accepted the 'impact-response schema', they also produced, over time, some of its sharpest critics. Keshab Chandra Sen, otherwise notorious for his loyalism to the British government, consistently disapproved of Western lifestyle or work methods. More importantly, his dissatisfaction with such matters seem to have been as strongly expressed during his visit to England as back in India.[131] By the late nineteenth century, the blighting of liberal hopes and growing bureaucratic opposition to political reform not only made Indians more wary of revealing their intellectual allegiance to the West, but also fall back on alternative sources of inspiration. Tradition thus became a new cultural site for agendas of change. The term 'Renaissance', too, was taken out of conventional historiography and given a new meaning. D.S. Sarma, a prolific writer on Hindu religion and culture, uses the term very differently when he: (*a*) sees the nineteenth-century Renaissance as nothing unique but only one in a series of successive developments in Indian history and (*b*) associates it not with early figures like Rammohan, as is usually done, but the late-nineteenth-century Hindu mystic, Sri Ramakrishna, who never went to a modern school or college.[132] Sarma's very distinctive use of the term 'Renaissance', as aptly pointed out by one scholar was meant to counter Farquhar's category of 'reform', through which this evangelist had tried to convey, in a superior way, the uniqueness of India's intellectual meeting with the West.[133]

A more decisive break with conventional historiography and with Renaissance analogues occurred in the 1970s when it could be established that understanding Indian experiences in the light of the European was based on a false reading of history that confused modernization with Westernization. This new historiography has drawn our attention to the colonial environment in which our reform movements were born and which raised hopes about bourgeois modernity without materially creating it, denied effective agency to the Hindu intelligentsia, and frustrated the heroic efforts of individual crusaders like Vidyasagar, who in his last days turned into a misanthrope.[134] It is also clear that the educated Hindus were quite selective in their acceptance of Western ideas, and that, in any case, Western Christian values, as disseminated in India were not always radicalizing in their intentions. Rev. Alexander Duff, a well-known missionary figure of the early nineteenth century, warned his Indian convert Krishna Mohan Banerjea of the 'terrible issues of the French Illumination'.[135] More recently, Heimsath had drawn our attention to the ambivalent uses of European thinkers like Herbert Spencer who could be appropriated by reformers and conservatives alike.[136] On the whole, it is only fair to say that, important as European rationalism was, it was by no means an unique or the only critical tool known to the modern Hindu. In any case, changes in the social and religious life of the Hindus were occurring under its own impulse. The socio-cultural regeneration of modern India, as the historian K.N. Panikkar puts it, 'was occasioned by the British presence, not created by it'.[137]

Certain tangential but interesting arguments have also come to light in the course of this debate. Not everybody felt that the 'false consciousness' theory could satisfactorily explain the complex maze of social responses and inconsistent social behaviour. Rajat K. Ray, to cite an important exception, did not think that Rammohan's outward conformity to caste or the widow marriage campaign favouring only child-widows had anything to do with the colonial nature of our state and society.[138] Colonialism by itself may not also explain why men made strange choices between otherwise related issues. Thus Peary Chand Mitra, a member of Young Bengal, who ran a woman's journal, *Masik Patrika,* wrote tracts supporting female education and opposed premature marriages, would not advocate the marriage of Hindu widows.[139] Even those individuals and institutions whom one might fancy rushing into reform sometimes made strange exceptions. The missionary journal, *Friend of India,* supported Vidyasagar's widow marriage campaign but opposed him on the issue of putting an end to polygamous marriages.[140]

[ii]

Within the world of social and religious reform, there has been persistent controversy on the use of broad identity labels such as 'reformer', 'revivalist', 'modernist', 'traditionalist', etc. To an extent, their use is unavoidable, notwithstanding inner nuances of meaning as also their somewhat changing definitions over time. Thus, the term 'reform' has always implied a change from the *status quo,* even as people sharply differed over the right pace at which this was to be conducted, or over the methods or strategies used. 'Revival' likewise, always tried to adapt modern conditions to an idyllic past, though just what that past was remained a matter of conjecture and debate.

However, conceptual problems are bound to arise when one attempts to fit complex historical changes into neat schematic packages. For the purpose of examining this problem more closely, I have chosen two recent and representative texts, namely, Kenneth W. Jones' *Socio Religious Reform: Movements in British India* (1994) and Bhikhu Parekh's *Colonialism, Tradition and Reform: An Analysis of Gandhi's Political Discourse* (1999). Jones' typologies of 'transitional' and 'acculturative' reform movements are insightful, but at times also a source of confusion. A contemporary critic sums up the problems in the following words:

> It is far from easy, however, to see quite how binding the distinction between the transitional and acculturative can be. Jones saw it in terms of timing. The transitional drew on an Indian heritage and was not a response to a colonial presence...Both transitional and acculturative are seen as drawing on the same tradition of protest and both are movements of return. Jones hedges his bets. 'There was no clear point of beginning or end,' he accepts, 'of the transitional movements of British India.' In many ways the acculturative were in no way new or modern, nor were they the creation of interaction with Christianity and Western civilization....The paradigms begin to look merely suggestive and unconvincingly defining.[141]

Problems of this nature, one imagines, are also bound to arise in the light of new information. The Swaminarayan cult of western India, which Jones labels as 'transitional', has now been shown to have borrowed organizational methods from Christian missionaries which would require rephrasing 'transitional' in respect of colonial society.[142]

Bhikhu Parekh reduces the omnibus, unproblematized categories of 'tradition', 'modernity', etc. into a more nuanced, four-fold classification of 'modernism', 'critical modernism', 'traditionalism', and 'critical traditionalism'. Modernism in this scheme represents the agenda of radical reconstruction and its exemplars are the Derozians, M.N. Roy (1887–1954), the early Dadabhai Naoroji (1825–1917), and the Nehrus, Motilal (1861–1931) and Jawaharlal. Critical modernism, by comparison, is said to be more inward looking, aiming to reorient cultures rather than reconstruct, and attempting in the long run a constructive synthesis of the West and India. Typical representatives of this trend are Rammohan Roy, G.K. Gokhale (1866–1915), and Keshab Chandra Sen. The schematic opposite of modernism is traditionalism, which is identified with an over-zealous and irrational defence of social malpractices like *sati*, infanticide, and child marriages. The major exponents of this position are the educationist Bhudeb Mukhopadhyay, the Hindu missionaries, Krishna Prosonno Sen (1849–1902) and Pandit Sasadhar Tarkachudamani (1851–1928), and the conservative Bengali daily, the *Bangabasi*. As an attitude, traditionalism is also believed to have been unpopular. Finally, there is critical traditionalism that represented a selective appropriation of European ideas and values, believed that each society was an autonomous, self-referential unit (thereby implicitly rejecting an universal criteria of judgment), and claimed that Indian civilization was primarily the work of Hindus. Included in this category are men like Bankim Chandra, Swami Vivekananda, Bipin Chandra Pal, and the revolutionary-turned-mystic, Sri Aurobindo.[143]

Parekh, of course, is nowhere rigid with his categories. They are, for him, categories of 'convenience' and each of them is said to refer not so much to the answers given by the Hindu leaders as *directions* (emphasis his) in which they looked for them.[144] All the same, this still leaves certain gaps in our understanding. The term 'critical', for example, does not tell us enough about the specific mode of questioning or its specific philosophical underpinnings. In the light of precisely which arguments and using which hermeneutical skills is tradition being critiqued? An interesting side to this problem is revealed by what Rammohan had once to say of a work by one of his opponents. It was Rammohan's feeling that in this particular case the methodological and interpretative error that the other party had committed was not authenticating his arguments with the aid of specific references and sources.[145] Here, the Raja was clearly hinting at text torturing and interpolation, and significantly enough, he considered 'truth' and not tradition per se to be the subject of debate and disputation. It would appear, therefore, that the mode of questioning was intimately connected with the social effectiveness of criticism. Would modern tools of analysis be effective or meaningful if social change was to be contingent on the approval of the *pandit* and the *shastri*? On the other hand, can typically traditional methods of exegesis be compatible with the increasing use of printed texts and the emergence of lay experts? Critical traditionalism and critical modernism may indeed be confused with one another, as Parekh admits,[146] but this is more likely to occur when the kind of questions asked within each are also comparable or similar.

Critical modernism, Parekh tells us, saw the state standing over and above society, and hence capable of pursuing collective and national goals.[147] This would explain Rammohan's or Keshab's actively soliciting government intervention in social matters. In a less conspicuous way, however, this also appears to be the position of Vivekananda and Bipin Chandra Pal, whom Parekh labels as critical traditionalist. On the whole, it is reasonable to conjecture that whether a Hindu thinker sought social legislation was not only related to specific issues but quite narrowly defined targets. Between 1868 and 1872, Keshab Chandra asked for government intervention in framing new marriage laws for Brahmos and a few other groups. But through this he proposed to bring about not a significant transformation in man–woman relationships, but the scrupulous rejection of idolatrous practices in respect of reformed marriages. Besides, people did not consistently adhere to one position on this question. Vidyasagar, who actively sought state intervention in respect of widow marriages, opposed it over the age-of-consent question.

Parekh's classification, it would appear, would have to be qualified at places with the aid of historical empiricism. Religious universalism, or an interest in the comparative study of religions, contrary to his suggestion, can be found as much in critical traditionalists as in the modernists. The ideas of a Universal religion and a positive appreciation of diverse religious cultures grew especially strong after the Western tours of Vivekananda, and at least at one place, the Swami even shows an inclination to syncretize cultures, as when he talks of a 'Vedantic brain' grafted atop an 'Islamic body'.[148] The difference between the two categories of critical traditionalist and modernist would not be so much of intentions as of methods. Rammohan knew the Muslim through his knowledge of Islam; Vivekananda, by comparison, got to know Islam through the Muslim. Finally, the categories of 'modernist' and 'traditionalist', as already demonstrated at several places, cannot be accepted without certain reservations. The researches of the historian Sumit Sarkar have revealed how the 'radicalism' of Young Bengal has to be qualified in some respects. One also fails to see how traditionalism could be an 'isolated', 'unpopular' phenomenon when men like Krishna Prosonno Sen and Pandit Sasadhar were the most popular Bengali orators of their time and how the *Bangabasi* sold about 20,000 copies a week.[149]

A rational and humanist critique of traditional society and religion was by no means unknown in premodern India. In 1802 Joshuah Marshman of the Serampore Mission reached the village of Chandooreah (district Hoogly?) where he reportedly met one Sitaram Das who had rejected Hindu idolatrous practices and commanded a following of 20,000 followers. Another contemporary observer, the Rev. Claudius Buchanan, mentioned a group of sceptics he met at Jessore (now in Bangladesh). Traditional paternalism coexisting with a palpable desire to reform can be seen in the life and work of the brahman reformer from Maharashtra, Vishnubawa Brahmachari (1825–71).[150] However, this self-criticism could not be related to a meaningful social transformation. It was precisely for this reason that traditional and indigenous ways of understanding the self and the larger society failed to produce a crisis in self-identity. Modern European rationalism by comparison proved to be a far greater challenge in this respect because in this case new patterns of thought were also accompanied by new structures of social organization. Traditional Hindu social theory, to cite an apt example, never produced a comparable emphasis on individuation and the autonomy of the private will.

Problems were further aggravated in modern India because whereas Western social theories considerably eroded older world-views, it did not provide other paradigms through which it might be possible to bestow meaning upon everyday human experiences. Beyond a point, modern rationalism, which had no real roots in the indigenist tradition, appeared unable to explain the growing fragility of the human condition. Utilitarianism was quite intolerant of tradition as 'Natural Religion' was of authoritative scripture or revelation. Above all, the indigenous intelligentsia lacked the social agency and political power to itself carry out modernization of tradition. This had the effect of counterposing tradition and modernity as mutually exclusive and incompatible categories. In the historical experience of modern Hindus, both reform and revival aimed at finding footholds in a rapidly changing world. They were, above all, the attempted seizure of initiatives.

Notes

1. B.C. Pal, 'The Present Social Reaction: What Does it Mean?'. Lecture at the Bethune Society, Calcutta, 5 December 1889. Excerpts from this lecture are reproduced in Part II.
2. *Speeches and Writings of Sir Narayan G. Chandravarkar* (L.V. Kaikini, ed.), Girgaon-Bombay, 1911, p. 8.
3. V.N. Mandlik in *Native Opinion*, 10 November 1867. Cited in Varsha S. Shirgaonkar, *Social Reform in Maharashtra and V.N. Mandlik*, New Delhi, 1989, p. 53.)
4. Ibid., p. 62.
5. For details see C.H. Heimsath, *Indian Nationalism and Hindu Social Reform*, New Jersey, 1964, pp. 22, 222; Shirgaonkar, *op. cit.*, pp. 53; Sivanath Sastri, *History of the Brahmo Samaj* (2 vols), Calcutta, 1974, pp. 173–81.
6. See excerpts from two public lectures by Vivekananda reproduced in Part II.
7. See excerpts from E.V. Ramasami Periyar's *Arivin Ellai* reproduced in Part II.
8. John and Karen Leonard, 'Viresalingam and the Ideology of Social Change in Andhra' in Kenneth W. Jones (ed.), *Religious Controversies in British India: Dialogues in South Asian Languages*, Albany, 1992, pp. 151–76.
9. See Appendix I to Goutam Chattopadhyay (ed.), *Awakening in Bengal in Early Nineteenth Century: Selected Documents*, Calcutta, 1965.
10. John and Karen Leonard, *op. cit.* The brahmanical *yuga* theory sees a cyclical movement of time. Of the four *yuga*s that follow each other in succession, *Kaliyuga* (said to have begun with the close of the Mahabharata war) is said to represent the most degenerate state of human existence. The early nineteenth-century Maharastrian reformer, Vishnubawa Brahmachari (1825–71), is said to have similarly diagnosed the ills of his society. His reference, interestingly, was to the preponderance of *mleccha* (denoting Western) opinion in *Kaliyuga*. See Frank F. Conlon, 'Hindu Revival and Indian Womanhood: The Image and Status of Women in the Writings of Vishnubawa Brahmachari', *South Asia*, 17(2), 1994, p. 47.
11. Heimsath, *op. cit.*, p. 27.
12. Ibid., 25, 7.
13. Cited in *Rammohan Rachanavali* (The Collected Works of Rammohan Roy) (Ajit Kumar Ghosh, ed.), Calcutta, 1973, p. 462.
14. As for example K.N. Panikkar, 'Socio-religious Reform Movements and National Awakening', in Bipin Chandra et al, *India's Struggle for*

Independence, Delhi, 1993, p. 82. This appears to be a somewhat toned down version of Panikkar's claim that Rammohan essentially saw religion as a mechanism through which to 'preserve existing property relations and to regulate social intercourse'. K.N. Panikkar, *Culture and Consciousness in Modern India: A Historical Perspective*, New Delhi, 1990, p. 7.

15. Cited in *Rammohan Rachanavali, op. cit.*, p. 435.
16. M.G. Ranade, 'The Cause of Excitement of Poona' (Speech before the Ninth Social Conference), reproduced in *Miscellaneous Writings of the Late Hon'ble Mr Justice M.G. Ranade*, New Delhi, 1992, p. 159.
17. *Rammohan Rachanavali, op. cit.*, p. 462.
18. Keshab Chandra Sen, 'Religious and Social Reformation' (1868) reproduced in Prem Sundar Basu (comp.), *Life and Work of Brahamananda Keshab*, Calcutta, 1940, p. 146; ibid., 'Lecture before the Bhavanipore Brahma Samaj' (1863), excerpts reproduced in Part II.
19. *Writings and Speeches of Dr Bahu Daji* (T.G. Mainkar, ed.), Bombay, 1974, pp. 255, 263.
20. See excerpts from the lecture reproduced in Part II.
21. See excerpts from Ambedkar's *Annihilation of Caste* reproduced in Part II.
22. Swami Vivekananda, *Notes of Class Talks and Lectures: The Complete Works of Swami Vivekananda* (Mayavati Memorial Edition, vol. 6), Mayavati, 1972, p. 144.
23. Heimsath, *op. cit.*, p. 4.
24. Chiranjiva Bhardwaja, *Light of Truth or an English Translation of the Satyarth Prakash: The Well Known Work of Swami Dayanand Saraswati*, Allahabad, 1927, p. 442.
25. See excerpts from his *Letters on Hinduism* reproduced in Part II.
26. See excerpts from Krishna Mohan Banerjea's lecture reproduced in Part II.
27. Chaturvedi Badrinath, 'Dissent, Protest and Reform: The Historical Context', in S.C. Malik (ed.), *Dissent, Protest and Reform in Indian Civilization*, Shimla, 1977, p. 45.
28. Heimsath, *op. cit.*, p. 34.
29. See the excerpts from Bankim's *Letters on Hinduism* reproduced in Part II.
30. For a very useful analysis, see Chaturvedi Badrinath, *Dharma, India and the World Order: Twenty One Essays*, Edinburgh, 1993, pp. 188–95.
31. A typical example of this occurs in the following statement from the Bengali reformer, Manmohan Ghosh: 'If the people of India could be made to feel that the English sympathized with them in the struggle

for social reform, the work will, I believe, be carried out much more speedily.'

'The Late Mr Manmohan Ghosh on Social Progress in Bengal during the Last Thirty Years', Reproduced in C.Y. Chintamani (ed.), *Indian Social Reform*, Part III, Madras, 1901, pp. 237–8.

32. M.G. Ranade, R.G. Bhandarkar, and K.T. Telang served on the advisory board of Sharada Sadan, the widows' home started by Ramabai. *Pandita Ramabai through Her Own Words: Selected Works* (Meera Kosambi, ed., comp.), Delhi, 2000, p. 11.
33. S.N. Mukherji, *Calcutta: Myth and History*, Calcutta, 1977.
34. See excerpts from N.G. Chandravarkar's 'The Mandlik School and Reform from Within', reproduced in Part II.
35. Y.M. Pathan, 'Mahatma Jotirao Phule and Satyasodhak Samaj', Malik, *op. cit.*, p. 241.
36. See excerpts from the *India Gazette*, cited by the *Calcutta Monthly Journal* reproduced in Part II.
37. Keshab Chandra Sen, 'An Appeal to Young India', reproduced in Basu, *op. cit.*, p. 83
38. For an useful account of Butler's influences on nineteenth-century Maharashtra, see Ellen E. McDonald, 'English Education and Social Reform in Nineteenth Century Maharashtra: A Case Study in the Transmission of a Cultural Ideal', *Journal of Asiatic Society*, 25 (November), 1965, pp. 463–8.
39. For a critical study of Bhudev's social theory, see Sudipto Kaviraj, 'The Reversal of Orientalism: Bhudev Mukhopadhyay and the Project of Indigenist Social Theory', in Vasudha Dalmia and H. von Stietencron, *Representing Hinduism: The Construction of Religious Tradition and National Identity*, New Delhi, 1995.
40. Cited in Heimsath, *op. cit.*, p. 226.
41. Ibid., p. 224, footnote 54.
42. See excerpts from Telang's speech reproduced in Part II. Also, Sudhir Chandra, 'The Problem of Social Reform in Modern India: The Study of a Case', in Malik, *op. cit.*, p. 288.
43. G.G. Agarkar, 'Samajik Sudharanes Atyanata Anukul Kal, Samprati Kal: Parts I & II' (The Present Times, the Most Favourable Time for Launching Social Reform), in *Agarkar Vangmay Khand* (Collected Works of G.G. Agarkar), (M.G. Natu and D.V. Deshpande, eds), Bombay, 1985, pp. 112–20.
44. John and Karen Leonard, *op. cit.*
45. Pal, *op. cit.*

46. Sitanath Tattwabhushan, *Social Reform in Bengal: A Side Sketch*, Calcutta, 1982, p. 19.
47. Srinivasa Row, cited in Tarashankar Banerjea, 'Social Reform Movements in Bengal in the Nineteenth and Twentieth Centuries: A Study in Social Change', in S.P. Sen (ed.), *Social and Religious Reform Movements in the Nineteenth and Twentieth Centuries*, Calcutta, 1979, p. 37.
48. See the excerpt from Aurobindo's piece on *Bande Mataram* reproduced in Part II.
49. See excerpts from Bentinck's Minute reproduced in Part II.
50. See excerpts from Ranade's speech reproduced in Part II.
51. See Phule's rejoinder to Malabari reproduced in Part II.
52. Cited in *Pandita Ramabai through Her Own Words, op. cit.*, p. 158.
53. For details, see Sen, *op. cit.*, Chapter 4.
54. Cited in Heimsath, *op. cit.*, p. 93.
55. Banerjea, *op. cit.*
56. See Bentinck's Minute, *op. cit.*
57. The minimum age for Hindu marriages was raised by Mysore in 1894, Baroda in 1904, and Indore in 1918. Some Rajput princes also initiated such reform. See *Writings and Speeches of Dr Bhau Daji, op. cit.*, pp. 276–7; Dayaram Gidumal, *Behramji M. Malabari: A Side Sketch*, London, 1892, pp. 224–5. In British India the question of determining the minimum age for marriages in respect to Hindus was debated in 1928–29, following a bill moved by the Arya Samaj leader, Har Bilas Sarda.
58. Sumit Sarkar, 'The Radicalism of Intellectuals in a Colonial Situation: A Case Study of Nineteenth Century Bengal', *Calcutta Historical Journal*, vol. 2 (July–December), 1977, p. 73.
59. For an excellent analysis of this case, see Chandra, *op. cit.*
60. See Ranade, *op. cit.*
61. See *Gidumal, op. cit.*, pp. 238–47, 217–22.
62. *Samachar Darpan*, 14 July 1821.
63. J.T.F. Jordens, 'Orthodoxy and Heresy: Reflections of the 1881 Calcutta Pandit Council', in Ganga Ram Garg (ed.), *World Perspectives on Swami Dayanand Saraswati*, Delhi, 1984, pp. 239–50.
64. See 'A Pamphlet of Rammohan Roy Containing Some Remarks in Vindication of the Resolution Passed by the Government of Bengal in 1829 Abolishing the Practice of Female Sacrifice in India (1831)', reproduced in J.K. Majumdar, *Rammohan Roy and Progressive Movements in India: A Selection from Records, 1775–1845*, Calcutta, 1941, p. 188.

65. See in particular his 'Bhattacharyer Sahit Vichar' (Disputation with the Orthodox Scholar, 1817), *Rammohan Rachanabali, op. cit.*, p. 33. Rammohan's attack was directed at Pandit Mritunjay Vidyalankar of Fort William College.
66. See Note 64 above.
67. The Petition of the Orthodox Community of Calcutta against the Suttee Regulation Together with a Paper of Authorities and the Reply of the Governor-General Thereto' (14 January 1830), reproduced in Majumdar, *op. cit.*, pp. 156–63. See particularly pp. 160–2.
68. See Note 64 above.
69. See Note 67 above.
70. Vidyasagar's plea for the validity of widow marriages in *Kaliyuga* was based on the canons of Parashar. For details on the category of *Kalivarjya*, see Batuknath Bhattacharya, *The Kalivarjyas or Prohibitions in the Kali-Age: Their Origin, Evolution and Their Present Legal Bearing*, Calcutta, 1943.
71. See J.D.M. Derett, *Religion Law and the State in India*, London, 1968.
72. See Note 67 above.
73. *Pandita Ramabai through Her Own Words, op. cit.*, p. 163.
74. Heimsath, *op. cit.*, p. 329.
75. See excerpts from the *Hindu Intelligencer*, 12 February 1855, reproduced in Part II.
76. Banerjea, *op. cit.*
77. Bankim Chandra Chattopadhyay, 'Vahubibaha' (Polygamy), reproduced in *Bankim Rachanabali* (J.C. Bagal, ed.), vol. 2, Calcutta, 1973, pp. 314–19. Also see excerpts from Bankim's *Letters on Hinduism* reproduced in Part II.
78. See excerpts from Chandravarkar's speech reproduced in Part II. Exactly the same argument had earlier appeared in 1885. See Debendranath Pakrashi, 'Samaj Samskar O Bartaman Hindu Samaj' (Social Reform and Contemporary Hinduism), *Nabyabharat*, 2, 10, Magh 1291 BS, 1885, pp. 471–7.
79. Sibnath Sastri, 'Sastre Deshachar O Dharma' (The Place of Custom and Religion in Shastras), *Nabyabharat*, Bhadra 1291 BS, 1884, p. 229.
80. For an analysis of Sri Ramakrishna's universalism, see Amiya P. Sen, *Three Essays on Sri Ramakrishna and His Times*, Shimla, 2001.
81. Swami Vivekananda, 'Reply to the Address at Madura', in *The Complete Works of Swami Vivekananda, op. cit.*, vol. 3, pp. 173–5; Sitanath Tattwabhushan, *op. cit.*, p. 4; Raja of Bhinga, 'The Modern Revival of Hinduism' (1902), in *Views and Observations: A Selection of Articles by Raja Udai Pratap Singh*, Calcutta, 1984, p. 45.

82. 'Pandit Gour Gobinda Roy's Lectures on Hindu Revival' Albert Hall, Calcutta, Tuesday, 17 March 1896, Reproduced in *Indian Mirror,* Supplement, 29 March 1896.
83. J.N. Farquhar, *Modern Religious Movements in India,* New Delhi, 1967, p. 445.
84. N.G. Chandravarkar, 'Hindoo Protestantism, Reform, Not Revival', *Speeches and Writings, op. cit.,* pp. 38–46.
85. M.G. Ranade, 'Revival and reform', *Miscellaneous Writings, op. cit.,* pp. 180–96.
86. See excerpts from Pal, *op. cit.* No less surprising is Heimsath's labelling Pal himself as a revivalist. Heimsath, *op. cit.,* p. 323. Such arguments, understandably enough, were also articulated by the social reformer from Bengal, Manmohan Ghosh (1844–96). See 'the Late Mr Manmohan Ghosh etc.', *op. cit.*
87. K.K. Gangadharan, *Sociology of Revivalism: A Study of Indianisation, Sanskritization and Golwalkarism,* New Delhi, 1970, p. 142.
88. Vasudha Dalmia, *The Nationalization of Hindu Tradition: Bharatendu Harishchandra and Nineteenth Century Benares,* Delhi, 1997, pp. 6–7.
89. Ibid.
90. Tapan Raychaudhuri, *Europe Reconsidered: Perceptions of the West in Nineteenth Century Bengal,* Delhi, 1998, p. 9.
91. See excerpts from Lajpat Rai's essay (1904) reproduced in Part II.
92. Sumit Sarkar, 'Rammohan Roy and the Break with the Past', in V.C. Joshi, (ed.), *Rammohan Roy and the Modernization of India,* New Delhi, 1975, p. 64.
93. See Note 91 above.
94. *India.*
95. See Note 77 above.
96. Chandra, *op. cit.,* p. 288.
97. See excerpts from Sister Nivedita's essay reproduced in Part II.
98. Asok Sen, *Iswarchandra Vidyasagar and His Elusive Milestones,* Calcutta, 1977, p. 107.
99. K.N. Panikkar, 'Historiographical and Conceptual Questions', in K.N. Panikkar, *Culture, Ideology and Hegemony: Intellectual and Social Consciousness in Colonial India.,* New Delhi, 1995, p. 69.
100. Ghulam Murshid, *The Reluctant Debutant: Response of Bengali Women to Modernization, 1849–1905,* Rajshahi, 1983.
101. R.C. Majumdar, 'Impact of Western Culture', in R.C. Majumdar *et. al.* (eds), *British Paramountcy and Bengal Renaissance: Part II,* Bombay, 1965, p. 260.

102. Geraldine Forbes, *Women in Modern India: The New Cambridge History of India*, IV.2, New Delhi, 1999, p. 113.
103. See excerpts from Mahesh Chandra Deb and Sumit Sarkar reproduced in Part II.
104. Bharatendu Harishchandra, 'Bharatvarsh ki Unnati Kaise Ho Sakti Hai?' (How Can One Improve India's Condition?), reproduced in *Bhartendu Granthavali*, (Collected Works of Bharatendu) (Vrajaratnadas, comp., ed.), Benares, VS 2070.
105. The most well-known cases here are those of Jogendra Chandra Basu, the founder of the conservative Bengali daily, the *Bangabasi* and his friend and co-writer, Indranath Bandopadhyay. For details see Amiya P. Sen, *op. cit.*, Chapter 3.
106. *Writings and Speeches, op. cit.*, 265.
107a. *Pandita Ramabai through Her Own Words, op. cit.*, p. 71.
107b. Speeches and Writings of Sarojini Naidu, G.A. Natesan and Co. Madras, n.d., 32, 100.
108. Neera Desai, *Women in Modern India*, Bombay, 1957, p. 124.
109. *Pandita Ramabai through Her Own Words, op. cit.*, p. 7.
110. *The Complete Works of Swami Vivekananda, op. cit.*, vol. 3, p. 246; 'Notes Taken Down in Madras', vol. 4: 115.
111. *Pandita Ramabai through Her Own Words, op. cit.*, p. 8.
112. See Deb, *op. cit.*
113. On details of the 1884 proposals, see B.M. Malabari, *Infant Marriage and Enforced Widowhood in India: Being a Collection of Opinions For and Against Received by Mr Behramji M. Malabari and from Representative Gentlemen, Official and Other Authorities*, Bombay, 1887.
114. See Phule's replies (2 parts) reproduced in Part II.
115. See *Bankim Rachanabali, op. cit.*, vol. 2, p. 921.
116. For a typical example, see Girish Chunder Ghosh, 'Social Reformation: The Condition of Women in India' (1854), *Selections from the Writings of Girish Chunder Ghosh: The Founder and First Editor of the Hindoo Patriot and the Bengalee* (Edited by his grandson Manmathnath Ghosh), Calcutta, 1912, pp. 183–5.
117. See in particular his essay 'Vibaher Boyos O Udeshya' (The Ideal Age for Marriage and the Aims of Marriage), *Bongodarshan*, Chaitra 1289 BS, 1883.
118. See excerpts from Tagore's lecture 'Hindu Vibaha' (Hindu Marriages), 1887, reproduced in Part II.
119. See Partha Chatterjee's essay reproduced in Part II.
120. Jawaharlal Nehru, *Autobiography: With Musings of Recent Events in India*, London, 1936, p. 383.

121. See for instance his 'Can't People Live without Religion?' (1927) and 'Why Should Religion be Abolished?' (1934), reproduced in *Religion and Society: Selections from Periyar's Speeches and Writings* (K. Veeramani, comp., intro.; R. Sundara Raju, trans.), Madras.
122. See excerpts from B.R. Ambedkar's *Annihilation of Caste* reproduced in Part II.
123. See M.K. Gandhi's rejoinder to Ambedkar reproduced in Part II.
124. Sudipto Kaviraj, 'On the Construction of Colonial Power, Structure, Discourse, Hegemony' in Dagmar Engels and Shula Marks (eds), *Contesting Cultural Hegemony: German Historical Institute*, London, 1994, p. 31.
125. K.N. Panikkar, *Presidential Address: Proceedings of the Indian History Congress* (Modern Indian Section), Delhi, 1975, p. 367.
126. Farquhar, *op. cit.*, p. 433.
127. *Hindu Patriot*, 6 April 1851. Reproduced in Benoy Ghose, *Selections from English Periodicals of Nineteenth Century Bengal*, vol. 3, 1970, p. 140.
128. Majumdar, *op. cit.*, p. 89.
129. P.C. Mozumdar, *Lectures in America and Other Papers*, Calcutta, 1995, p. 178.
130. Chandravarkar, *op. cit.*
131. See K.C. Sen, *Lectures in India*, Calcutta, 1954; *Keshub Chunder Sen in England. Diaries, Sermons, Addresses and Epistles* (Navabidhan Century edition), Calcutta, 1980 (1st English edition 1881).
132. D.S. Sarma, *Renascent Hinduism*, Bombay, 1989, pp. 8–9, 46.
133. Wilhelm Halbfass (ed.), *Philology and Confrontation: Paul Hacker on Traditional and Modern Vedanta*, Albany, 1995, p. 229.
134. Sen, *op. cit.*, pp. 84, 86.
135. Cited by Sumit Sarkar, 'The Complexities of Young Bengal', *Nineteenth Century Studies*, 4 October 1973, p. 506.
136. Heimsath, *op. cit.*, p. 50.
137. Panikkar, *op. cit.*
138. Rajat K. Ray, 'Man, Woman and the Novel: The Rise of a New Consciousness in Bengal, 1858–1947', *Indian Economic and Social History Review* 16(1), 1979, pp. 2–3.
139. Sarkar, 'The Complexities of Young Bengal' *op. cit.*, p. 516; Brajendranath Bandopadhyay, *Peary Chand Mitra: Sahitya Sashak Charitramala*, (vol. 2), Calcutta, 1970.
140. *Friend of India*, 3 July 1856, reproduced in Ghose, *op. cit.* (vol. 3), p. 89.
141. Antony Copley (ed.), *Gurus and their Followers: New Religious Reform Movement in Colonial India*, Delhi, 2000, pp. xii–xiii.

142. Ibid, p. xiii. The new information about the Swaminarayanis is taken from Raymond Williams, *A New Face of Hinduism: The Swaminaryan Religion*, Cambridge, 1989.
143. Parekh, *op. cit.*, p. 332, Note 35, pp. 68, 329, Note 1, p. 72.
144. Ibid., p. 42.
145. Rammohan Roy, *op. cit.*
146. Parekh, *op. cit.*
147. Ibid., pp. 68, 75.
148. Vivekananda's letter to Mohammed Sarfaraz Hussain, dated 10 June 1898, Almora. *The Complete Works of Swami Vivekananda*, (vol. 6), *op. cit.*, p. 415.
149. Sarkar, 'The Complexities of Young Bengal', *op. cit.*, 'The Radicalism of Intellectuals in a Colonial Situation', *op. cit.* On the activities of Sen, Pandit Sasadhar and the *Bangabasi*, see Amiya P. Sen, *op. cit.*, chapters 4 and 5.
150. Kamal Kumar Ghatak, *Hindu Revivalism in Bengal: Rammohan to Ramkrishna*, Calcutta, 1991, pp. 3–4. On Vishnubawa Brahmachari, see Frank W. Conlon, 'The Polemic Process in Nineteenth Century Maharashtra: Vishnubawa Brahmachari and Hindu Revival', in Kenneth W. Jones (ed.), *Religious Controversy in British India: Dialogues in South Asian Languages*, Albany, 1992.

Part Two

2

The Conceptual Nuances of Reform

The Inadequacy of Reform

Growth, not Reform

[i]

For nearly the past hundred years, our country has been flooded with social reformers and various social reform proposals. Personally, I have no fault to find with these reformers. Most of them are good, well-meaning men and their aims, too, are laudable on certain points, but it is quite a patent fact that this hundred years of social reform has produced no permanent and valuable result appreciable throughout the country .... The reason is not hard to find. It is the denunciation itself ....

We must try to keep our historically acquired character as a people .... We have to earn many lessons from outside, but I am sorry to say that most of our modern reform movements have been inconsiderate imitations of Western means and methods of work; and that surely, will not do for India ....

In the second place, denunciation is not at all the way to do good. That there are evils in our society even a child can see and in what society are there no evils? .... In comparing the different races and nations of the world I have been among, I have come to the conclusion that our people are, on the whole, the most moral and the most godly, and our institutions are, in their plan and purpose, best suited to make mankind happy. I do not, therefore, want any reformation. My ideal is growth, expansion, development along national lines .... I am no preacher of momentary social reform. I am not trying to remedy evils. I only ask you to go forward and to complete the practical realization of the scheme of human progress that has been laid out in the most perfect order by our ancestors .... They also were breakers of caste, but they were not like our modern men. They did not mean by the breaking of caste that all the people in the city should sit down together for dinner of beef-steak and champagne, nor that all fools and lunatics in the country should marry when, where, and whom they choose .... Nor did they believe that the prosperity of the nation is to be gauged by the number of husbands its widows got. I have yet to see such a prosperous nation ....

[ii]

To the reformers I will point out that I am a greater reformer than any one of them. They want to reform only little bits. I want root and branch reform. Where we differ is in the method. Theirs is the method of destruction, mine is that of construction. I do not believe in reform; I believe in growth. I do not dare to put myself in the position of god and dictate to our society: 'This way thou shouldst move and not that' ....

The history of the world teaches us that whenever there have been fanatical reforms the only result has been that they have defeated their own ends .... The whole problem of social reforms, therefore, resolves into this: where are those who want reform? Make them first. Where are the people? The tyranny of a minority is the worst tyranny that the world has ever seen. A few men who think certain things are evil will not make the nation move. Why does not the nation move? First educate the nation, create your legislative body, and then the law will be forthcoming. First create the power, the sanction from which the law will spring. The kings are gone, where is the new sanction, the new power of the people? Bring it up. Therefore, even for social reform, the first duty is to educate the people and [for that] you will have to wait till the time comes. Most of the reforms that have been agitated for during the past century have been ornamental. Every one of these reforms only touches the first two castes and no other. The question of widow marriage could not touch 70 per cent of Indian women ....

That is not reform. You must go down to the basis of the thing, to the very root of the matter. That is what I call radical reform. Put the fire there and let it burn upwards and make an Indian nation. And the solution of the problem is not easy as it is a big and a vast one. Be not in a hurry, this problem has been known for several hundred years.

We must grow according to our nature. Vain is it to attempt the lines of action that foreign societies have engrafted upon us .... I do not condemn the institutions of the other races; they are good for them but not for us.

> (Excerpted from Swami Vivekananda, 'The Mission of the Vedanta' [no date] and 'My Plan of Campaign' [no date] respectively, in *The Complete Works of Swami Vivekananda* (Mayavati Memorial edition), (vol. III), Mayavati 1973, pp. 194–6 and 213–20.)

Social Reform or Social Revolution?

The problem facing the nationalists, self-respecters, and socialists is, to my mind, not social reform but really what may be called destructive work undertaken with courage and resolution.

Social reform is like cleaning the water with insecticide or baling out the water to clean the tank. To close the pond is to destroy it. I am a destructionist only in this sense. I say this only because social reform has had its day in our land. I do not refer to the modern types of reform, which are really not worth the name, as they are indulged in by some educated people and some plutocrats merely to hoodwink the innocent common man. They are not calculated to improve his lot ... the principal reason for this state of affairs is that the people who are really responsible for the degradation of the masses have come out as reformers for purely political reasons. But the reformers I have in mind are the great Siddas, Buddhas, Thiruvallavar, Ramanuja, and the like who were reputed to have attempted social reform but yet failed miserably .... The most important item of social reform in our country refers to the inequality based on birth .... It is impossible to say that any reform was done by our reformers genuinely for the benefit of the masses.

The obstruction posed by belief in God, religion, Vedas, *Shastras* is the main reason for the lack of any initiative or effort on the part of our reformers. However, the divisions in Indian society have benefited and still benefit certain castes who have all along turned a deaf ear to all talk of reform ....

It must be understood that god and religion are erected on the foundation of the superstitious beliefs of the people. Our daily life is regulated by superstition .... It cannot be said that it is outside the pale of social reform to preach against blind faith and superstitious beliefs. On the other hand, these are the targets for destructive attack in social reform .... I am firmly of the opinion that if anything of old, based on blind faith and superstition is sought to be retained or tolerated, the result will be the total failure of reform. I am not one of those who feel that social reformers must necessarily be refrained by moderation and traditional rules. Instead, they should be ready to sweep away everything before them .... It is possible that sermons from the lips of savants like Vivekananda and Gandhi would be quoted against me. I am certainly opposed to their views. Instances are related in the Puranas of a few pariahs being admitted into the temples, where the all-king god is stated to have given them grace and outright salvation. If it is asked why such things never happen these days, the reply is that those pariahs were different from those we see now. If that is really so, where is the need to preserve these old arts and letters? Untouchability may be pardonable in view of human ignorance, yet we have stories to say that even god recognizes untouchability ....

Of the things that cry out for reform the principal ones are, to my mind, god and religion, for the simple reason that these are the two things that are invariably put in opposition to all reform .... No religion appears to have given man peace and prosperity. Yet, in the name of religion, war and propaganda have filled man's history to the brim. Every particular religionist is convinced that salvation is possible only through his own creed .... It is impossible to find out who is representing the truth ....

If it were said that religion is meant to give a code of conduct to people of each region or country and variable according to time and age, there might be some excuse for it. Instead of that it is said that the religious prescriptions are divine expressions not susceptible to any change ....

Women in general have been treated as sub-humans in society. [The] woman has been taken for granted as man's slaves. The status given to women all over the world is bad; more so in India. The rules of chastity imposed on them make one shudder ... woman's freedom and equality with man is therefore a desideratum for civilization, and this is what a reformer should strive for ....

Chastity enforced under compulsion is really no chastity. Love and companionship should alone condition chastity .... [The] government has also a responsibility in this regard. They can no longer take shelter under the plea of tradition and religion, any more than social reformers. Turkey, Afghanistan, and China have already given the necessary lead in this matter. There does not appear to be any sense whatever in compulsory widowhood. One does not know who is actually benefited by this enforcement, unless it be that some *sadhus* and *sanyasins* felt the need for the existence of such a group of women. It cannot also be that the ancient state feared a disproportionate growth of women and the consequent difficulty of matrimony among girls .... Widows should henceforth strive for their freedom, find husbands for themselves, and take lessons from many of the lower castes in which widows do marry ....

Caste is proof of the fact that our people are not really a civilized people .... All men are born equal and equality enforced in after life is contrary to nature itself .... I do not hope to witness any change through pious persuasion, searching of hearts, or national need. The institution can be attacked only at the government level through representation in all things in proportion to strength of population of each caste. Equality in the enjoyment of material goods will ultimately lead to equality in status .... Some nationalists raise the objection that claims based on caste would only perpetuate caste. They patriotically plead for equality of treatment, knowing fully well that it is the high-caste man who will benefit .... One wishes that a country in which such a system [of untouchability] obtains should be destroyed by fire or earthquake or floods .... Would it not be desirable for the untouchables to free themselves by force or violence and perish in the attempt? .... The cause of untouchability is not political slavery. It is the Hindu religion, pure and simple. Social reformers have perforce to kill the demon of untouchability if necessary by killing the Hindu religion ....

Education should particularly be diverted to women, untouchables, and other backward classes, and denied altogether to those who credit themselves with divinity or intelligence through their birth itself. At least for some 15 years, high-caste pupils should be denied admission in all colleges and technical schools ....

Since I have lost hope in social reform through constitutional, persuasive methods, I feel that a totalitarian government pledged to rationalism and socialism alone will be able to do something .... More than all, it is necessary for reformers not to be afraid of being labelled atheists .... All religionists sail in the same sinister boat. A change of religion is no solution to man's ills. No religion is the solution.

(E.V. Ramasami Periyar, 'Social Reform or Social Resolution?' [Translated from *Arivin Ellai* by A.M. Dharmalingam], Madras, 1965, pp. 1–19.)

Religion as the Basis of Social Reform

Social Reformation in India

In the present transition age of Hindu society it behoves all who are interested in India's welfare seriously to observe the signs and the tendencies of the age, and suggest and adopt such measures as may tend to establish a pure system of social and domestic economy on the principles of true religion. That a revolution of great magnitude awaits us, ordinary sagacity may predict .... Let us as the representatives of young India, take lessons from the premonitory symptoms of revolution and do all that lies in our power, individually and collectively, to turn the course of events towards truth .... Let us see how the enlightened among the rising generation stand at present in relation to social reformation and how the influences of the education which they have received affect the cause of the country. Young Bengal may be said to consist of four sections or parties, distinct in their character and tendencies: (1) the Sceptical, (2) the Speculative, (3) the Ultra, and (4) the Moderate. The Sceptical Party is composed of those who are lost to religion, and have therefore no spiritual anxiety for the welfare of others .... Next in order stands the Speculative Party. Excellent in its own sphere of thought and speculation, it lies at a considerable distance from practical reformation. It observes with the keen eyes of logic, the main principles of moral and social reformation ... but fails always, for want of moral heroism, to act up to them. Hence, for practical purposes, it is to a great extent useless. We now come to the third or Ultra Party. This is composed of those minds [that] are seen to be intensely interested in the country's good, and who are always clamorous for reforms. In the frenzy of over-patriotic ardour, they leap beyond the bounds of discretion, and advocate measures of a rather impracticable or impolitic character .... The last is the Moderate Party. Free from sceptical recklessness and obnoxious extremes of the other parties ... the

Moderates are best fitted to take the lead in social reformation. The very fact that they possess a steady religious principle and a strong sense of moral obligation affords the best proof that the task of regulating the social life of a large population belongs to them .... This party is identical with the Brahmo Samaj ....

The mission of the Samaj is essentially a religious one. Hence, social reformation must be based upon religion. It is true that the reformation of social customs and usages may, to a great extent, be accomplished independently of religion; but it is not true that social reformation can be thorough and complete without religious advancement. Religion, by improving the mind and investing conscience with supreme authority, lays the axe at the very root of corruption, whether in the individual character or in the institutions of society. Social reformation must, therefore, be preceded by and based upon religious reformation. The Hindu meets his religion at every turn. In eating, drinking, moving, sitting, standing, he is to adhere to sacred rules, to depart from which is sin and impiety. Under such circumstances, how is it possible to overthrow all the social evils of Hinduism, when faith in its authority is suffered to reign undisturbed in the heart? The Samaj does not seek to destroy caste as an institution distinct from Hinduism by setting up a purely secular movement to oppose its laws and principles. It seeks to establish the equality of man on religious grounds, and thus indirectly abolish caste distinctions. It wages a purely religious war with all evils, theological and social.

I now proceed to treat the second principle of social reformation, namely the necessity of securing positive social reforms by making the destructive and constructive agencies work together. Reformation signifies forming anew. Every reformer should, therefore, not only destroy absurd and corrupt institution, but build up positive institutions of undoubted usefulness and purity .... The thorough reformation of native society is the object of the Brahmo Samaj. It proposes to give it a reorganization upon the basis of pure faith, and adorn it with useful institutions ....

The third rule of social reformation is to harmonize independence and authority. It is our duty in legislating for social administration of a country to institute a system of salutary restraint which will prove a safeguard against license in matters in which conscience demands absolute subjection and at the same time withhold from encroaching upon the freedom of the people in matters of taste and judgement.

The fourth and last principle I have to describe is the union of courage and deliberation. Courage without due deliberation degenerates into rashness; deliberation without courage is synonymous with weakness and cowardice. Before you take any step against the usages of your country, you should seriously consider its expediency ... you must shape your course in such a way that you may neither miss your object nor give unnecessary offence to those around you.

I proceed to describe and discuss those domestic and social ceremonies which may be adopted by the reforming party .... The three ceremonies—subscription, marriage and funeral rites, may be regarded as necessary institutions of society, and require considerable amount of solemnity in form proportionate to their moral significance. They partake of both religion and custom, and involve the interests of church and society, as well as individuals. They are [of] religious importance and national importance, and, therefore, unlike other ceremonies, should be left as little as possible to individual judgments, or the mere sentiments and predilection of the parties concerned. In references to these, society as a corporate body has a ruling authority and to that each individual member should yield. That authority is certainly not identical with the supreme authority of conscience; nevertheless, for private and public morality's sake, it should be obeyed. In the momentous matter of matrimonial union, little choice can be given to individuals; the form must be the same in all cases, minor matters of course excepted. Followers of the same religion must marry according to a fixed formula prescribed by the church. So also in regard to subscription and funeral ceremonies the necessity of a fixed ritual is in the individual is incontestable. Although it is true that religion, whether in the individual or in a community, is not to be sought in external forms, but in the convictions and acknowledgements of the heart, yet it must be admitted that some form should be prescribed in accordance with which youths, after receiving the knowledge of religious truths, are to be admitted with solemnity into the True Church and made to understand the great responsibilities to be undertaken in connection with it .... I now proceed to inquire how far they [ceremonies] are morally obligatory, how far the question of duty is involved in them. This is the great question which is being agitated with much force at the present stage in our community. Some even have gone so far as to believe that the introduction of *anusthans* [ceremonies] is but the revival of idolatry and superstition. In order to solve this vexed question, it is necessary to remember the material difference which exists between form and essence in religion, and the connection which they have with our sense of duty. Each of the ceremonies under review is but an application of religion to the affairs of social and domestic life. This is the essence of the ceremonies and has a moral import. But this application is external and necessarily involves some amount of form which should not be confounded with the essence. To be grateful to God for every temporal blessing is a duty, and carries with it the weight of moral obligation; but the form in which and the accompaniment with which that gratitude is displayed cannot be morally binding, but constitute the peculiar province of each man's individual judgment and taste. Brahmoism holds that only to be obligatory and binding which has the sanction of conscience; all the rest it leaves to the free judgment of every individual. This is the grand difference between it and idolatry, which exacts religious conformity even with the non-essential matters of reform .... It is now clear, I trust that the reformed ceremonies denote essentially the fulfilment of certain domestic and social morality. But there is another standpoint from which we may observe their moral bearing on society. At the present time, when so many and varied sweeping innovations and revolutions calculated only to destroy prejudices and pernicious usages and customs are in progress around us, any movement for positive reforms must be warmly hailed by all interested in the social and moral welfare of India. Such positive reforms are to be found in these ceremonies .... Rest assured that the best foundation for the prosperity of a nation is pure faith, and that unless this is deep in its life, mere secular measures, however much they may tend to produce superficial refinement, will fail to effect any substantial or lasting improvement.

> (Excerpted from Keshab Chandra Sen's lecture at the Bhavanipur Brahmo Samaj, 21 February 1863. Reproduced in Prem Sundar Basu (comp.), *Life and Works of Brahmananda Keshav*, Calcutta, 1940, pp. 60–8.

Religion as a Social Mission

The movement of the Arya Samaj, with which the Arya Kumar Sabhas are so closely connected, has a double mission. It is humanitarian as well as national. The Arya Samaj is humanitarian in so far as it aims at making men and women better, mere[ly] truth loving and nobler. The Samaj believes in certain truths which it preaches in all its sincerity to mankind in general without any distinction of creed, colour, or climate. It believes in a certain type of civilization, the propagation of which will, in its opinion, benefit mankind in general and add to their progress in the spiritual and on the moral plane, and also to their physical happiness. The Arya Samaj believes that the Vedic religion affords the best solution of world's difficulties and is best calculated to promote better understanding between man and man. As such the mission of the Arya Samaj is worldwide and makes no distinction between one nationality and another. But intimately and inseparably connected with this mission is the task of reforming and regenerating the people who have from times immemorial believed in the teaching of the Vedas .... These people are the Hindus and the Arya Samaj has special obligation towards them. In this sense, the mission of the Arya Samaj, is 'national' .... The Arya Samaj stands for solid progress and it realizes that in the prevailing conditions of Indian public life, the rate of progress cannot be slow. It is useless to deny that it has a strong nationalizing influence with a religious mission all-embracing and universal. It has a social mission which from the very nature of its teaching tends to strengthen and solidify all those who revere the Vedas and accept them as their scriptures, and are not only proud of what[in] the present day goes by the name of Hindu culture but sincerely mean to stand by that culture and make it the basis of their future greatness ....

As such the first thing that is necessary for an Arya Kumar is to have a preliminary *grounding* in the religious teaching of the Arya Samaj. This does not at all imply that he should encumber his mind with all the subtle niceties of religious philosophy, nor is it advisable for him to give too much importance to the controversial side of religion ....

I am very strongly of opinion that a young man studying religion ought to avoid the habit of mind which results in affection of religion. Some young men begin to imitate the pose of religious men simply because they have read a few books on religion or simply because they have taken to conform themselves to the outer forms of religion. To my mind, this impairs the development of a true religious spirit and as such I deprecate the premature encouragement of a spirit of religious controversy or empty observances of ritual in youths, and much more do I deprecate attempts to thrust controversial religion down the throats of boys and girls before they have grown into men and women. I am strongly in favour of a few broad religious truths being included in the school education of every boy and girl, but beyond that any attempt to introduce the subtleties of dogma in the scheme of studies is likely to injure the eventual development of manly frankness in them .... [It] is desirable if every Hindu boy and girl knows by heart a few select Vedic hymns, singing the glory of God, laying an emphasis on the necessity of mutual goodwill, and cooperation in social life .... But to initiate boys and girls into the mysticism of religion or into the intricacies of Vedanta is, in my humble opinion, positively harmful .... Constantly to din into the ears of the boys and girls of the nation that this world is unreal, illusory, or that secular things are of no importance as against religious asceticism ... is positively mischievous ....

Over and above this what is needed is that the beauties of the Hindu social culture should be explained with special emphasis on the abuses which have crept in the later days of darkness and ignorance, and which require to be purged out. With this religious grounding and the mental equipment, what should be expected of Hindu youths is clear and unequivocal conception of the absolute necessity and desirability of physical strength and fitness .... No Hindu youth should allow himself to be compelled to marry against his will nor should he allow his physical growth to be checked by the foolish desires of his parents to see him in wedlock at an early age ... the Arya Kumar Sabhas can be very helpful in the work of social uplift, in disseminating the principles of social reform, in bringing elementary education to the depressed classes, in famine relief work ....

No man is really great and good who is solely devoted to the pursuit of selfish ends. No nation can be great, the competent parts of which suffer from a lack of public spirit. *No one can be truly religious* who does not feel that the service of God's creatures is the highest and the most sacred of a man's obligations ....

The founder of the Arya Samaj, an ascetic who had been brought up in a school which propounded that highest bliss lay in 'self-realization' without any relation to the world outside, found by long study and experience that we had misunderstood the teachings of our ancestors on the subject of self-realization, and the 'self-realization' preached by the vast number of *sadhus* and *sanyasis* going about in the country was nothing but consecrated or magnified selfishness, and that it had destroyed the grand structure of social and public duties which had been reared by our ancestors in the *Shastras* for the good of the individual and the society. The *Varna Ashram Dharma* had been completely undermined, misinterpreted, and misused. He, therefore, exhorted us back to the old ideals of duty and laid the foundation of a splendid public life by inaugurating the Arya Samaj. His clarion call having been stilled for a time, we are perhaps again falling into the state of *omne torpor* and adding to the volume of our guilt ....

The work is difficult, uphill, full of risks and danger, yet there is no escape from it. The times have changed, and escape from pain and sorrow by sheer resignation can no longer be held to be the proper object of life.

(Excerpted from Lajpat Rai, 'The Mission of the Arya Samaj' presidential address delivered at the Third All India Arya Kumar Sammelan, Saharanpur, UP, on 18 and 19 October 1912. Reproduced in Lajpat Rai, *Writings and Speeches*: 1888–1919 (vol. 1),(ed.) V.C. Joshi, Delhi, 1966, pp. 185–98.)

The Past as a Cultural Resource and Reformist Demands of the Present

Reform Civil and Social

The subject of my intellectual offering to you upon the present occasion is *reform, civil and social,* among the educated Hindoos, and the reasons which led me to its adoption are its absolute necessity on the one hand, and the want of attention, on the other, which is paid to it, and consequently the spacious room there is for improvement and exhortation respecting it. Few matters are of more solid importance so far as the sublunary interests of our country are concerned; and therefore few topics can deserve more immediate and constant attention from the members of a society which is composed of the flower of the rising generation .... Before domestic, civil, and social reform in a moral point of view takes place in our community, it would be preposterous to expect our rise as a nation, and the advantages which might accrue from our exertions in other respects would be greatly hindered and interrupted by the countless spots which stain our lives as a body and which nip every effort at our advancement in the very bud.

In order the more clearly to open my thought on this subject, I must take the liberty of asserting that the *reform* of which I have spoken implies the improvement of our *civil* and *social* institutions—and it is these to which we must chiefly attribute the national evils under which our community labours at present and which stand as a bar to our rising in eminence and civilization .... The attentive inquirer into the human mind and the diligent student of human history must have been struck at the influence which the opinions of the few exercise upon the minds of the many—and at the strictness with which institutions that have had the sanction of antiquity are observed by the great majority of our species. The respect which talent commands leads us to attach importance to the opinions of the man who broaches them—and so the institutions of philosophers meet with easy reception from the vulgar .... Men are fond of reposing under the sanction of eminent predecessors whose memory they revere, and a sufficient answer they think is given to those that would lead them otherwise, when an appeal is made to antiquity and custom.

Not that the principle of being guided by the decisions of those whom we respect and especially of our own revered ancestors is wrong in itself. So many are the mistakes and inadvertencies to which uncultivated minds are liable to fall that society could never enjoy order and prosperity if some difference were not allowed to the erudite and learned. The generality of men have neither time nor ability to frame laws for the proper regulation of their lives as members of society, and therefore, the duty of drawing up rules for the guidance of civil and social life devolves upon the few that are capable of discharging it with any success. And when customs are found to have been set on foot by wise men and have prevailed from time immemorial, the favourable voice of venerable antiquity may justly attach some degree of importance to them. That a law has been in force from times past is a presumption that it ought to continue; and the examples of those whose collections are precious to us are justly entitled to our regard unto a limited extent. Did we act upon the principle of discarding everything that was ancient, society would rather retrograde than advance in point of civilization and enlightenment. Unless we availed ourselves of the improvements made by our predecessors, we should always have to set out from the first point; and since our short lives would leave our efforts unfinished, man could never attain to the consummation of any desirable object .... Those persons therefore that would sap the foundation of existing systems *vi et armis,* advocate a most pernicious principle, and would if they succeeded overturn the main pillar of human happiness. But when corruptions are actually found to prevail, they ought by all means to be buffeted, and all real rubbish ought to be speedily removed [so] that a sound superstructure may have room for its foundation and be raised to the prosperity of nation and individuals .... The indolent and lazy habits of the mind which thinks not for itself but solely depends upon the decisions of others and to which our constitutional imbecility renders us constantly liable, has always checked the course of improvement in many countries. Civilization meets with a dead stop when it is not allowed to make any further progress than antiquity chose to assign to it—and men live and die as if they were only capable of being led by others .... It is therefore a point of peculiar importance to be constantly reminded of our natural right to think and act for ourselves—and to study non-submission to any system which we may have discovered to be pernicious to the interests of humanity .... The origin of institutions in our country is a striking illustration of the remark we have already made that the few lead the many. Individuals succeed in enforcing their opinions upon the belief and observances of whole tribes and bodies, and as darkness covered over the minds of the vulgar, who in an ignorant age, had neither time nor ability to help in the organization of society, the glimmering light of a few twinkling stars rendered passage through this stage of life somewhat tolerable. But what was useful in a barbarous and grossly dark age may be a plague in times that are more cheering .... And it is criminal now to submit to a demoralizing system when we can strike out one more worthy of our age, as it then would be to refuse obedience to the only rule, however corrupt, that was available .... Whatever may have been the reasons which dictated the adoption of the institutions which have prevailed in our country, it is certain that they have retarded the course of human improvement. It is not for us to sit in judgment over our ancestors so far as their wisdom and probity are concerned. We may take both these for granted if we choose without any injury to our practical advancement. They have left us certain maxims and ordinances for our observance, and these we may try before the bar of our reason without any slur upon their characters. We have to do with the customs and opinions which are at present in vogue, and not with the characters of the persons from whom they originated. Only in matters of history is it necessary to consider the *character* of the author upon whose testimony we receive them as facts, but in matters of opinion, since we are not bound to repose implicit faith in the judgment of any earthly teacher, we are at liberty to think for ourselves and to follow the dictates of our own reason .... Much as the assertion of our privilege of thinking and acting for ourselves is needed wherever there is human breath, it is particularly called for in our own country where custom has long been everything and where the progress of improvement has been considerably retarded by a servile obedience to prevailing institutions .... So much of positive evil has been bequeathed to us by our forefathers that it is necessary to call all the powers of the mind to break upon the task, and not only unsparingly to eradicate whatever has a tendency to upset the well-being of society among us, but also energetically to introduce and uphold whatever is likely to prove a better and more useful substitute. It is impossible for us to see happy days dawning over our country if we continue idle and inactive ....

I pass on, therefore, to the ultimate object of my discourse, which is to call upon you to set seriously upon their improvement. The necessity of achieving this object on your part arises from the advantage which providence has vouchsafed to you of a liberal education by which you have been enabled to detect some of the diseases that kept our society in an unhealthy and enfeebled condition. Did you not possess better notions and had you no knowledge of the abuses which exist, you could not be called upon to reform what you did not feel required reform .... Who will come forward to India's relief in this respect if her enlightened children indulge [in] supine indolence and thoughtless inactivity? .... Can the blind lead the blind? No! gentlemen, that shall not, that cannot, be .... The work of domestic and moral reform must begin with and be conducted by the inhabitants of the soil. Foreigners may at best aid and encourage you, but you must personally bear the heat and brunt of the battle .... Reform at home must commence with and be carried on, by those who are at hone, and before this reform can take place, and before you act your own parts, you cannot with good grace enforce your claims upon the sympathy of those that are abroad .... It so happens that the most influential members of the Hindoo community are extremely averse to the idea of reform, and desire fervently the continuance of [the] plagues which custom has introduced. The educated portion, therefore must meet with opposition and, in some cases, with persecution too if they attempt a renovation .... This prospect, however, should not dampen your spirits .... Where have you known of a reformation springing naturally from the abuses it was intended to destroy? Where have you known of a renovator lull together in a bed of down? ....

No reformer in our country will perhaps be ever called upon to suffer at the stake or scaffold, nor have to pay even the price of confiscation and exile for the sake of principle. Shall then mere threats silence you? .... Your course becomes easier when you consider that in the prosecution of your views as respects civil and social reform, you shall not be necessarily called upon to transgress the dictates of the Shasters and as your combat will principally be against customs and practices which the corruptions of time have invented, you shall be unassailable even upon the enemies' own ground. In fact, even if you did transgress the limits of their revered writings, still no human contemporary could with any grace proceed against you since there are numberless practices now tolerated and sanctioned by your opponents which are open violations of the law they hold sacred. My call, however, at present is of a civil and social character and so I pass over those things which are connected with religion.

(Excerpted from Rev. Krishna Mohan Banerjea, 'Reform Civil and Social', lecture before the Society for the Acquisition of General Knowledge, no date. Reproduced in *Awakening in Bengal in Early Nineteenth Century: Selected Documents* (vol. 1) (Goutam Chattopadhyay, ed.), Calcutta, 1965, pp. 128–98.)

The Essentials of Hinduism

Not only is Hinduism, under the name of the Hindu religion, held to include all Hindu religion, past and present, all things Hindu whether religious or secular, but also much that never has had any connection with 'anything Hindu, religious or secular'. Non-Aryan customs and observances retained by non-Aryan tribes converted into Hinduism, non-Aryan fetishism, popular superstitions without any warranty in Hinduism, and only similar to those that are to be found in every country, Christian, Mussulman, or heathen, nursery legends disseminated by old crones for the edification of class-going children, and such every other subject of popular or juvenile belief is pressed by the critic of Hinduism into his service, and a monstrous caricature of a national faith is thus manufactured and described, in eloquent language 'as a tangled jungle of gods, ghosts, demons, and saints', and other monsters, language which admiring statisticians call upon all students of Hinduism to learn by heart.

Let us eliminate all these sources of error. Let us rid our conception of Hinduism of this 'tangled jungle of ghosts, demons, and saints' and such other articles of belief which are to be found in every country and among peoples of all creeds, and which are no more essential parts of Hinduism as they are of Christianity. Let us free it also of all that is not properly religion but social polity or domestic morality and unwritten law of the country, of general culture. Something of this no doubt will have to be included in Hinduism, if you conceive religion as I think you do, to be a system of social culture .... There will still remain a vast quantity of matter utterly foreign to religion which will have to be excluded. Thirdly, the term Hinduism has to be restricted to the articles of religious belief accepted by Hindus generally at the present day in exclusion of the Vedic and the Brahmanic faiths out of which Hinduism evolved itself. Lastly, we have to remember that these articles of faith vary from province to province, differ in different sects in the same province, and even among individuals in accordance with the culture or the mental constitution of the individuals concerned. Yet among all these varieties and divergences will be found some common features, certain fundamental principles which form the basis of all. These fundamental principles will be found sufficient to constitute a religion in themselves, and this religion is Hinduism.

In thus restricting the application of the term Hinduism, I do nothing which is arbitrary. I merely insist that if you wish to denote by it an existing religion, you must confine its application to an existing religion and exclude all that does not properly belong to the existing religion .... It will exclude ... much that is popularly considered to be a portion of Hinduism even by Hindus themselves. That, however, is not and ought not to be an objection against the definition. It is precisely popular delusions of this sort that have encrusted Hinduism with the rubbish of ages—with superstition and absurdities which subvert its higher purpose, and which it is the duty of every true Hindu actively to assail and destroy .... Hinduism is in need of a reformation—not an unprecedented necessity for an ancient religion. But reformed and purified it may yet stand forth before the world as the noblest system of individual and social culture available to the Hindu even in this age of progress. I have certainly no serious hopes of progress in India except in Hinduism—in Hinduism reformed, regenerated, and purified. To such reformation it is by no means necessary that we should revert, like the late Dayananda Saraswati, to old and archaic types. That which was suited to people who lived 3,000 years ago may not be suited to the present and future generations. Principles are immutable but the modes of their application vary according to time, to circumstances. The great principles of Hinduism are good for all ages and all mankind—for they are based on what Carlyle would call the 'Eternal Verities', but its non-essential adjuncts have become effete and even pernicious in an altered state of society .... Let us not be awed and silenced by the imposing authority of ancient names, or be led away by pretended learning and antiquated jargon. Let us look steadily and bodily into the face of things; discard falsehood whenever we meet with it hoary and hallowed by time though it may be; and if in our search we meet with truth, let's drag it out of darkness under which it was hid, and enthrone it in the light of heaven. Let us revere the past, but we must, in justice to our new life, adopt new methods of interpretation, and adopt the old eternal and undying truths to the necessities of that life.

(Excerpted from Bankim Chandra Chattopadhyay, *Letters on Hinduism* (Letter II). Reproduced in J.C. Bagal (ed.), *Bankim Rachanavali* (Collected Works of Bankim Chandra Chattopadhyay) (vol. III), Calcutta, 1969, pp. 229–36.)

3

The Debate over Strategies

The Road to Reform: Individual Moral Courage vs Cautious Deference to Tradition

Social Reform with Picnics and Tea-parties!

Ram Mohan Roy, Daya Nund, Syed Ahmed belong to those generations who did not owe much to English education, and represents a type of character that is becoming rarer day by day. Ram Mohan Roy and Daya Nund are gone; and Syed Ahmed according to the ordinary calculations of human life belongs to the past rather than the present; but when we look to their successors in various departments of our national activity the decay of character becomes apparent. With the steam of progress we seem to have glided into an age of peace and comfort—of loud disputations and weak convictions—an age in which everybody seems to be prepared to play the *role* of reformer with a light heart, in which the fair promises of materialistic advancement have thrown the ascetic elements of life into the background, and a race of reformers has sprung up, of weak resolve and weaker initiative—fighting shy of the difficulties of the situation, shrinking from self-sacrifice and pain:

> Waiting to strive a happy strife,
> To war with falsehood to the knife,
> And not to lose the good of life.

The glorious vision of modern culture which has suddenly gleamed upon our sight and the general mental ferment to which it has given rise do not for the present enable us to realise fully and properly the deterioration of character which has overtaken us, but to those who can look beneath the surface, its symptoms are perfectly legible.

Now that the conflict of Eastern and Western civilizations has utterly wrecked the old order, and our oldest beliefs and institutions have been cast into the melting pot to come out in some fresh mould, the reconstruction of our political, social, and religious life upon a new basis is the grand duty of the hour. But who are the men who have undertaken it and what are their qualifications for the task?

The religious sentiment has been most deeply affected by the change, and there are loud complaints from all sides that religion is in danger. My belief is that Hinduism is in a critical condition. I do not believe in the immortality of any thing under the sun except the Spencerian Unknowable; and whatever may he the hold of Hinduism upon the masses, if it is permissible to dream of a day when these masses will have been raised to the mental level of the educated classes, and if English education will have the same effect upon the former as it has had upon the latter, then it is perfectly legitimate to hold that when that day comes the knell of Hinduism, as we know it, and as it has existed through centuries, will have sounded. Be the result of this speculation what is may, true it is that while a profound religious change is taking place in India, we look in vain for any master spirit among ourselves to guide the master currents of this change. The hour is said to bring the man, but of modern India we may say, inverting the words of Carlyle, that while the hammer in the horologue of time has been pealing through the universe that there is a change from era to era, the man who would incarnate in himself the tendencies of transition and lead his people safely though the changes is not forthcoming. We have able and earnest workers in the Brahmo Samaj, the Arya Samaj and in several other religious organizations; but is there any one now living upon whom may be said to have fallen the mantle of Daya Nund or Ram Mohan Roy, or Chaitannya? Among an extremely religious people, and in an age when belief is engaged in a life-and-death struggle with unbelief, we have no religious teachers and reformers of commanding genius, who may be said to have any strong and durable hold upon the national mind. There can hardly be any greater proof of the decay of Indian genius in the field of action.

We turn to social and political reform, and we find the spectacle discouraging. The new conditions of life have made the reform of certain social abuses not only an indispensable step to further progress, but an important element of personal happiness. Female education, the abolition of early marriage and forced widowhood, the training of children, the organization of public charity on some rational basis, the restrictions of caste, specially in relation to sea voyage—these are some of the important questions pressing for a wise and speedy solution. The nation will not improve so long as these questions are not solved, and they will not be solved so long as some of us do not fight the forces of opposition with all our might and main. Keshub Chunder Sen, Vidya Sagar, Dr Bhandarkar, Mr Justice Ranade, Dewan Rughu Nath Rao, Mr Malabari are among the most prominent names in the rank of our social reformers and the country owes them a large debt of gratitude. But I am not sure if with the exception of Keshub any one of these has any large following in the country; and even Keshub's influence is religious rather than social. Indeed Keshub lies under the serious change of having been found wanting when weighed in the balance in the case of his own daughter's marriage. Of the rest it may be said that while they are everything that men of culture and strong national sympathies should be, they hardly come up to the level of those fanatics of Reform whose whole life is a protest against the established order—who have a mania for change—those leaders of forlorn hopes, whose voice is half-battle and who strike the blow while the wise and the prudent remain calculating in their armchairs the final chances of the war. Men like Clarkson and Granville Sharp, Diderot and Condorect, Shankracharj and Nanak have by sheer force of their character, by their dauntless courage and inflexible will by an utter disregard of social expediencies and a complete sacrifice of the most coveted prizes of life—reformed and renovated human society in other countries and other times; and in our country at the present time the saviours of society will be those who will be born revolutionists, burning with an enthusiasm for progress—prepared to follow without fainting or faltering, their ideals, like the vision of immortality, through death and the grave. Such characters do not exist in India, but in their place we find Social Conferences and Associations—very good things in their way—meeting periodically—more zealous in settling the question where they should meet than what they should do when they meet—passing resolutions which nobody heeds—and thus going on from year's end to year's end with an amount of patience which is truly admirable. These modern representatives of Sysiphus are really a sight for gods and men. And even this game of social reform with its picnics and tea-parties some times becomes too serious for most of us when any question like that of the Age of consent crops up, and then we have anti-reform demonstrations threatening to smother all reforming spirits under the files of the *Patrika* and the *Patriot* while that brilliant swordsman of Indian radicalism—Surender [sic] Nath Banerji—may be seen huzzaing the mob from his Editorial chair. What wonder if the hostile critic talks of the superficial vineer of our modern enlightment?

(Excerpted from Pt Bishan Narain Dar, *Speeches and Writings*, vol. 1, (part I and II) H.L. Chatterji (ed.), Lucknow, 1921, pp. 56–9. Originally appeared under the title 'The Decay of Genius in Modern India' published in NWP and Oudh Educational Magazine, 1896.)

Social Reform: The Virtues of Discretion

Our reader must have perceived from various recent indications and discussions that considerable excitement has for some time existed among the more intelligent and educated classes of the native population of Calcutta. Here as well as elsewhere there is conflict going on between light and darkness, truth and error, and it is because we cannot fully approve of the temper and proceeding of those who have our best wishes that we now advert to the subject in the hope of leading them to a more correct appreciation of the circumstances in which they are placed and to the adoption of better adapted means for the promotion of their object ....

The first objection we have to make to their proceedings is that instead of limiting their attention to the essentials they lessen their own influence and strengthen the cause of their idolatrous opponents by unnecessarily running counter to the customs and institutions of native society. We take it for granted that their object is what it ought to be—to make a stand against the folly, the vice, and the impiety of idolatry .... But the attainment of these objects, instead of being furthered, will be retarded by certain views which in their minds appear to be combined with them. For instance, indiscriminate eating and drinking that is eating and drinking not in conformity with the rules of caste are inconsistent with the enjoyment of respect in Hindoo society as at present constituted ... yet most of those of whom we are speaking despise the rules of caste and refuse all conformity to them by which means they not only banish themselves from Hindoo society and lose all influence over it, but even supply their enemies with a handle against themselves .... We are far from thinking that the institution of caste is harmless, but the observance of its rules in respect of eating and drinking need not trouble any man's conscience .... Another instance occurs to us of the way in which popular prejudice is unnecessarily offended and native customs broken down. Everybody knows that good manners according to the etiquette introduced by Moosulman courts require a native to have his head covered in the presence of others, but some of our youthful Hindoo reformers, from a weak imitation of English customs, are now in the practice of going about with their heads uncovered ....

Another way in which they are acting unworthy of themselves and creating among the English community at least a moral impression against their cause is by treating with scorn and contempt, the praiseworthy literary exertions of the idolatrous opponents. The example which we have here in the case of Raja Kali Kishen who lately published a translation from the Sunskrit of the *Neeti Sunkulun*, or collection of Sunskrit *sloka*s of enlightened *Moonee*s .... The work itself doubtless contains many puerilities, but to our apprehension, it also contains some beauties and unfolds a page of human nature from which we acknowledge that we have derived both amusement and instruction .... Raja Kali Kishen is an evidence and representative of one of the beneficial effects that have been produced upon the wealthy Hindoos by the progress of education .... Fifty years ago a Hindoo of this description would have plunged into sensuality and expended his superfluous riches in the most evanescent gratification .... We shall advert at present to only one other point .... Even in opposing what is wrong they do not pursue that temperate and consistent course which would satisfy the mind of the observers that their opposition is founded on sound principles and good feeling .... We may refer also in illustration of what we mean to the pages of the *Enquirer*, the chief organ of the party. There we find almost everything that is calculated to irritate and inflame, scarcely anything to persuade or convince. When it is considered that the writers are young and inexperienced, imperfectly acquainted with the language in which they write, superficially informed of the religion of their forefathers which they have forsaken, and not even professing to have any system of their own to substitute for it, we may conceive with what feelings the assumptions of this tone is regarded by their countrymen and must conclude that until it is abandoned they must abandon all hope of being useful in the cause of truth and virtue.

(Excerpted from the *India Gazette* quoted by the *Calcutta Monthly Journal*, October 1831. Reproduced in Jatindra Kumar Majumdar (ed.), *Raja Rammohun Roy and Progressive Movements in India: A Selection from Records, 1775–1845*, Calcutta, 1941, pp. 88–90.)

Reform from Within

The present generation is accustomed to thinking of him [V.N. Mandlik] as a man of the old and unbending school of orthodoxy, but there was a time in his career when he fought the good fight of reform, and tried in his way to beard orthodoxy in his own den. In the sixties he championed the side of the great social reformer Karsandas Mulji, when the latter was sued for defamation for boldly and fearlessly writing against the Vallabhacharya Maharajas in the columns of the *Rast Goftar* and *Satya Prakash*; and he was also one of the foremost Hindoos of his time who sowed the seeds of female education in this part of the country. At heart, however, he was a man of the old school—he worshipped his idols, believed in caste, and hated change. But he was a man of convictions. There was no eyewash in his idol worship, and he did not try to make a trade of idolatry, as some do who praise it as the only true mode of worship, though they believe in neither God or gods. He was true to his faith in the caste system, for he did not know the art of dining in 'hotels' and at the same time posing as a true casteman. There was a true ring about Rao Saheb Mandlik's orthodoxy, however much one might feel inclined to reject it as a faith .... If I were asked why he deserves to be remembered as one of our great and good men that have passed away, leaving fond memories behind, I should answer that his resolute and manly spirit, his genuineness of convictions, and his faithful devotion to his wife made him a moral man, worthy of reverence in our eyes—in the eyes of even of those who differed from him on the question of social and religious reform ....

It is within the memory of all who witnessed the events of 1886 that the opposition to Mr Malabari's notes on 'Infant Marriage and Enforced Widowhood' in which he appealed to government for legislative interference with some of our social customs culminated in a monster meeting at Madhavbag, consisting of thousands of Hindoos of all castes and classes, headed by Rao Saheb Mandlik, and entered a very emphatic protest against the proposed legislation .... The orthodox party thought 'the so-called reformers' a very mischievous but a very imbecile set of men, who were playing into the hands of Mr Malabari, because, instead of adopting the true method of social progress by effecting 'reform from within', they were seeking to force 'reform from without' on an unwilling community. The reform party retorted that all the talk of 'reform from within', which came from the party headed by Rao Saheb Mandlik, was mere moonshine, and if that party was sincere, it ought not merely to oppose 'the reform party', but ought to go a step further and show how 'reform from within' could be effected. Rao Saheb's school charged the reformers with doing nothing but talking, and with making the cause of reform stink in the people's nostrils by irritating discussions, violent articles in newspapers, and high-flown lectures. The 'reform party', in return, demanded to know what their opponents were going to do to further the cause of reform; and it was told in answer that the proper procedure to follow was to approach the *swami*s and *guru*s, the spiritual heads and *shastri*s of the castes, to win them over by gentle persuasion, not to irritate them or set them at naught, but take them in confidence, and proceed with the work of reform with their sympathy, support, and cooperation. And all would go on then as merrily as a marriage bell .... Each party said it had the true key to reform, and each denounced the other as insincere, impractical, and bidding for cheap reputation .... The good old Rao Saheb did try to put his hand to the plough of reform. His school had gone too far in the controversy to recede .... Young and well-educated Brahmin gentleman had just then returned from England, and the Rao Saheb set himself to the task of inducing those known to be learned in the *Shastra*s, and acknowledged by the orthodox as authorities on the sacerdotal laws and customs of the Hindoo community, to throw the weight of their influence on the side of reform by readmitting the England-returned gentlemen into caste after the performance of some penance which they might prescribe .... He [Mandlik] got several *shastri*s to meet him at a conference and then, well, they took fright and proved stubborn. There was one at least I knew of who thought Rao Saheb Mandlik's attitude was a bolt from the blue. Mahamahopadhyay Bhimacharya Zhalkikar, then a Sanskrit *shastri* in Elphinstone College, was among others approached by the Rao Saheb, but he suspected the whole movement and thought its promoter was going to sell them all and their religion. I had it from *shastri* Bhimacharya himself that when he was consulted and entreated to prop up the reform, he refused because he could find nothing in the *Shastra*s to justify the proposed change. Said the *shastri* to me in giving an account of the experiment, 'We *shastri*s know the tide is against us and it is no use opposing. You people should not consult us, but go your own way and do the thing you think right; and we shall not come in your way. But if you ask us and want us to twist the *Shastra*s for your purpose and go with you, we must speak plainly and we will oppose.' There was thus a division in the camp. Preparations were made for giving the England-returned gentlemen penance and dinner. The *shastris* did not turn up. The Rao Saheb presented himself at the ceremony for *pan-supari*, but did not dine and yet the dinner was the crucial part of the test. The experiment failed and we never heard after that of 'reform from within'.

And yet there was a meaning in that phrase which I have learnt to link with Rao Saheb Mandlik's name. Apart from the question whether he was right in denouncing state legislation in matters of social reform, we owe it to him and his opposition that he drew attention to what he called a cheap class of reformers—'Luthers', he said, 'of lavender and rose'. He was perhaps too hard on those who, in the midst of tremendous difficulties, were trying to expose social evils .... But one good effect at least of the controversies of 1884–87 has been this—that both 'reformers' and 'reactionaries' have learnt something worth learning from each other. The Rao Saheb by his opposition enabled the reformers to search their own conduct and their conscience and to see more clearly than before that they must be prepared for solid work and self-sacrifice if they wanted to win .... Rao Saheb Mandlik put too much faith in moving with the *shastris* and the masses, but the experiment he made has proved that the *shastris* and the masses will not move unless responsible leaders, men of light and leading, who have seen the light of reform, grasp it, walk themselves by the light of it, and set an example for others to follow ....

'Private repentance', individual moral energy, deep personal faith in some great conception of duty or religion are the prerequisites and causes of all social amelioration. *Swamis* and *shastris* are wedded to old and worn out ideals, and it is expecting too much of them to give up beliefs in which centuries of custom and tradition have nurtured them. They will follow the new reform when they find they must, or else there is no chance for them. They will, of course, try to throttle the cause and its upholder, begin to kick and curse, but the cause gains all the more on that account. The reformer has to make himself heard and the majority are listless. They will neither hear nor see; but once the *swamis* rise in opposition, all eyes and ears are turned to the reformer .... Rao Saheb Mandlik was often accustomed to warn[ing] reformers against what he called 'the rocks ahead', and a warning of that kind even the best of reformers may at times need .... But in India, where the principle of conservatism is born with us and deep-rooted, the warning seems to me to be a little too superfluous, if it is not coupled at the same time with words of hope and encouragement .... 'Not to break off our moorings', 'not to break away from the past', 'to be cautious and slow' are all fine phrases and good advice so far as they go. But human nature is so full and fond of the past, at least in India, so inert and supine, that there is no danger of any reformer running headlong and revolutionizing society .... The past is too strong in the present, and it has tremendous energy to take care of itself; what is wanted is force to mould it and that can come from 'reform within'. And 'reform from within' is impossible so long as the enlightened and educated individuals will sit still and in the hope that something may turn up and that they will *then* help in the regeneration of their kind. Persecution there will be, and they must be prepared for it.

(Excerpted from N.G. Chandravarkar, 'The Mandlik School and "Reform within"'. Reproduced in *The Speeches and Writings of Sir Narayan G. Chandravarkar* (L.N. Kaikini, ed.), Bombay, 1911, pp. 32–8.)

The Problem of Social as Against Political Reform

The Line of Least Resistance

The subject of the address in not altogether new to me. It attracted my attention many months ago when I was writing a letter to my friend Mr B.M. Malabari in reference to his 'Notes on Infant Marriage and Enforced Widowhood'. When I was writing that letter, Sir Auckland Colvin's communication to Mr Malabari had just been published in the newspapers. And the view had been expressed in it that we ought to turn our attention to social reform in preference to the endeavours we were making to teach our English rulers what their duties were in the government of the country. In my letter to Mr Malabari I ventured briefly but emphatically to express my dissent from this view of Sir Auckland Colvin ....

At first, when we asked to give precedence to social over political reform, it is necessary to consider whether there is such a sharp line of demarcation between social and political matters as must be in order to give effect to this demand. I confess, I think that such a line cannot be logically drawn .... Those matters which are mainly and to a great extent social have most important political aspects and vice versa .... And, secondly, even if the preference suggested be justified in theory, it would not be feasible to enforce it in practice .... I have endeavoured to follow the whole controversy as it has been going on for some time past. And I have come across only to reason in favour of the preference thus suggested. First, it is said that slavery at home is incompatible with political liberty. Now when understood in its true sense, I have no quarrel with this principle .... But I apprehend that for the application of this principle, you must have a conscious tyranny on the one side and a slavery that is felt to be slavery on the other .... Have we in truth got to deal with a case of conscious tyranny and felt slavery? I say certainly not .... So far as we have tyranny and slavery ... we have only a case of the tyranny of the past, the present being bound in slavery to it. It is not, as is often represented, a case of male tyrants and female slaves to any notable extent .... As regards all these burning questions which just now trouble us in connection with social reform—as regards enforced widowhood, infant marriage, voyages to England, and so forth—the persons who are supposed to be our slaves are really in many respects our masters. You talk of the duty that lies upon us, the breaking of the shackles, and they decline to let us break them. They protest against an interference with and desecration of their ancient and venerable tradition, which from their point of view is involved in the course of enfranchisement. Therefore, I hold that the phrase 'household slavery' as used in the controversy is an entire misnomer. It is these so-called slaves within our households who form our great difficulty. And in these circumstances, I venture to say that the sort of 'household slavery' in truth prevails among us is by no means incompatible with political liberty. The position in fact is this. Here we have what may for convenience, be treated as two spheres for our reforming activities. There is slavery on the one side and there is slavery on the other, and we are endeavouring to shake off that slavery in the one sphere as well as in the other ....

Let us now go to the next reason alleged in favour of the precedence claimed of social over political reform. It is said that a nation [stagnant] cannot be politically great .... Now if this means that political and social progress are [placed] together, that the spirit of progress working in the political sphere always manifests itself in greater or less vigour in the social sphere, I at once admit it .... But this is a very different thing indeed from the proposition involved in the present argument. It is not enough, as thus understood, to justify the preference demanded. For that it is necessary to prove that any social condition that is at any given period in history, political greatness in unattainable and political progress not to be achieved. To this proposition I confess I cannot say that history offers any support. And I hold, indeed, that the lessons to be deduced from history run exactly counter to this. Look at that brilliant episode in the history of India which is connected with the names of Shivaji and the subsequent Maratha rulers .... I cannot find that the social condition of that period was very much superior to the social condition now prevailing .... It is plain, I think, that the claim of superiority cannot be awarded to the period covered by the achievements of the great Maratha power. Yet there can be no doubt that politically, those achievements were very brilliant and that they implied great political progress .... In this England of ours, this England where political reform was advanced by leaps and bounds, where political affairs attract such attention as is shown by the commotion of the General Election ... in this England there are still social evils awaiting remedy. To them attention is not directed with anything like the force and energy bestowed on political affairs .... Where then is the lesson of history which we are asked to deduce and act upon? ....

I will now proceed to state the arguments which appear to me to support the negative answer to that question. First, it seems to me plainly a maxim of prudence and common sense that reform ought to go, as I may say, along the line of least resistance. Secure first the reforms which you may secure with the least difficulty, and then turn your energies in the direction of those reforms where more difficulty is to be encountered .... This is the principle which we actually act upon within the sphere of political activity itself .... Now if this principle is correct, it leads manifestly to the conclusion that more energy ought just now to be devoted to political than to social reform .... Political reform is entitled to greater share of our energies than social under the circumstances we have got to deal with. Every one of us can not devote himself to every one of the numerous reforms which are wanted. Extraordinary natural gifts may enable any person like, for instance, my friend Mr Ranade, to devote himself successfully to many modes of activity at one and the same time. but this is not possible for us all .... What are the forces opposed to us? .... On the one side, we have a government, by a progressive nation, which is the benign mother of free nations ... [and is] ready to admit us to political rights when we show that we deserve them well. On the other side we have an ancient nation, subject to strong prejudices, not in anything like full sympathy with the new conditions now existing in the country, attached perhaps 'not wisely but too well' to its own religious notions with which the proposed social reforms are closely, intimately, and at numberless points intertwined, loving all its hoary traditions and some of its very modern ones ... yet often failing to understand the true meaning and significance of both classes of traditions. As between these two groups of what I have called, only for convenience of phrase, opposing forces, can there be any reasonable doubt how the line of least resistance runs? If we compare the government of India and the Hindu population as two forts facing the army of reform, can there be any doubt that the wisest course for that army is to turn its energies first towards that represented by the government where we have numerous and powerful friends among the garrison and which is held against us only in order to test first whether we shall be able to properly use any larger powers that may be conceded to us there? .... The soldiers in the old garrison are not in the least ready to 'give up', and in some respects we have yet got even to forge and to learn to wield the weapon by which we have to fight them.

Again, in politics, argument goes a big way, in social reform, it goes very little ... where feeling and tradition are the authorities appealed to, logic is almost impotent. You must then make up your minds to still use logic of course, but only as a subordinate agency—and you must rely on the long, patient, toilsome process of diverting feelings or to express it differently .... In one word, to go back to our old political phraseology, we have here got, like Disraeli, to educate our party which must always be ... a long and laborious operation .... In political matters we can all unite at once ... Hindus, Mussulmans, Parsis .... The evils, or supposed evils, are common .... The remedies ... are also the same, and intelligent Indian opinion is necessarily unanimous. In regard to social matters, the conditions are all altered. The evils for one are not identical ... and the remedies, therefore ... are almost of necessity different. It is plain then, that the advantages to secure which we can all unite ought to be tried for first so that we may obtain the benefit of the traditional feeling which must be generated by such cooperation. If political reform is thus secured by the concerted action of all the educated classes of India, this must and inevitably will tell favourably on the advancement of social reform ....

In political matters we are learning, and learning more easily than we should do in any other department of activity .... To this end we must give and take, and sink smaller differences for the one common purpose. This lesson like others ... will form the best possible equipment for the work of social reform that lies before us .... These we shall have to apply in the performance of duty in the social sphere. Let us remember further that with political independence, to a certain extent, goes a greater capacity for social advancement. This is not an empty speculation. It is a theory in support of which historical testimony can be advanced ....

Admitting that we are miles and miles away from the goal in social reform, I hold that we are as yet equally far in political. We have made and are making preparations in both and in both we have made a similar amount of progress ....

I venture to repeat that we cannot fairly be censured for giving too exclusive attention to political at the expense of social reform .... It is not possible to sever political from social reform altogether, the two must go hand in hand although the marriage may not, in the case of both, be with equal celebrity .... We ought to devote the greater portion of our energy to political reform, but so as still to keep alive the warm sympathy for social reform .... In my judgement they are both duties, and must both be fairly attended to and discharged according to our circumstances and opportunities.

(Excerpted from K.T. Telang, 'Must Social Reform Precede Political Reform in India?' Speech before the Student's Literary and Scientific Society, 22 February 1886. Reproduced in C.Y. Chintamani (ed.), *Indian Social Reform: Part. IV*, Madras, 1901, pp. 292–309.)

Does Social Reformation Require Political Moderation?

The *Indian Social Reformer* has discovered that the moderate programme needs revisions. Moderation is defined by this authority as a desire to preserve the British *Raj* until social reform has accomplished itself, for the reason that an indigenous government is not likely to favour social reform so much as the present rulers do. The *Reformer* would therefore like the moderate programme to be modified in order to tally with its own definition of moderation. We presume that, in its view, the Congress instead of demanding legislative councils, should ask for the forcible marriage of Hindu widows; instead of the separation of the judicial and the executive, the separation of reformed wives from unreformed husbands or vice versa; instead of the repeal of the Arms Act, the abolition of Hindu religion. This introduction of social details unto a political programme is a fad of a few enthusiasts and is contrary to all reason. The alteration of the social system to suit present needs is a matter for the general sense of the community and the efforts of individuals. To mix it up with politics in which men of all religious views and various social opinions can join is to confuse issues hopelessly. It is not true that by removing the defects of our social structure we shall automatically become a nation and fit for freedom. If it were so, then Burma would be a free nation at present. Nor can we believe that the present system is favourable to social reconstruction or that self-government would be fatal to it. The reverse is the case. Of course, if social reform means the destruction of everything old or Hindu because it is old or Hindu, the continuance of the present political and mental dependence on England and English ideals is much to be desired by the social reformers; for it is gradually destroying all that was good as well as much that was defective in the old society. With the programme of becoming a nation by denationalization we have no sympathy. But if a social development be aimed at, it is more likely to occur in a free India when the national needs will bring about a natural evolution. Society is not an artificial manufacture to be moulded and remodelled at will, but a growth. If it is to be healthy and strong it must have healthy surroundings and a free atmosphere.

(Aurobindo Ghosh, 'The "Reformer" on Moderation', *Bande Mataram* 1 May, 1907. Reproduced in Sri Aurobindo, *Bande Mataram: Early Political Writings,* Pondicherry, 1973, pp. 312–13.)

The State and the Question of Social Legislation

A Legislator for Hindus

To consent to the consignment year after year of hundreds of innocent victims to a cruel and untimely end when the power exists of preventing it, is a predicament which no conscience can contemplate without horror. But, on the other hand, if heretofore received opinions are to be considered of any value, to put to extinguish at once all hopes of these great improvements affecting the condition not of hundreds of thousands, but of millions, which can only be expected from the continuance of or supremacy, is an alternative which, even in the light of humanity itself, may be considered as a still greater evil. It is upon this first and highest consideration alone, the good of mankind, that the tolerance of this inhuman and impious rite can, in my opinion, be justified on the part of the government of a civilized nation ....

In venturing to be the first to deviate from this practice [*sati*], it becomes me to shew [show] that nothing has been yielded to feeling, but that reason and reason alone has governed the decision .... So far also from being the sole champion of a great and dangerous innovation, I shall be able to prove that the vast preponderance of present authority has long been in favour of abolition .... Prudence and self-interest would counsel me to tread in the footsteps of my predecessors. But in a case of such momentous importance to humanity and civilization, that man must be reckless of all his present or future happiness who could listen to the dictates of so wicked and selfish a policy? ....

We have now before us two reports of the Nizamat Adalut, with statements of *sati*s in 1827 and 1828, exhibiting a decrease of 54 in the latter year as compared with 1827, and a still greater proportion as compared with former years .... The decrease, if it be real, may be the result of less sickly seasons, as the increase in 1824 and 1825 was of greater prevalence of cholera. But it is probably in a greater measure due to the more open discouragement of the practice given by the European functionaries in later years ....

It seems to me the very general opinion that our interference has hitherto done more harm that good by lending a sort of sanction to the ceremony .... Under the present position of the British Empire moreover, it may be fairly doubted if any such underhand proceeding would be really good policy. When we had powerful neighbours and had greater reason to doubt our own security, expediency might recommend an indirect and more cautious proceeding, but now that we are supreme, my opinion is decidedly in favour of an open, avowed, and general prohibition, resting altogether upon the moral goodness of the act and our power to enforce it; and so decided is my feeling against any half-measure, that were I not convinced of the safety of total abolition, I certainly should have advised the cessation of all interference.

Mr Wilson considers it to be a dangerous evasion of real difficulties, to attempt to prove that *suttee*s are not 'essentially a part of Hindu religion'. I entirely agree in this opinion. The question is not what the rite is, but what it is supposed to be; and I have no doubt that the conscientious belief of every order of Hindus, with few exceptions, regards it as sacred.

Mr Wilson thinks that the attempt to put down the practice will inspire extensive dissatisfaction .... I must acknowledge that a similar opinion as to the probable excitement of a deep distrust of our future intention was mentioned to me in conversation by that enlightened native, Ram Mohun Roy, a warm advocate for the abolition of *suttee*s

.... It was his opinion that the practice might be suppressed quietly and unobservedly by increasing the difficulties, and by the indirect agency of the police. He apprehended that a public enactment would give rise to general apprehension that the reasoning would be, 'While the English were contending for power, they deemed it politic to allow universal toleration, and to respect our religion, but having obtained the supremacy their first act is a violation of their professions and the next will probably be, like the Mahomedan conquerors, to force upon us their own religion' ....

It might be very difficult to make a stranger to India understand, much less believe, that in a population of so many populations of people ... so great is the want of courage and vigour of character, and such is the habitual submission of centuries, that insurrection or hostile opposition to the will of ruling power may be affirmed to be an impossible danger .... Few of the natives of the Lower Provinces are to be found in our military ranks. I therefore, at once deny the danger in toto, in reference to this part of our territories, where the practice principally obtains. If, however, security were wanting against extensive popular tumult or revolution, I should say the Permanent Settlement, which, tho' a failure in many other respects, and in its most important essentials, has this great advantage at least of having created a vast body of rich landed proprietors, deeply interested in the continuance of the British Dominion, and having complete command over the mass of people, and, in respect to the apprehensions of ulterior views, I cannot believe that it could last but for the moment ....

Ere the scene of this sad destruction of human life laid in the Upper instead of the Lower Provinces, in the midst of a bold and manly people, I might speak with less confidence upon the questions of safety ....

It is stated by Mr Wilson that interference with infanticide and the capital punishment of Brahmins offer a fallacious analogy with the prohibition now proposed. The distinction is not perceptible in my judgment. The former practice, though confined to particular families, is probably viewed as a religious custom; and as for latter, the necessity of the enactment proves the general existence of the exception, and it is impossible to conceive a more direct and open violation of their Shasters, or one more at variance with the general feelings of the Hindu population. To this day in all Hindu states the life of a Brahmin is, I believe, still held sacred ....

The first and primary object of my heart is the benefit of the Hindu. I know nothing so important to the improvement of their future condition as the establishment of a purer morality, whatever their belief and a more just conception of the belief of God. The first step to this better understanding will be dissociation of religious belief and practice from blood and murder. They will then, when no longer under this brutalizing excitement, view with more calmness, acknowledged truths .... Thus emancipated from these chains and shackles upon their minds and actions, they may no longer continue, as they have done, the slaves of every foreign conqueror, but that they may assume their just places among the great families of mankind. I disown in these remarks or in this measure any view whatsoever to conversion to our own faith. I write and feel as a legislator for the Hindu, and as I believe many enlightened Hindu think and feel.

(Excerpted from Lord William Cavendish Bentinck's Minute on *Sati*, 8 November 1829. Reproduced in Jatindra Kumar Majumdar (ed.), *Rammohun Roy and Progressive Movements in India: A Selection from the Records, 1775–1845*, Calcutta, 1941, pp. 139–48.)

Reservations on the Propriety of State Interference

To

Captain R. Benson,

Military Secretary to the Governor General.

Sir,

I have the honor to acknowledge your letter of the 10th instant, requiring me to submit through you, to the Governor General, my sentiments on the subject of self-immolation of Hindu widows.

My opinions are adverse to any authoritative interference with the practice. I am aware that this avowal may expose me to the imputation of the absence of Christian charity and common humanity, but I should be unworthy of the reference made to me by the Governor General if I suffered the fear of undeserved detraction to restrain the honest acknowledgement of the sentiments I entertain ....

Before inquiring how far the practice of the *suttee* may be put a stop to, or the consequences that may attend its suppression, the subject I conceive should be freed from the extraneous matter with which it has been blended, and which, whilst it seems to illustrate, serves only to perplex the question. The practice should be considered by itself: not in connection with rites, to which it bears no analogy, and form the successful counteraction of which no safe guide can be derived.

The sacrifice of infants at Sagor was not only unauthorized by any part of the Hindu code, but was found upon inquiry to be 'neither countenanced by the religious orders nor the people at large, or at any time sanctioned by the Hindu or Mahomedan governments'. It was also necessarily of rare and restricted occurrence. This therefore affords no parallel to the performance of an act observed throughout India for many ages, under every form of government, and enjoined texts which all Hindu regard as holy.

The practice of female infanticide was, in like manner of very limited observance, being confined to a few castes in one or two districts. Its suppression also was, in the first instance, the work of persuasion and personal influence ....

The capital punishment of Brahmins is alluded to in your letter as an instance of safe interference with Hindu prejudices. It is true that no open opposition has been made to the execution of such a sentence, but it is less true that the law is far from popular, and that whenever is spoken of by the natives in communication with those to whom they are not afraid to express their real sentiments is pronounced by the violation of their religious code ....

These considerations, therefore, appear to me of little weight. The analogies are fallacious, and it seems a dangerous evasion of the real difficulties attending the question of abolishing the *suttee* to adduce them as proofs of the impunity with which its abolition may be effected.

Of a similar character is the attempt to represent it as not essentially a part of Hindu religion. A widow, it is true, is not commanded to burn in every case, and Manu is silent on the subject of concremation. Other authorities, however, of equal sanctity are sufficiently explicit, and the act is enumerated by them amongst the duties of a faithful widow just as much as chastity is held to be the duty of a virtuous wife .... The injunctions are set forth not by writers of recent date or disputable authority, but those whose whom the Hindus universally class amongst the divine and inspired founders of their system. They have, therefore, the weight of commands, as far as weakness will admit of their being obeyed, and they cannot be directly opposed without violence to the conscientious belief of every order of Hindus.

This is the only light in which, in my estimation, the question can be regarded. The *suttee* cannot be put down without interference with the Hindu religion ....

I do not imagine that the promulgated prohibition of *suttee*s would lead to any immediate and overt act of insubordination or violence. It would create very general alarm .... The people will not regard the prohibition, and *suttee*s will be attempted in spite of the law .... Again, supposing the rite is performed, what penalties are to be inflicted on the parties concerned who have acted under the impulse of religious incitement. If they are slight, they will be ineffective, and if severe, they will occasion great heartburning and discontent ....

I cannot offer any reply to the queries more particularly regarding the effects which the abolition of the practice may have on the native army. I should conclude, however, that the Hindu portion of it would share the feelings of their countrymen, more especially as it consists very largely of men of high castes .... It must be necessary for me to suggest in what a painful and anxious situation the native soldiery must be placed if it should ever be necessary to call upon them to give effect to the orders of the government, and to array their duty and allegiance against their social prejudices and religious beliefs.

Even if I may be mistaken in regarding the abolition of *suttee*s as actual interference with the Hindu religion, I think it will scarcely be denied that it will be so considered by the Hindus themselves. One or two individuals in Calcutta ... may hold a different persuasion, but the vast body of the population will concur in the same impression and the government has to legislate not for a handful of sectaries but for the Hindus at large.

Calcutta I have &ca

25 November 1828 [Sd] H.H. Wilson

(Excerpted from a letter from H.H. Wilson to Captain R. Benson, Military Secretary to Governor General, Lord William Bentinck. Dated 25 November 1828. Reproduced in Jatindra Kumar Majumdar (ed.), *Raja Rammohun Roy and the Progressive Movements in India: A Selection from Record, 1775–1845*, Calcutta, 1941, pp. 133–7.)

A Note from Sir Steuart Bayley

It will be easier for the government to deal with the question of widow marriage where protection against caste persecution only is wanted than with that of child marriage where the question really seems to lie mainly in the leaders of the society themselves.

(Excerpted from 'Note by Sir Steuart Bayley', Member, Government of India in the Home Department, Simla, 7 July 1884. Reproduced in B.M. Malabari, 'Infant Marriage and Enforced Widowhood in India: Being a collection of Opinions for and against Received by Mr Behramji Malabari from Representative Gentlemen, Official and Other Authorities', Bombay, 1887, p. 19.)

A Note from A.P. McDonell

In dealing with such subjects as those raised in Mr Malabari's 'Notes', the British government in India has usually been guided by certain general principles .... When caste or custom enjoins a practice which involves a breach of principles which involves a breach of criminal law, the state will enforce the law. When caste or custom lays down a rule which is of its nature enforceable in civil courts but is clearly opposed to morality or public policy, the state will decline to accept it. When caste or custom lays down a rule which deals with such matters as is usually left to the option of citizens, which does not the need the help of civil or criminal courts for its enforcement, state enforcement is not considered either desirable or expedient .... There is one common sense test which may often be applied with advantage in considering whether the state should or should not interfere in its legislative or executive capacity with social or religious questions .... The test is 'can the state give effect to its command by the ordinary machinery at its disposal?' If not, it is desirable that the state should abstain from making a rule which it cannot enforce without a departure from its usual practice or procedure .... The Governor General in Council, as at present advised, would prefer not to interfere ... until sufficient proof is forthcoming that legislation is required to meet a serious practical evil and that such legislation has been asked by a section, important in influence or number, of the Hindu community itself.

(Excerpted from the 'Note by A.P McDonell', Officiating Secretary to the Government of India. Extract from 'Proceedings of the Government of India in Home Department (Public)', Simla, 8 October 1886. Reproduced in Malabari, *op. cit.,* p. 108.)

Sir Andrew Scoble's Speech before the Legislative Council

The Hon'ble Sir Andrew Scoble, Law Member, moved the 'Report of the Select Committee on the Bill' to amend the Indian Penal Code and the Code of Criminal Procedure, 1882, be taken into consideration:

.... The discussion that has taken place with regard to the Bill during the last ten weeks has had many good effects. It has shown, among other things, that outside Bengal there is very little opposition to the measure; that for Bengal itself the extent and importance of the opposition have been by no means so great as represented, and that as regards the objection raised to the Bill, its supporters have everywhere had very much the best of the argument .... And if I may judge from the minute of dissent which my hon'ble friend Sir Romesh Chunder Mitter[1] has appended to the 'Report of the Select Committee ', it has satisfied him that the bulk of the argument with which he assaulted the Bill, on the occasion of its introduction into this Council, are not tenable and must be abandoned .... I fear I must occupy the Council for some time in going over the old ground, and showing how slight is the foundation either in fact or reason upon which the objections to the Bill are based and what little justification there is for the outcry which has been raised against it ....

My hon'ble friend Sir Romesh Chunder, while assuming for the purpose of his argument that 'the rule of premature intercourse with girl wives exists to a culpable extent in Bengal' states that this assumption, so far as the knowledge of Hindu society in Bengal goes, is not fairly tenable. I can understand my hon'ble friend's reluctance to admit the existence of a state of things so degrading to his countrymen, and I should have been glad had I been able to accept his testimony on this point. But what are the facts as stated in official documents which have been laid before the Council? ....

It has been stated that the case of Hari Maiti[2] is an isolated case and my hon'ble friend asserts that after the most searching enquiry not a single case resulting in conviction of a husband for rape during the last thirty years has been found out ....

[Here follows a description of cases of similar brought to the notice of the courts in the years immediately preceding.]

I might multiply cases of this kind, which shows not only that Hari Maiti's case is not exceptional, but that the present law, though not absolutely a dead letter, does not go far enough to efficiently protect this helpless class of children ....

And what of those cases in which neither death nor grievous hurt, nor other physical injury cognizable under the Penal Code, is caused? What of the case in which motherhood is attained and which are relied on by the opponents of the Bill in justification of their demand that things will be allowed to remain as they are? In a paper read by Dr Bolye Chunder Sen before Calcutta Medical society, it is stated on the authority of Dr Doyal Chunder Shome ... 'that of 21 cases of labour of girls between the ages of eleven and thirteen, ten of which were under his immediate care, while he did the genera; supervision of the other eleven natural delivery took place in five cases and stillborn children were born in six cases ... [and that five of them dies] of pernicious anaemia after prolonged suffering from fever and diarrhoea, and two died of phthisis' ....

Upon these facts, I think I am justified in asserting that the necessity for further protective legislation is established .... I pass on now to consider an argument of importance originally urged by my hon'ble friend, but which he does not now seem disposed to insist on. He disapproved of the Bill as being 'a departure from the non-interference policy hitherto observed by the government and carried by the Great Proclamation of 1858' ....

Now, this is too serious an indictment to be felt unnoticed even if my hon'ble friend as upon mature consideration thought fit to abandon it. There is absolutely no justification for the contention of my hon'ble friend, and it is intolerable that Her Majesty's gracious words should be perverted, as they have been on many platforms and in many newspapers in order to support to charge the breach of duty by the government of India. If my hon'ble friend had had the candour to read all those parts of the Proclamation which bears upon the argument ... [he would have found that] there is here no such undertaking of absolute non-interference as my hon'ble friend suggests, and if there were any room for doubt on the subject, Parliament would have given a fatal blow to the construction which he would adopt, by enacting under Section 19 of the Indian Councils Act, that with the previous sanction of the Governor General, measures affecting the religion or religious rites and usages of my class of Her Majesty's subjects in India may be introduced not only into this Council, but into the Provincial Councils whatever they may be established ....

So far as the sanction of religion or religious usages is claimed for the practice [of premature sexual cohabitation], which the Bill seeks to prohibit, it seems to me that the argument may be disregarded if the Council is of the opinion that the practice on grounds of humanity and morality ought to be prohibited. I am disposed to agree with my hon'ble friend that no legislative body [whether constituted as at present or in any other way] can satisfactorily deal with the question of the Shastras in the way of giving an authoritative opinion on them. But no member of this Council who has invaded, as I have done through a mass of dissertations on the subject which this controversy has called forth, cannot have come to the conclusion that the construct put upon the shastras by the Bengal *pandits* has not been accepted by the other parts of India, and that the balance of argument and authority is in favour of the supporters of the Bill .... Were I a Hindu, I would prefer to be wrong with Prof. Bhandarakar, Mr Justice Telang[3], and Dewan Bahadur Raghunath Row[4] than to be right with Pandit Sasadhar Tarkachudamani[5] and Mr Tilak,[6] and I should agree with His Highness, the *Maharaja* of Jeypore, in thinking that had the Indian sages whose authority is invoked by the so-called orthodox party lived now, they would have taken upon themselves the responsibility (as His Highness himself has done) of legislating with a view of protecting society from the pernicious consequences of early marriage and the consummation of marriage before the child-wife has scarcely any idea of what marriage means. It seems to me, moreover, unwarrantable to claim for Bengal an orthodoxy, and for its Shastras, an authority superior to that of the rest of India. It can hardly be contended that a doctrine which is non-essential elsewhere becomes essential because it is held in Bengal ....

I can equally understand that there may be men who place religious duty above all earthly loss, but these men are few; and I think Pandit Iswar Chunder Vidyasagar is nearer the truth when he says that the punishment that the Shastras prescribe for violation of a rule is of spiritual character and is liable to be disregarded ....

I pass on now to the only ground upon which my hon'ble friend appears now to base his opposition to the Bill and that is its inutility. I may observe at the outset that the utility of a measure of the kind depends to a very great extent on this support given to the more influential members of the community .... Consider how helpful an Act of this kind will be to them if they are really sincere in desiring an improvement in their marriage custom .... I have no sympathy with the pseudo-reformers who talk glibly on the subject and do nothing. If they honestly believe their marriage customs are bad, let them follow the example of the Sardars of Rajputana and amend them. If the legislature is to wait for their action before undertaking a measure of protection of this kind, the necessity for which I think, I have amply proved, the fate of child-wives in Bengal will never be ameliorated. My hon'ble friend says that the Act will be a dead letter; it is for him and for those who support him to make it so, not by throwing itself in the way of prosecution, but by lending their whole influence so as to modify caste rules and domestic practice that prosecutions may become unnecessary. No one will hurt by this Act who does not break it, who shall say that the punishment likely to be awarded is too severe? ....

No doubt the adoption of the age limit of twelve years will not cover all the cases which it would be desirable to protect, but it will go a long way in that direction ....

In many parts of India and among other classes, the practice is established or is gaining ground of not sending wives to live with their husbands, until they are at least twelve years old, and as the Chief Commissioner of the Central Provinces observes, 'The theory of the law still, by the proposed amendment, be brought into harmony with the practice of the people on a point in which the morality of the people is in advance of the morality of the law' ....

It is said that the offence [of premature sexual intercourse with child-brides] when committed by a husband against the wife ought not to be classed as rape and should be visited by a limited punishment. I do not think it is desirable that the gravity of the offence should be minimized in this way .... It is an offence affecting the wife not as wife but as human creature, and I should greatly regret if this Council were to weaken the effects of the Bill by drawing a distinction in favour of a brutality on the part of the husband.

Notes

1. Sir Romesh Chunder Mitter was one of the two Hindus (and four Indians) who were members of the Imperial Legislative Council.

2. Hari Maiti caused the death of his wife, Phulmoni, through forcible intercourse. The courts, however, refused to convict the offender on the grounds that he was the victim's husband, thus pointing to the need for amending existing penal laws.
3. K.T. Telang (1850–93), Judge and public figure in Maharashtra.
4. Reformer from south India, associated with the National Social Conference.
5. A prominent spokesperson of the Hindu orthodoxy in Bengal who strongly opposed the Age of Consent Bill.
6. B.G. Tilak (1856–1920) too opposed the Consent Bill in 1890–91.

(Excerpted from Sir Andrew Scoble's speech before the Imperial Legislative Council. Reproduced in 'Speeches on the Age of Consent Bill [Indian Penal Code of Criminal Procedure, 1882 Amendment Bill]', Calcutta, 1891, pp.14–25.)

Ranade on State Legislation in Social Matters

This question really reduces this to two points of enquiry: first, whether or not the institution assailed produces on the whole, more evil than good; and, second, whether the evil that is in them admits of speedier and far more effective remedy than is employed in the advice of those who would drift along with the stream of events, but neither exert themselves nor permit others to make an effort to regulate the current and make it run steadier and stronger in the desired direction. On the first point, taking the general sense of those who have spoken out on both sides, there appears to be a general agreement. The dispute here is confined to the alleged extent of the evils, which are freely admitted to be real. On the second point the difference of views is radical and there does not appear to be any great likelihood of an agreement ever being arrived at which will satisfy both parties. When one sees how men who had grown grey [under] the denunciation of these evils, turn around immediately a suggestion is made for practical action and join the orthodox majority in praise of the existing arrangements, the political *rishi*s' warning about the defects of the Hindu character seems to be more justified. There appears to be no ground for hope in such circumstances of seeing any genuine reform movement springing up from within the heart of the nation, unless the heart is regenerated not by cold calculations of utility, but by a cleansing fire of religious revival ....

[The] early celebration of child-marriages, the forcible disfigurement of widows, and absolute prohibition of remarriage in the higher castes ... are all admittedly corruptions of recent growth unknown to the best days of our country's history .... Internal dissensions, upheaval of non-Aryan races, and the predominance acquired by the barbarous Scythian and Mahommedan conquerors degraded the condition of the female sex, deprived them of the rights of inheritance and freedom, and made women dependant on man's caprice instead of being his equal and honoured helpmate .... Fortunately, the causes which brought on this degradation have been counteracted by providential guidance, and we have now, a living example before us of how pure Aryan customs, unaffected by barbarous laws and patriarchal notions, resemble our ancient usage .... [On the question of legislative intervention in social matters] several objections have been urged by the advocates of the let-alone school .... The first objection is that these are social questions, which it is not the duty of the state to regulate. We answer that this argument is not open to those who welcome, as the vast majority of these classes of opponents freely do, state regulations for the abolition of *sati*, of infanticide, suicide by *jogee*s on the banks of Ganges, and self-torture by hook-swinging ... or to those who propose compulsory education and compulsory vaccination and sanitary precautions generally. Individual liberty of action is no doubt a great force, but this liberty has its limits imposed by the fact that no man's liberty should encroach upon those who surround him .... The state in its collective capacity represents the power, the wisdom, the mercy, and charity of its best citizens .... The regulation of marriageable age has, in all countries, like the regulation of the age of minority or the fit age for making contacts, been a part of its national jurisprudence ....

The next argument urged on the other side is that the evil is not so great as some people think and that it really needs no state action. There can be no doubt that to some extent Mr Malabari has laid himself open to this side attack .... But this does not go to show that, making due allowance for all exaggeration, the residue of unaddressed wrong which calls for remedy is not sufficiently great to justify action. Much the same thing was said when it was proposed to prohibit *sati* or infanticide .... A third way of stating the same objection is that the parties who suffer do not complain and strangers have, therefore, no business to intervene. This is a very old line of defence. It was urged as an argument against the abolition of slavery ....

And if the state contemplated forcible action in spite of the wishes of the victims, arguments may be urged with the same effect. But nobody in his senses can or does contemplate any such method of procedure. Widows and children are not proper persons who can seek their own relief for the wrong that is done to them and to society, and the argument therefore falls to the ground ....

This jealousy of foreign interference in social matters is not altogether a bad sign and if the interference was of foreign imitation, the force of the argument would be irresistible. In this case, however, the foreign rulers have no interest to move of their own accord .... Imitation is to be our own and based chiefly upon the example of our venerated past and dictated by the sense of the most representative and enlightened men in the community, and all that is sought at the hands of the foreigners is to give to this response sense, as embodies in the practices and usages of the respectable classes ... and the sanction of law .... If we are to abjure such help under all circumstances, we must perforce fall back behind Parsis, Mahommedans and Christians, who have freely availed themselves of the help in recasting their social arrangements. Further, as it is likely that foreign rule will last over us for an indefinite length of time, we refuse ourselves by accepting this policy to the extreme absurdity of shutting out very useful help for many centuries to come. In such matters, a distinction of foreign and domestic rulers is a distinction without difference .... The change is sought not as an innovation but as a return and restoration to the days of our past history. Those who advocate it justify it on the authority of texts revered and admitted to be binding to this day.

> (Excerpted from M.G. Ranade, 'State Legislation in Social Matters', [no date]. Reproduced in *Religious and Social Reform: A Collection of Essays and Speeches by M.G. Ranade* (collected and compiled by M.B. Kolasker), Bombay, 1902, pp. 92–102.)

The State as Executor of Popular Will

Governments cannot afford to lead to matters of reform. By their very nature, governments are but interpreters and executors of the expressed will of the people whom they govern, and even a most autocratic government will find itself unable to impose a reform which its people cannot assimilate .... Well-ordered, persistent agitation is the soul of healthy progress and so, if it were not, I would not let the government to rest till this reform was carried through. Not allowing the government to rest does not by any means mean embarrassing the government. A wise government welcomes and needs the support, warmth and encouragement of such an agitation.

Reformers in any country are to be counted on one's fingertips and I know that the brunt of all such reforms falls upon the devoted heads of that small band of reformers. What are the reformers then to do in the face of this evil of such long standing [untouchability] is really the question one has to solve. The reformers all over the world have resorted to one or other of the two methods that I am about to mention. The vast majority of them have drawn attention to evils by creating wild agitation and resorting to violence. They have resorted to agitation that embarrasses the government, that embarrasses the people, that disturbs the even tenor of the life of the citizens. The other schools of reformers which I would call non-violent school resorts to agitation of the gentle type .... It draws attention by simple suffering. It never exaggerates. It never departs by a hair's breadth from truth and whilst impatient of evil, does not mean ill even to the evil-doer [satyagraha] ....

In my opinion, the government [of Travancore] is on the side of reform; only the initiative will have to come from you and not from the government.

(Excerpted from M.K. Gandhi, 'Speech at Trivandrum'. Reproduced in *The Collected Works of Mahatma Gandhi* (vol. 35), Ahmedabad, 1969, pp. 102–5.)

Hindu Shastras and Social Reform

The Shastras as a Guide to Reform

There are those who maintain that the cause of ... reform must be placed on what is called the Shastric basis and that we must appeal to the *religious* instincts of the masses. The view is that we must plead for those reforms not on the grounds of natural justice but on the grounds of Shastric injunctions. In his *Republic,* Plato has mentioned this as one of the grounds of human improvement and he speaks of the method as 'noble falsehood'. Prof. Macmillan of Elphinstone College, Bombay, hints at it as a valuable method of reform when he says that 'religion is much more teachable than morality to large masses of people'. And dealing with this question Mr Mckenzie in his work on 'Social Philosophy' remarks that 'at a certain age, both religion and morality can hardly be taught except in the form of myth' ....

Seeing that religion has so large a hold on the human mind, larger than anything else, and that we, Hindus, have been essentially a religious people, there is some force in the view that we must approach their minds and their hearts by means of the Shastras by which they profess to be guided. But the Shastras themselves are not agreed upon many points. Those of us who are familiar with Canarese know the proverb which ... translated into English, means that the 'Shastras make the din of the marketplace' and another proverb which means that the Puranas are all chaos and confusion. This very circumstance, however, ought to be our help in the promotion of reform. If the Hindu Shastras are wide and comprehensive enough to include any measure of reform, the social reformer ought not to omit to derive support from them and base his cause on them so far as he can base it. but our very Shastras have given us a free hand in changing with the times, by agreeing upon one point more than upon anything else—that is, by pronouncing without *any* hesitation that *custom or usage can supersede the injunction of the Shastras.* The whole history of the Hindu society has been a history of tumultuous departure, whenever the departure was rendered necessary or expedient from the laws laid down in the Shastras. Every custom marks the beginning of such a departure; and if the Shastras themselves say that we can make new customs, I do not see why the social reformer should confine himself to the Shastras alone. By all means let us not make light of our sacred books; like the Christian nations of modern Europe who owe much to the Bible and cannot, therefore, do away entirely from the influences they have derived from it, we Hindus cannot free ourselves from the influences we have derived from our Shastras. The Shastras have been more liberal than we care to be by giving us a free hand to deviate from them when necessary. It is this fact which the social reformer must incessantly din into the ears of the masses; that the Shastras are a valuable means of showing that our history has been a history of change. As Dr Bhandarkar[1] pointed out to you in his address from this place two years ago, there was a period when our women were not only educated but learned, when infant marriages did not prevail, widow marriages were not unusual, and caste distinctions did not exist in the aggravated and absurd form in which they exist now. That period was followed by another and we have gone on changing. We made no doubt *bad customs,* we made customs nevertheless and got the Shastras to adapt themselves to those customs. Let us now reverse the process and try to make good custom, and call to our aid the Shastras when and where we can, and appeal to the liberty of making customs which they have given us where the injunctions are against us.

Note

1. Dr Ramkrishan Gopal Bhandarkar (1837–1925), prominent Indologist and social reformer, who was on the side of the reformers during the protracted controversy regarding the suitable age of marriage and consummation.

(Excerpted from the presidential speech by N.G. Chandravarkar on the occasion of the fourth anniversary meeting of the Madras Hindu Social Reform Association on 28 November 1896. Reproduced in C.Y. Chintamani (ed.), *Indian Social Reform* (part IV), Madras, 1901 pp. 328–30.)

The Inner Ambivalence of Hindu Shastras

We have received a small brochure in Bengallee from the pen of Iswarchunder Bidyasagar, principal of Sanscrit College, treating upon the question of the remarriage of Hindu widows, which he tells us on the authority of a text of Parasara, is not opposed to Hindu law, adding that Parasara expressly prepared his code of laws for the use of people in this iron age, and what his ordinations should, therefore be followed by us in preference to those of any other legislators of the olden time. But strange, nay passing strange, that though nearly 5,000 years have passed away since the beginning of what we call the *Kali Yug,* the law of Parasara which is said to have been especially directed for observance in that period, continues practically a dead letter, throughout the length and breadth of Hindusthan. It would have been well had the learned principal of the Sanscrit College, who is regarded by foreigners as a man of enlarged views and deep research, afforded us some explanation of the circumstance, but the desideratum can be easily supplied; and the same arguments, which would have availed him in tracing out the cause of the apparent rejection of the Parasara's law, hold us good in pointing out the difficulties attending the remarriage of Hindu widow.

Matrimony is one of the 10 rites prescribed by Hindu religion, which every individual professing that religion must undergo at certain periods of his or her life. None of them, when once administered, can be repeated under any circumstances. They impose certain solemn obligations, which are binding for ever. If you break off those obligations, you are no longer within the pale of Hinduism. Hence, we presume, the views of Parasara, if they were such as have been interpreted to us by the author of the brochure under notice, have never been adopted by the Hindus, and will yet continue to be discarded by the people of this country for a long time to come. The Hindu society is not yet ripe for such a radical innovation in its nature and constitution. But the text of Parasara, on which so much stress has been laid by Iswarchunder Bidyasagar, admits of a different interpretation, which appears to us to be the more reasonable. Parasara merely says that a woman whose husband is dead, or had become an apostate, or has long been unheard of, or is an hermaphrodite, or has become an outcaste, might in any of these five cases lawfully take another man for her consort. This does not show that she might regularly go through the ceremony of a second marriage, which is expressly prohibited in all our codes of laws, both ancient and modern. It would hardly be natural to suppose that Parasara, living in an age in which Hinduism was in full force in India, could have the boldness to ordain what he knew was at variance with public opinion, and would never be followed by the people, or that he would ordain a new law without laying down specific injunction for its proper observance. But it would be far more reasonable to conclude that he merely responded to the opinion of those who had preceded him in the work of legislation and held valid a practice, which appears to have been common in those days, as well among the natives of India as among the Greeks, Egyptians, Persians, and other nations of antiquity, and is still in vogue among the lower orders of the people of Hindustan. It would not be fair to infer that because the ancient Hindus repudiated the remarriage of widows, they were not cognizant of the miseries caused to them by the loss of their husbands and happiness. On the contrary, there are numerous instances on record, which show that they not only alleviated of the sufferings of widowhood, but also relieved those of other women whose husbands had either been long absent from home or become renegades and outcastes. The lives of Mandodari, the queen of Ravana; of Tara, the consort of Bali; of Kunti and her sister-in-law Madri, the mother of five Pandavas, and of the wives of the Chitrangada and Vichitravirjya, as well as a host of other females, afford examples of a custom which is sanctioned by the Hindu law. They were not married again according to the ceremonial of the Hindus, but lived as wives with their husbands' next of kin without incurring in the least infamy; and their issues enjoyed the same respect as was shown to the other members of their families. This custom no longer prevails among the natives of the higher orders as it did in former times, but it is still followed by those of the lower grades; and it is to this custom we are inclined to think that Parasara alludes in his book, where he says that a woman may take another man for her husband under certain special cases. The learned principal of the Sanscrit College must know that Parasara wrote at the beginning of the *Kali Yug,* and both he and his son Vyasa, were particularly interested in upholding a practice which had not only descended to them from time immemorial and been recognized by their predecessors in their compilation of Hindu law, but was also one which they themselves followed. But if our modern reformers contend that the text of Parasara, which forms the basis of Iswarchunder Bidyasagar's dissertation, does not refer to the custom we have adverted to, but inculcates a new law providing for the remarriage of the Hindu widows—a provision which the learned principal of Sanscrit College labours to prove was especially made for this iron age—will they tell us whether they are prepared to go the whole hog and adopt the law of Parasara as it stands? Will they marry girls whose husbands have apostatized from the Hindu faith, or become outcastes by reason of their conduct being against the dictates of the religion? We can easily perceive that they do not intend to do this, then why do they talk of Hindu Shastras and ransack them for some absolute texts to support their views? Granting for the sake of argument that the remarriage of Hindu widows, ordered by the Hindu law, still, as it has never taken place during the five thousand years which have rolled away since Parasara wrote his book, and as it is not known that it was never resorted to, in the three preceeding ages, it is quite useless to cite that law in its favour at such a distance of time, when our social and domestic institutions have been so materially altered from what they were in the days of Parasara. These changes have assumed a certain form and consistency; and it is no easy task to create such a revolution among them as the remarriage of Hindu widows is likely to produce. But as we have said before, there are many other evils which might be removed with less labour, and to which our reformers should direct their attention, leaving the settlement of the question, which they have now taken up, to time and education, as any such innovation in our domestic economy as that question involves, will be the very last thing to take place.

12 February 1855

(Originally appeared as an editorial entitled 'Remarriage of Hindu Widows', *Hindu Intelligencer*, 12 February 1855. Reproduced in Benoy Ghose (ed.), *Selections from English Periodicals of the Nineteenth Century* (vol. III, 1849–56), Calcutta, 1980, pp. 111–14.)

The Tactical Unity of the Orthodox

Some years ago I happened to be in Benaras and, as I was driving through the narrow city streets, my car was held up in a crowd. A procession was passing through and, apart from processionists, there were many sightseers and little boys intent on sharing the fun. Crowds interest me and I got out of the car to find out what was afoot. The procession was certainly an interesting one and had certain unique features. We saw Brahmans ... marching shoulder to shoulder with bearded Moulavies ... and one of the standards they carried in triumph bore the flaming device '*Hindu–Muslim ekta ki jai*' (victory to Hindu–Muslim unity)! Very gratifying, we thought. But still, what was all this about?

This was a joint protest by the orthodox of both religions against the Sarda Act (or perhaps it was a Bill at the time) which prohibited marriages of girls under fourteen. The pious and the holy of both faiths had joined ranks and hands to declare that they would not submit to this outrage on their deepest convictions and their most cherished rights ....

Offensive slogans were hurled at us and there was some jostling about. Just then, the procession arrived at the Town Hall and, for some reason or other, started stone throwing. A bright young person thereupon pulled some crackers and this had an extraordinary effect on the serried ranks of the orthodox. Evidently thinking that the police or the military had opened fire, they dispersed and managed [this] with exceeding rapidity.

A few crackers were enough to put the procession to flight, but not even a cracker was required to make the British government in India surrender on this issue. A little shouting in which, oddly enough, the Muslims took the leading share, was enough to kill and bury the Sarda

Act. It was feeble enough at birth with all manner of provisions which hindered its enforcement, and then it gave six-month grace which resulted in a spate of child-marriages. And then, after the six months were over? Nothing happened; child-marriage continued as before, and government and magistrates looked the other way while the Sarda Act was torn to shreds and cast to the dogs ....

What were we doing all this time? We were in prison. For six years now, we have been mostly in prison, sometimes as many as sixty or seventy thousand at a time. Outside, a strict censorship prevailed, meetings were forbidden and an attempt to enter a rural area was almost certain to lead to prison, if not worse. The various emergency laws and denial of civil liberties were certainly not aimed at preventing support of the Sarda Act. But in effect they left the field clear to the opponents of that measure. And [the] government, in its distress at having to combat a great political movement directed against it, sought allies in the most reactionary of religious and social bigots. To obtain their goodwill, the Sarda Act was sat upon, extinguished. '*Hindu–Musalman ekta ki jai*' ....

This instance of the Sarda Act was a revealing one, for it showed that all the shouting about Hindu–Muslim friction and disunity was exaggerated and, in any event, misdirected. That there was such friction nobody could deny, but it was the outcome not so much of the religious differences as of economic distress, employment, and a race for jobs, which put in a sanctified grab and in the name of religion, and deluded and excited the masses. If the difference had been essentially religious, one would have thought that the orthodox of the two faiths would be the farthest removed from each other and the most hostile to each other's pretensions. As a matter of fact, they combine frequently enough to combat any movement of reform, social, economic, and political. Both look upon the person who wants to change the existing order in any way as the real enemy; both cling desperately and rather pathetically to the British government, for instinctively they realize that they are in the same boat with it ....

I have no doubt that this process will continue and will lead to the toning down of the communal and religious animosities, to Hindu–Muslim unity of a kind. The communalists of various groups, in spite of their natural hostility, will embrace each other like long-lost brothers and swear fealty in a new joint campaign against those who are out for radical change, politically or socially or economically. The new alignment will be a healthier one and the issues will be clearer. The indication to some such groupings are already visible, though they will take some time to develop .... Sir Muhammad Iqbal, the champion of the solidarity of Islam, is in cordial agreement with orthodox Hindus in some of their most reactionary demands. He writes: 'I very much appreciate the orthodox Hindu's demands for protection against religious reformers in the new constitution. Indeed, this demand ought to have been first made by the Muslims.' He further explains that 'the encouragement in India of religious adventurers on the ground of modern liberalism tends to make people more and more indifferent to religion, and will eventually completely eliminate the important factor of religion from the life of the Indian community. The Indian mind will then seek some other substitute for religion, which is likely to be nothing less than the form of atheistic materialism which has appeared in Russia.' ....

Sir Muhammad Iqbal's argument, however, takes us very much further than merely anti-communism or anti-Socialism .... His position on this issue of suppression of all reformers is, it should be remembered, almost the same as that of the Sanatanist Hindus .... I am afraid I cannot bring myself to agree with Sir Muhammad Iqbal and the Sanatanist party. The reason perhaps is a personal and a selfish one. I do not think I will get on at all under their joint regime; I may even land myself in prison .... It is an astonishing thing to me that while our millions starve and live like beasts of the field, we ignore their lot and talk of vague metaphysical ideas and the good of their souls; that we shirk the problems of today in futile debate about yesterday and day before yesterday; that when thoughtful men and women all over the world are considering problems of human welfare and how to lessen human misery and stupidity, we, who need betterment and raising most, should think complacently of what our ancestors did thousands of years ago, and for ourselves should continue to grovel on the ground. It astonishes me that a poet like Sir Muhammad Iqbal should be insensitive to the suffering that surrounds him; that a scholar and thinker like Sir Muhammad should put forward fantastic schemes of states within states, and advocate a social structure that may have suited a past age but is a hopeless anachronism today. Does his reading of history not tell him that nations fell because they could not adapt themselves to changing conditions, and because they stuck too long to that very structure which he wants to introduce in a measure in India today? We were not wise enough in India and the other countries of the east, and we have suffered for our folly. Are we to be so singularly foolish as not even to profit by our and others' experience?

(Excerpted from Jawaharlal Nehru, 'Orthodox of all Religious Unite!' (Written at Almora District Jail, 23 August 1935), *Modern Review*, December 1935.)

Objections to Hindu Code Bills

Preamble

To amend and codify: It is not at all expedient either to amend or codify the Hindu Law, all at once or in successive stages:

Reasons: The Hindu laws of succession are to be found in the Smritis. They are a part of our Sashtras and the sanction at the present moment is one of religion.

To amend such laws by votes taken in the legislature is an act sacrilegious in itself, and the laws will not command that respect and obedience which alone can make it endure the test of time.

Moreover, if we take to amending Sashtric laws, those portions which we seek to retain, will gradually lose their sanctity and will be disobeyed with a lighter heart.

According to Hindus, the moral codes of conduct are obeyed and respected more because these are Shastric injunctions to that effect than because [of] an infringement of those rules has been made punishable under the Indian Penal Code.

It may be argued that with material progress and change of circumstances a change in the laws is called for. This may be conceded. But the change should come gradually, imperceptibly, by the growth of healthy and reasonable customs modifying the law where it has become archaic, or by judicial interpretation of old texts. The Hindu Law allows the growth of usages and customs to suit the altered conditions, and when proved, such usage and customs will outweigh the written text of law.

The general mass of the Hindus, most of whom though illiterate are not uneducated, have never been asked to send representatives to the Central Assembly for the purpose of altering, amending, or codifying their personal laws. If they had been so directed, they would certainly have chosen quite a different class of representatives—people on whom they could rely as persons conversant with the Smritis, the difficulties if any which they were feeling regarding the application of Shastric rules, people who are learned in the Shastras and able to reconcile conflicting texts and to indicate the course to be adopted if any change was desired. Instead, they have sent to the legislatures those whom they thought fit to fight the British bureaucracy and wrest political, economic, and material advantages for themselves. It would almost be a breach of trust for these legislators to attempt tampering with the Hindu laws based on Smritis and Shastric sanction.

Regarding codification, it presupposes knowledge of the entire body of laws which is sought to be codified. Now, the Hindu Law of which there are many schools with sub-schools, and which also comprise the special rules of succession, marriage, transfer, etc., sanctioned by usage and custom of particular localities, sects, subsects, and families is so vast a subject that it is no disparagement to admit want of knowledge of the entire Law.

Then again the only benefit of codification is the easy reference to particular rules. But being vast and varied, the codification of the Hindu law can never be perfect, and will leave some rules or usages uncodified which will have to be proved otherwise than by reference to the proposed codes.

The codification will, therefore, be of doubtful benefit. In fact, it will not serve the purpose better than the textbooks on Hindu law now in use.

There is another serious objection to the amendment and codification of the Hindu law by these Bills. As section 1 of the Bill provides the Hindu Code with its amendments, etc., [it] will apply to those living in British India. Under the Government of India Act the authority of the legislature does not extend beyond British India. But there is a very large population of Hindus living outside British India. It not infrequently happens that members of the same family—father, son, or brother—are living under different sovereigns, but they are all Hindus and previous to the Code, the same personal law used to govern them all. Now after the Code, instead of there being simplicity, there will be confusion. The father will be governed by one law, the son by another; lands and properties within British India by one law and those within the states or elsewhere by another law. This result is to be avoided at all costs.

Coming to the question of the object of laws according to the Hindu law (*dharma*) is that which holds (*dharyate*) the society. Looked at from that angle, it is evident that the proposed laws, far from holding together the Hindu society and benefiting it, will within fifty years completely disrupt the same, by dividing and subdividing laws and introducing incompatible and very often unsympathetic, if not actually hostile, co-sharers. We have the object lesson of the Mahomedan society before our eyes. That they still have property is due to special features of the personal law—which by the way they are determined to protect from legislative attacks—namely, the right of making *wakf* for the benefit of children, which by making the properties inalienable, keep their properties intact. The Hindu law has no such safeguard; even if it had, it surrendered the same when the Transfer of Property and Succession Acts were passed. So the Code is objectionable as being positively harmful to Hindu Society.

In our opinion amendments and changes in the law are neither desirable nor have they [had] the desired effect unless those for whom such changes are intended feel that they are necessary. The zeal of reformers often leads them to make changes without reference to the actualities of the situation. They should take a lesson from the Hindu Widow Remarriage Act which, although placed on the statute book in the 50s of the last century, is not even now widely availed of. We would earnestly request the Government of India and the law member to cry halt and try to ascertain from the published judgments, proceedings of caste meetings, Hindu *sabha*s, and other public bodies whether there is any real demand on the part of the Hindus for a change in their personal laws of inheritance and marriage, before circulating the Bill or setting the legislative machinery in motion. We can assure them that the Hindu population is not feeling any such difficulty and there is no general demand for any change in their laws.

We, therefore, oppose this attempt to amend and codify the Hindu law.

(Sanat Kumar Chaudhury [ex-mayor of Calcutta], 'Objections to Hindu Code Bills', *Modern Review*, September 1942, pp. 256–7.)

4

The Typologies of Reform and Revival

Revival as Reform

We thought that with the fall of the old class of *pandit*s we had done with those wars of words which were formerly carried on with all the weight of great learning and accompanied by a demonstrative show of deep erudition, but we had evidently counted without our hosts, the great body of Indian reformers that are the products of English education, who owe nothing to the old school of *pandit*s and for whom the old school of *pandit*s have incurred no responsibility whatever. Before the spread of English education in this county there were only two classes of public literary or intellectual entertainments to which the people were treated now and then, and which supplied some diversion from the otherwise dull, monotonous, or in some places extremely hazardous lives which they generally led. The one was the most popular and useful practice of reciting the *katha*s to mixed and general audience consisting of all classes of people, from old men to boys and from old ladies to young girls. The ancient epics of the land—the chronicles of the life of Rama and his consort, and the great *Mahabharta*—were very often the books that were thus recited.

These *katha*s were greatly instrumental in keeping the national spark alive through so many vicissitudes of national fortune, when on occasions it had almost reached the point of total extinction. The second were the periodical religious discussions, which in most instances originated with the advent of a learned *pandit* from the outside.

Very often the new *pandit*'s discourse had caught the popular ears and the local *pandit* or *pandit*s thought their dignity, prestige, and even emoluments were in danger, to prevent which calamity, they considered it their duty to come out and give a challenge to the newly arrived, to prove his superiority in the knowledge of the Shastras by an open discussion. Or it might be that the newcomer thought his success depended on drawing out the local theologian and giving him a defeat. Be it as it may, the invariable result was that the discussion began with words, the accuracy of certain expressions used by one or the other, the applicability or the non-applicability of certain rules of grammar, and ended often, if not always, in words and sometimes in blows. I am sorry to observe that the present quarrel over 'reform or revival' between the reformers seems to me to resemble, at least in parts, the above-mentioned wordy polemics between the *pandits*. The reformers claim to be the leaders of the community. They have occupied the place of the *pandits* and divines of former times. They profess to lay down rules for the guidance of the general mass of people. They are agreed that the state of Hindu society is bad and rotten, that it needs great and radical changes, and that without these changes the whole social fabric stands in danger of giving way and burying the nation down in its debris. They have remedies, ready, patent, and infallible. On most of these they agree, only to differ on the name by which the same is to be styled. Their agreement as to the remedy disappears in their differences about the wordy habitat to be given to the proposed and contemplated changes. One class of people who have already established a name for themselves, do not like to give up the name they have patented and by which they have gained distinction. These latter gentlemen call themselves reformers and insist upon certain social changes being introduced in the name of 'reform' and reform only. The other class, who have lately come into prominence, call themselves 'revivalists', and they swear that any change in the social customs and institutions of the community can only be introduced under the shadow of revival. They think they cannot tolerate reform. The result is that while the former taunt the latter as 'revivalists and reactionaries', the latter mock the former as 'reformers and revolutionists'. Both classes contain amongst them great and good men, men with pure motives and noble intentions. They are generally prominent men—well read and deep in the lore of history. Both classes are to all appearances sincere in their convictions and efforts, but to the great misfortune of the country and the nation they cannot join their heads and work amicably. The wordy weapons are sometimes changed, and while the reformers take their stand on 'reform on rational lines', the revivalists plead for 'reform on national lines'. Here, for once at least, they seem to agree on reform, as the force of the difference is centred on the words 'rational' and 'national'. The result is that much ink and paper are uselessly spent in dilating upon the necessary soundness of reform, and the danger and risk of revival, and vice versa. Unfortunately, no one ever sees and deplores the great waste of valuable time and precious energy which this quarrel involves—time and energy which could be usefully employed in, nay, which is imperatively demanded by, so many other things that are the sine qua non of national progress and that should be done but are not done from want of working hands. On both sides are arrayed tough warriors armed with the knowledge and experience which is gathered by deep study and growing years. On both sides are arrayed sturdy and stout soldiers possessed of and carried by the enthusiasm of youth, full of ambition, and proud of credentials gained by academical successes and literary achievements. On both sides the pen and the tongue are being used with strength and vigour not totally devoid of grace. It is very perilous to come between such daring, bold, and determined fighters, specially for a comparatively ill-provided and poorly circumstanced man like myself who can wield neither the pen with the dexterity that comes of practice nor the tongue with that skill which is the outcome of discipline. In fact, I am rather inclined to think that it is positively dangerous for recruits who have not had the advantage of regular lessons in drill or of the discipline that comes out of exercises at the manoeuvres, to interfere between such veteran combatants. But the interests at stake are so great, the field is so vast, the workers in the field are so few and far between, the amount of energy available is so little, and the resources are so limited, that on better thought I have decided to take the risk and raise my voice against what to me looks sheer waste of opportunities and misapplication of energy.

I will begin by examining the respective programmes of reformers and revivalists, and see if there are any vital and real differences which justify so much contemptuous talk of each other. On both sides I believe that the social reform programme begins, and very rightly too, with the questions of early marriage. I confess I am unaware of any radical difference between the views of the reformers and the revivalists on the point. In provinces other than the Punjab, Mrs Besant is believed to be the leader of the latter. Now, who does not know that she is opposed to early marriages and denounces them as un-Shastric and disastrous? She has in fact taken pains not only to definitely pronounce against this evil custom, but to give force to her utterances, has shut the doors of a department of her school at Benares against those who might have been or might be by the improvidence of their guardians married at a tender age. The Arya Samajists also, may to a certain extent, be called revivalists, but in this matter of early marriage and the marriageable ages of boys and girls, they go a step further than even the most radical reformer is prepared to just now. They say and preach, and try to enforce their precept, that no girl be married under 16 and no boy under 25. Now let us ask if there is anything irrational in saying that the institution of child-marriage is not only condemnable by reason, but is actually opposed to the letter as well as the spirit of the Shastras. From the question of child-marriage, we may proceed to the great evil of the present divisions and sub-divisions of caste. Mrs Besant and her school have already pronounced against the subdivisions in the main castes. Her defence of the original Hindu conception of four castes principally coincides with the views of the Arya Samajists in the matter and practically knocks the present caste system on the head, though in theory only. In practice, neither the Arya Samajists nor the reformers can go further than denunciation. All of them agree that a beginning should be made with the subdivisions. The subdivisions having been swept away (which is not likely to be achieved very soon or very easily) the time will then come to think of the remoulding or the fusion of the main castes on Shastric or rational lines. For the present, we are all agreed that the existing arrangement is an unmixed evil, and the sooner it is done away with, the better. From castes let us proceed to the question of foreign travel, and here again we find a practical unanimity. Of course, there are and there shall continue to be ultra-orthodox people who will not give up their opposition to any of these measures and will continue to say that they are un-Hindus; but just now we are not concerned with them, as we dare say there is no one who can justly or even contemptuously be called a revivalist who condemns foreign travel on the plea of revival and not reform. Then let us take up the great question of female education. I know of no sensible man in the country, not to speak of the revivalists only, who is a man of culture and education, who is opposed to it. The school of Mrs Besant, the Arya Samajists, and the reformers are all pledged to it. There may be and there are practical difficulties in the way of educating our girls and sisters and wives, but nobody questions the desirability, nay, the necessity, of giving, if possible, the very highest education to girls. People may differ on the modus operandi or may have different views about schemes of education to be enforced in the case of females, but there are no two opinions on the question of principle. There may be some among the so-called revivalists who are not favourably disposed to an exact copy of European customs and usages relating to females being adopted by the Hindus, but surely there is none who can in the name of revival defend the existing *purdah* system or the universal ignorance of women. Similarly, we do not think there is much difference of opinion, at least so far as practical measures feasible at present are concerned, on the necessity of raising the social status and bettering the condition of low castes, if Hinduism is not bent upon social indifference and mad neglect of vital interests which might result in disastrous consequences. With the exception of some apparently spurious passages in Manu and other Smritis, there is absolutely nothing in the more ancient literature to justify the inhuman and cruel treatment to which the low castes are at present or were till lately subjected. We think we have almost exhausted the list of prominent subjects comprised in the list of reforms advocated by the social reformers, having reserved one important matter to be discussed last, namely, the question of widow remarriage.

On this question there exists undoubtedly real difference of opinion between the so-called reformers and the so-called revivalists. We grant that the question is a very important one; but still we are not prepared to admit that a difference on this single question justifies all that bitterness which characterizes the writings of these two classes about one another. The real and important differences are on questions of religion and worship which the social reformers profess to exclude from their curriculum of school and college education. Here in the Punjab, fortunately, we have been spared that bitter fight over these words which is going on in the western and southern presidencies, although we are not unaware that of late attempts have not been wanting to introduce it in collegiate and inter-collegiate debates. We cannot but deprecate these unwise attempts and will warn our young men from throwing themselves into the vortex of this absolutely unnecessary and uncalled for fight over words. We may be pardoned for pointing out that to us, the fight seems to be generally on the same lines and on the same grounds which marked the polemics of the old class of *pandits*. The real truth is that the so-called reformers are mostly in faith and in religion, Brahmos. They were the earliest in the field and fought for reform when the revivalists had not yet come into existence. The revivalists are the products of a wider diffusion of Sanskrit literature which has taken place principally within the last quarter of a century. This study has afforded them sufficient and strong evidence of their ancestors having enjoyed a great and glorious civilization from which most of the present evil practices and customs that are the bane of modern Hinduism were absent. They, therefore, naturally look to the past for light and guidance, and plead that a revival might lead them into that haven of progress which is the object of all. They have found that most of the social evils existing in their society were not to be found in the ancient Hindu race and they have, therefore, begun to appeal to the authority of the past and the Shastras for the introduction of these very reforms for which reformers had been pleading with much force though with scanty success on grounds of utility and natural justice. The revivalists are naturally popular in Hindu society as they take their stand on the authority of the Hindu Shastras and thus threaten to oust the reformers from their hard earned position. Then, to add insult to injury, their exposition of the popular religious beliefs of the Hindus is so injurious and cunning as to justify a reasonable fear in the minds of the reformers that they are taking the nation back to superstitions and low and debased forms of worship from which English education, contact with Western religion, and a study of the masterminds of the West was just extricating them with so desirable a success. The reformers had thus based their religious propaganda on the same basis on which their social programme rested, namely, grounds of rationality. The revivalists, having taken to the defence of the so-called national, have extended the same base to the removal of social evils and thus the fight began between 'reform on national lines' and 'reform on rational lines'. But, as I have pointed out above, so far as real social reform is considered, both lines of work lead to a common conclusion. It is not, therefore, fair to entangle social reform in this quarrel which is really based on differences in religious views. Let the 'reformers' by all means if they like, ridicule the religious views of 'the revivalists', and criticize or hold them to derision, but it is not, to say the least, graceful and fair to talk of them contemptuously in matters of social reform. The same should we say to the revivalists. Happily, here in the Punjab, as we have already said, there is not much difference between reform and revival. By far the strongest reforming agency in the Punjab appears to accept both. To them reform is revival and revival is reform. It is true they attach much importance to nationality or to national lines, but subject to the important proviso *that they are not irrational.* The Arya Samajists shall have nothing *irrational,* though it may even have the look of being national. They want everything national which is rational as well. They even go in for things national if only they are not irrational, but no further. According to them, nothing can be either national or rational which is against the letter or the spirit of the Vedas. So far there seems to be no danger of the Punjab being involved in this meaningless distinction between reform and revival, but we think it is better to take time by the forelock and sound this note of warning to guard against any contemplated or impending mischief. But over and above that, it is our earnest request to the leaders of the Hindu community in the western and the southern provinces to abjure this absurd distinction and to work harmoniously for social reform, at least so far as all are agreed upon. Lately, I had occasion to listen to an address on social progress by an esteemed friend of mine who is a pronounced social reformer. In the course of his remarks, he treated the revivalists with scant respect and in support of his views read the following quotation from the Amraoti speech of that great reformer, the late Mr Justice Ranade:

> On the other side, some of our orthodox friends find fault with us, not because of the particular reforms we have in view, but on account of the methods we follow. While the new religious sects condemn us for being too orthodox, the extreme orthodox section denounce us for being too revolutionary in our methods. According to these last, our efforts should be directed to revive and not to reform. I have many friends in this camp of extreme orthodoxy and their watchword is that revival and not reform should be our motto. They advocate a return to the old ways, and appeal to the old authorities and the old sanctions. Here also, as in the instance quoted above, people speak without realizing the full significance of their own words. When we are asked to revive our institutions and customs, people seem to be very much at sea as to what it is they seem to revive. What particular period of our history is to be taken as the old? Whether the period of the Vedas, of the Smritis, of the Puranas, or of the Mahomedan or modern Hindu times? Our usages have been changed from time to time by a slow process of growth, and, in some cases, of decay and corruption, and we cannot stop at a particular period without breaking the continuity of the whole. When my revivalist friend presses his argument upon me, he has to seek recourse in some subterfuge which really furnishes no reply to the question. What shall we revive? Shall we revive the old habits of our people when the most sacred of our caste indulged in all the abominations, as we now understand them, of animal food and drink which exhausted every section of our country's zoology and botany? The men and gods of those old days ate and drank forbidden things to excess in a way no revivalist will now venture to recommend. Shall we revive the twelve forms or sons, or eight

> forms of marriage which included capture, and recognized mixed and illegitimate intercourse? Shall we revive the Niyoga system of procreating sons on our brothers' wives when widowed? Shall we revive the old liberties taken by the Rishis and by the wives of the Rishis with the marital tie? Shall we revive the hecatombs of animals sacrificed from year's end to year's end, and in which human beings were not spared as propitiatory offerings? Shall we revive the *shakti* worship of the left hand with its indecencies and practical debaucheries? Shall we revive the *sati* and infanticide customs, or the flinging of living men into the rivers, or over rocks, or hook-swinging, or the crushing beneath Jagannath car? Shall we revive the internecine wars of the Brahmans and Kshatriyas or the cruel persecution and degradation of the aboriginal population? Shall we revive the custom of many husbands to one wife or of many wives to one husband? Shall we require our Brahmans to cease to be landlords and gentlemen, and turn into beggars and dependants upon the king as in olden times? These instances will suffice to show that the plan of reviving the ancient usages and customs will not work out salvation, and is not practicable. If these usages were good and beneficial, why were they altered by our wise ancestors? If they were bad and injurious, how can any claim be put forward for their restoration after so many ages? Besides, it seems to be forgotten that in a living organism as society is, no revival is possible. The dead and the buried or burnt are dead, buried, and burnt once for all, and the dead past cannot, therefore, be revived except by a reformation of the old materials into new organised beings.

Now, if it be permissible for a comparatively young and inexperienced man without laying himself open to a charge of disrespect for one of our revered leaders whose great wisdom, deep learning, and general judicial-mindedness are accepted all around, I will, with due deference to the late Mr Ranade, beg to point out the injustice of the observations quoted above. Cannot a revivalist, arguing in the same strain, ask the reformers into what they wish to reform us? Whether they want us to be reformed on the pattern of the English or the French? Whether they want us to accept the divorce laws of Christian society or the temporary marriages that are now so much in favour in France or America? Whether they want to make men of our women by putting them into those avocations for which nature never meant them? Whether they want us to substitute the legal *niyoga* of the Mahabharata period with the illegal and immoral *niyoga* that is nowadays rampant in European society? Whether they want us to reform into Sunday drinkers of brandy and promiscuous eaters of beef? In short, whether they want to revolutionize our society by an outlandish imitation of European customs and manners and an undiminished adoption of European vice? The revivalists do not admit that the institutions which they want to revive are dead, burnt, and gone. The very fact that they wish to revive them goes to show that they believe that there is still some life left in them and that, given the proper remedy, their present unhealthy and abnormal state is sure to disappear, and result in the bringing about of the normal and healthy condition of affairs. In fact, in an earlier part of the same address, Mr Ranade summed up the position of the revivalists in a few well-chosen and apt words when he admitted that, 'In the case of our society especially, the usages which at present prevail amongst us are admittedly not those which obtained in the most glorious periods of our history. On most of the points which are included in our programme, our own record of the past shows that there has been a decided change for the worse and it is surely within the range of practical possibilities for us to hope that we may work up our way back to a better state of things without stirring up the rancorous hostilities which religious differences have a tendency to create and foster.' It is exactly this working up our way back which the revivalists aim at. No revivalist has ever pleaded for the institutions selected by Mr Justice Ranade as the butt end of his attack against them.

The real significance of these words—'reform' and 'revival'—if any, seems to be in the authority or authorities from which the reformers and the revivalists respectively seek their inspiration for guidance in matters social. The former are bent on relying more upon reason and the experience of European society, while the latter are disposed to primarily look at their Shastras and the past history, and the traditions of their people and the ancient institutions of the land which were in vogue when the nation was at the zenith of its glory. On our part, we, here in the Punjab, are prepared to take our inspiration from both these sources, though we prefer to begin with the latter and call in the assistance of the former mainly to understand and explain what is not clear and ambiguous in the latter. But so long as our conclusions are principally the same, I think the fight is not worth being continued and may be dropped for good.

(Originally published in the *Hindustan Review* and *Kayastha Samachar Volume x* (1904), pp. 474–82. V.C. Joshi (ed.), *Lala Lajpat Rai: Writings and Speeches, 1888–1919*, vol. I, pp. 445–54, Delhi, 1966.)

Revival as Reaction

That a strong tide of reaction in favour of the old ideas, the time-honoured customs, and the superstitions of our society ... began very strongly to flow in our midst must be too plain to all .... What is the genesis of the movement? It owes its origin in Bengal .... And in Bengal, this movement owes its origin to the violent action of the first batch of our social reformers with those whose freaks and fancies that previous little Bengalee book of Babu Rajnarain Bose *Sekal O Ekal* (The Past and the Present) has made the readers of Bengalee literature so familiar .... The Brahmo Samaj, reconstructed by the solid piety and steadfast devotion of Devendranath Tagore, was the first factor in the development of this reactionary spirit .... The next factor in the development of this reaction was the ancient Sanskrit literature .... And so far this reaction was a perfectly healthy one ....

[But following the controversy surrounding the Ilbert Bill] we naturally turned around and began to defend those evil customs with that subtle sophistry of which we are unrivalled masters, and what was at first a mere tactic, a mere manoeuvre in a political war, gradually attained the strength and tenacity of a social creed ....

[A] careful analysis of this movement will show that there are about five classes and kinds of reactionists .... The first class consists of those gentlemen who were at one time really earnest and sincere friends of reform but who ... have discovered that they do not work so smoothly and a fall here ... an obstacle in another, have now led them to conclude that things are best as they already exist in our society. The next class ... consists of men who had been drawn to the reform movement by the magnifying rhetoric of some powerful and popular leader, and, naturally enough, as one tide of sentiment had brought them to the side of reform, so another tide of sentiment had taken them back to the enemies' quarters .... The third class consists of men ... who although not really opponents of reform, have ... sought alarm at the general disruption of society .... The fourth class ... is recruited from the ranks of those weak men who, not being able in the face of social persecution to embrace thoroughly the cause of reform, have with a view to quiet their uneasy conscience, gradually led themselves to believe that cause to be unjust and false .... The fifth and the last class ... who are also the most numerous, the most important, and the most powerful supporters and leaders of that movement, owe their faith to the growth of a particular form of political life in the country. It mainly consists of those amphibious creatures ... the political Democrats and the social Tories of the country—of that large number of our countrymen whose patriotism is simply another name for an universal hatred of everything foreign and who have lent support to this reactionary movement not because they believe ... this movement to be true and good, but because they find it an excellent means for enlisting recruits for the political agitations of the country ....

[T]he present social reaction—what does it mean? It means, then, in the first place that the various reform movements of the country have not as yet found their true and eternal basis .... [W]ith regard to the question of child-marriage, for instance, far more attention has been paid by our reformers to the numerous inconveniences arising out of it than to the injustice and unrighteousness upon which the evil custom is based .... [N]othing short of the entire and absolute eradication of this pernicious custom could meet the demands of reform .... And, gentlemen, with regard to widow marriage, it seems to me that the basis of this reform has been most sadly misinterpreted by a large number of its advocates and has been grossly misunderstood by its opponents, for the real question in the matter is not the introduction of widow marriage but the removal of disabilities under which the Hindu widow labours. I do not believe that widow marriages have any particular virtue of their own ... but because I think that the disabilities inflicted upon them by Hindu social custom is an unjust encroachment upon individual rights and liberties .... I shall fight against [it] ....

But, gentlemen, this spirit of social reaction does not only indicate the shallowness of the case of social reform ... it means as well that our political agitations have not as yet been founded upon a sound and rational basis. I can very well understand, sir, why political activity in this country should have precedence over the activities towards social reform, for it is due entirely to the law in statics that all forces must work along the line of least resistance. But I do not understand the position of those, who, in the same breath, clamour for the political enfranchisement of the people and defend their social slavery .... It means that we have yet to realize the truth of the principle that the growth of political institutions in a nation absolutely depends upon the growth of ideas, and the progress of thought and culture in all the departments of the nation's life ....

I am afraid that unless this reaction is soon checked and brought under control, even the political agitations of the country that have done so much to foster and strengthen this spirit will ultimately die a violent death in the hands of this very reaction. For the one essential condition of the success of all constitutional political agitation in this country is loyalty to the British government, and unshaken confidence in the sense of justice and right of the British nation. But the anti-English spirit of which the socials reaction is an outcome and which again this reaction is materially helping to grow in strength tends to destroy this one essential condition of the success of our political movement....

[I]t is said even by those who are no friends of the cause of social reform that all reforms must grow from within and not [be] imported from without. And I believe the enemies of reform whether social or political must believe in ... a new synthesis of life.

> (Excerpted from B.C. Pal, *The Present Social Reaction: What Does It Mean*? [substance of lecture delivered at Bethune Society, Calcutta, 5 December 1889], Calcutta, 1889.)

The Underlying Unity of Reform and Revival

'How did the Pope go to Avignon?' says an European proverb. '*En Protestant*'—as a Protestant.

Even the Pope, then, in the face of an usurper, may, till he is reinstated, act the part of a Protestant. Even a Hindu, in a similar place, may call himself a reformer. It would be sad, however, if the Pope, in love with the attitude of a protestor, were permanently tinged with the originality and discontent of that character. The great church of which he is the head, divided thus against herself, could no longer stand intact under the blows that would then be dealt her by her chief pastor. And similarly of the reformer. The work of reform is always limited in any given direction, and nothing can be more mischievous than the temper of the professional reformer. One reform there indeed is which may be pursued day and night, in season and out of season, but this is the reform effected by pure ideas. The same universality does not belong to reform proper, that is to say, to the displacement of one institution by another. Never, for instance, can we sufficiently realize, never can any sufficiently aid us to realize, the highest ideals of faithfulness in woman. But who could presume to dictate to another the form in which this could be pursued? Picture the folly of one who tried to force the exclusive imitation of the Blessed Virgin on unwilling followers in the east, or that of Sita on equally reluctant disciples in the West! Imagine the disastrous removal of all familiar exemplars in order to spread submission to the ideal of the preacher. It is clear that the result would be moral and social chaos. Only the pure idea, the concept of faith and purity itself, can be universal. The form must always be of localized application. Only the crusader of the ideal, then, can claim passports without limitation. The rights of the reformer of institutions are definite, and have a beginning and an end.

It follows that the ideal itself binds together both reforming and unreforming. For, if it be universal, it must be common to these two. In the great ends of human striving, the orthodox and the modern are at one. Both alike are struggling to reach the ideal. Both alike recognize good as good and evil as evil. We may take it, however, that the reformer is often one who understands the reality of a need to which the rest of his society is blind ....

We are usually very one-sided in our perceptions. All the world must prostrate itself in admiration before women who were capable of performing *sati*. But Ram Mohan Roy was indubitably right when he took any means that lay to his hand to forbid women in future that liberty. The patriot admires the heroic wifehood and admires also the lion-hearted reformer. Hinduism has appropriated in this matter, the labours of the agitator. Hindus know well that his stern prohibition must be eternally enforced. They only hold that in his person—original as was his impulse, national as was his whole upbringing—it should be recognized that a Hindu, and not foreigners, put an end to the custom. Ram Mohan Roy's was the apostate. The response of his own people was the sanction. All that foreigners contributed was the assistance of the police, on definite occasions.

This is indeed the mode of all social progression. Custom grows rigid or becomes exaggerated. Protest arises in the person of the saint or teacher, and society opens her arms, embraces her rebel son, and takes her stand henceforth on that wider basis which his work has built for her. Or, to put it otherwise, a healthy reform group represents an experiment in the laboratory of social growth ....

The Pope went to Avignon as a Protestant. True. But he came back. And when he did return, it was as a good Catholic, glad to be at home, in familiar places, glad to be freed from the necessity of protesting against anything. So the reforms in general. A good deal of dust is stirred up by their inception. A good deal of antagonism and mutual conflict is required at first, partly to weed the ranks of recruits who might not be helpful. But in the end, there assuredly comes a time when the pioneer-stage of the labour is ended. Then a new duty arises on both sides. On society, it is incumbent to appropriate consciously, all that the social experiment has achieved and evolved. On the reformers, it is desirable to draw closer the bonds that unite them to the old fold, and to sun themselves once more in those communal thoughts and sentiments from which, for a while, they were necessarily isolated.

Then arise fresh and still more living ideals. The divided consciousness of conservatism on one side and new moulding on the other gives place to the sense of a great task of upbuilding to be performed in common. Men realize that they are after all but the children of their own fathers; that should they reach the fullest significance of their institutions, the achievements would be tantamount to the most perfect reform. The radical sees that his own moral fervour and love of integrity were handed down to him from his orthodox forebears, who must have been to the full, good men as himself. The orthodox man, on his side, realizes that a mere religion of the kitchen could never represent *dharma*. Instead of casting stones at others for their errors of sympathy, it is his duty to widen his own activity. The Brahmo is no longer to be blamed for abandoning the ancient forms of caste, and neither is the orthodox to rest content with his own petrification of custom. For nationality has arisen, as the goal of all sections of society alike, and side by side must work brothers of all shades of opinion, of all forms of energy, for the recreating of the *dharma*, for the building anew of the modern world, of *Maha-Bharata*, Heroic India.

Our watchword then is no longer 'reform'. In its place, we have taken the work 'construct'. We have to recreate the *dharma*. We have to build again the *Maha-Bharata*. It was said that the church and its protestants, society, and the reformer, we are now to exchange achievements and become fused once more. For, after all, humanity is greater than any church. Society was made for man, not man for society ....

We are working comrades, not because we speak the same language or believe the same creeds. Should I cease to be the brother of my own mother's son because he went abroad and learnt a foreign tongue, or took up the worship of Mahadeva instead of that of Vishnu or Parthasarathi? We are working comrades on no basis so limited as that of creed or language, which after all would limit us geographically to a province and spiritually to a single line of development. Our task is one, the rebuilding of Heroic India. To this, every nerve and muscle of us tingle with response. Who is so foolish as to imagine that a little political petting and pampering can make a nation forget its kinship with the other half? We have not to become one. We *are* one. Our sole need is to *demonstrate our unity.*

(Excerpted from Sister Nivedita, 'Revival or Reform', originally appeared in the *Indian World,* January–July 1907. Reproduced in *Sister Nivedita's Lectures and Writings,* Calcutta, 1975, pp. 82–8.)

5

Imperatives within Social Reform

The Social Agitation on the Woman Question

The Pressing Need for Emancipation

Gentlemen, had not my theme been of such paramount moment to the progress of civilization and refinement in our dear native land and did I not feel myself called upon by the voice of humanity to agitate it, I should have hardly thought of obtruding upon your notice this crude and feeble attempt. But I am sustained by the conviction that however crude and feeble it may be, it cannot fail to awaken your attention and rouse your sympathies in behalf of a class of your fellow-beings whose wretched situation makes upon you the most emphatic call enforced by ties of blood and country .... You will admit, gentlemen, that habit renders us callous and indifferent, and reconciles us in a great measure to those disadvantages which we have been accustomed to endure from our very birth. This is likewise equally true of those blessings with which we have been surrounded and which we have enjoyed from our infancy .... It is natural, therefore, that under this peculiar tendency of the mind to accommodate itself to whatever privations it has long been subjected, we should to a great extent overlook and become habituated to those evils under which we are born and have grown up. It is under this conviction and not to enlighten you with what you already know, that I have undertaken to embody in language the miseries of our countrywomen and to paint them in vivid but faithful colours. The first step towards the redress of these grievances under which we have groaned for ages but which long usage has in a manner taught us to regard with apathy, is to annihilate this lethargy of habit under which the mind labours by frequently exposing to it those grievances. The only way, therefore, that seems to me calculated to direct our attention to the degraded and miserable condition and to enlist our sensibilities in favour of the companion of man in this country is to depict as often as we can her sufferings with all the eloquence of truth and feeling ....

It is much to be regretted and no less to be wondered at that a subject of so much vital importance, so intimately connected with the welfare and regeneration of fallen unhappy India, should have so long remained untouched. It is equally a matter of great sorrow and astonishment that no powerful impulse has yet been given to the cause of these miserable and unhappy creatures; that no efficient project has yet been set on foot to ameliorate the condition of the Hindoo women ....

Woman, who has allotted to man as his inseparable companion during his journey through life, to participate [in] his dangers and sorrows, to alleviate his distress, and share his joys and happiness, leads indeed a wretched life in this country. Penned up in her eternal prison house she is doomed to pass her days in misery and confinement .... Her occupations during the day are confined to those of a low menial .... Notwithstanding all their laborious drudgery to please and win the stubborn hearts of the inhuman wretches with whose fates *their* destinies are indeed identified, I say notwithstanding all this they are very often wantonly left to enjoy a *solitary bed* during the night, for I blush to confess, that owing to the low ebb to which morality is reduced, adultery is looked upon by our countrymen as a crime, high and fashionable. They suppose women are born only to minister to their comforts and luxuries, and consider that man is absolute lord not only over the fishes of the sea, the fowls of the air, and the beasts of the forest, but over the female world ....

The cause of that state of seclusion and imprisonment in which the females of this land are preserved may be traced to the tyranny of the Mehommedan emperors .... The state of constant alarm and anxious suspense in which the poor natives left made them regard their safety always at the expense of their other duties and occupations; the fear of brutal ravishment suspended the social intercourse between females. To shield them from the hand of ruthless power, they were withdrawn from society by their fond parents, and from that time they were kept in a state of strict seclusion in a *zenana* which since ratified by time, has now become an irresistible and fatal custom ....

The state of their [women's] mind is indeed lamentable .... They know of no other enjoyments beyond the gratification of the senses.

They are strangers to the pleasures of novelty of imagination and of intellect. They derive no enjoyment from a contemplation of the sublime and the beautiful .... The influence of superstition over their minds cannot be better exemplified than in reference to the horrid and revolting rite which they perpetrated so often but lately. I allude to the self-immolation which they committed on the funeral pyres of their deceased husbands .... The only ambition which they seem to be actuated by is to gain the name of a 'good cook', and indeed she is looked upon in the limited circle in which she moves as a woman of no ordinary accomplishments! They are entirely destitute of all those refined intellectual attainments which render women doubly amiable, makes her society a delightful refuge from the thrall and tedium of business, and add double force to the resistless and captivating charms of beauty ....

I have perhaps too severely animadverted upon the Moslem rule as the most prominent cause which has induced those sad and deplorable effects that I have faintly and partially portrayed above .... I should notice one or two circumstances which, as is vouched by experience, have proved no less prejudicial to the interests and well-being of the Hindoo women .... I allude to the existence of Hindoo Shastras. It is these religious codes of our countrymen which render their wives literally slaves both in body and mind to their will and caprice. By this I do not mean to condemn that refined piety which every female ought to show towards husband and which it is her bounden duty to maintain, not only because it is one of the highest recommendations and one of the brightest ornaments in a woman, but it is ordained by nature. But I am free to declare that I abhor from the very core of my heart, those abominable principles, the inculcation of which makes women emphatically called the better half of our species merely 'the slaves to a tyrant's will' ....

The last topic with which I shall trespass upon your time, gentlemen, on this occasion is that which entails the heaviest evils, moral and physical, upon the Hindoo women and crowns their unhappy situation. I mean that execrable marriage system which prevails in this country. You will in vain look for anything similar in the domestic economy of any nation .... [W]e are married at an age when neither the graces of the mind nor of the body are sufficiently developed. We have not a single opportunity of judging for ourselves with respect to either of these until it is too late .... I need not tell you that personal or intellectual accomplishments are of secondary moment to our parents. Whatever be the physical and mental recommendations of a youth, they are scarcely taken into account, if unaccompanied by that most important qualification *kul*.... The result of these incongruous matches is that absence of all conjugal love and consequently of domestic felicity which is so universally observable amongst the natives. It is, however, the women that are by far the greatest sufferers from these ill-assorted marriages. When the grievances are on the side of men, they resort to various means to indemnify themselves. The world is open to them .... They have recourse to licentious gratification which is, however, not confined solely to those who have been unhappy in their marriage. I may here remark, by the way, that this circumstance is independently a source of bitter suffering to the women. You cannot but be painfully aware of the general prevalence of that most detestable crime of adultery, the avowed practice and open toleration of which strikingly marks the utter degeneration of our country .... The Shastras concede to the men, the privilege of wedding more than one woman. They often take advantage of this invidious right not only on the score of connubial infelicity, but from various other motives such as passion, prejudice, and the like. There is no creature more impatient of a rival than a woman .... Yet our countrymen too often forget the impossibility of reconciling two rivals to each other and making them live in harmony under the same roof .... I now come to another source which produces unmingled suffering to the Hindoo women .... I allude to the prohibition of the remarriage of widows .... The death of their husbands cuts them off from every comfort and enjoyment .... They are condemned to additional household drudgery and drag on their existence a burden alike to themselves and their surviving relations .... But the most trying evil which they are obliged to undergo is the perpetual celibacy to which they are subjected .... Gentlemen, there remains but one topic connected with the sufferings of the Hindoo women. I mean the marriage system which prevails amongst the *kulin* Brahmins. This is another prolific source of the most heinous crimes and the most poignant miseries. But I refrain from entering upon it tonight.

(Excerpted from a paper read by Mahesh Chandra Deb, January, 1839, before the Society for the Acquisition of General Knowledge, Calcutta, and entitled 'A Sketch of the Condition of the Hindoo Woman'. Reproduced in Goutam Chattopadhyay (ed.), *Awakening in Bengal in Early Nineteenth Century: Selected Documents* (vol. 1), Calcutta, 1965, pp. 89–105).

A Crusader's Testament

Question: Judging from results, you seem to have been well rewarded?
Malabari: Certainly. I have cause to be profoundly thankful. At first it was an uphill work and get at the right sort of supporters, the old superstition about 'religion' being still prevalent in most quarters. I saw this rock ahead at a glance, and determined not to knock my head. I divested my proposals of all 'religious' or 'social' complexion, confining myself entirely to the anomalies and absurdities of British-made laws in India bearing on the relations between the sexes, and to an exposition of the doctrines of false neutrality the government had been led into adopting. Here, I would repeat once more what I have said a hundred times over, namely, that my proposals have nothing to do with religious, social, or domestic reform as such. They simply deal with some of the defects of their own laws and policy for which the British government in India are responsible. It has been the one war cry of the anti-reform party that a foreign government should not interfere with the domestic concerns of our people. I say *amen*. Thank you very much, gentlemen, for deprecating foreign interference. We go with you. So far reformers and anti-reformers now occupy the same platform ....

Let us look at the proposals themselves. As regards the protected age being raised to at least 12. There was practically no objection that I could find in England. On the contrary, some of the most competent authorities ... demanded a larger increase .... In India I do not think there can be two opinions about the question now. The old argument about the interference of the police and so on is suicidal for our few remaining opponents. As a Bengali friend pointed out the other day, if there was no police interference when the age stood at 10, there ought to be less than none of the danger apprehended when the age is raised to 12. The other argument, that the age for completion of marriage in India is 16, is equally suicidal. If that age is 16, why object to the protected age being raised to 12 or for that matter to 14? As a matter of experience, however, the average age for completion of marriage amongst Hindus stands below 14. Is it too much, then, to fix the protected age at 12 in the case of husbands and 13 in the case of strangers? ....

As regards [the restitution of conjugal rights] also I heard not a single dissentient voice in England once the case was fairly stated. Some of the friends of that hateful importation disowned it, and agreed to have the coercive process abolished without further delay ....

The proposal regarding arrangements for infant marriage is apt to be misunderstood. Let the critic be so good as to remember that my appeal was addressed to the British public and British authorities, and directed not against the religious or social customs of the people in India ... but the share which the 'neutral' British government in India have had in aggravating the lot of victims of those customs, by legally recognizing and enforcing those customs on the weaker sex, while yet professing a policy of non-interference .... I was bound to submit that the 'neutral' government ought at least to decline to have anything to do with the results of unnatural social arrangements ... My first object was to pin the government of India to their declared policy of neutrality. To be practical, I had to add that as a foreign government could not prohibit infant marriages, let them by all means permit such marriages to be contracted at any age, subject to only to ratification before the parties coming of age ....

Let me tell my Hindu bretheren frankly that the object with which I have framed this proposal is three-fold: firstly, to discourage baby marriages, secondly to leave the parties free in case of extreme need, and thirdly to save infant wives from the status of widowhood. Is it too much for such an object to ask that the 'neutral' British government shall remain neutral; in fact, that they shall neither prohibit nor recognize infant marriages? ....

All that I need to say about the Widow Marriage Act is that the government be just and consistent. It is their own business ....

What then becomes of the 'revolution' which a certain meddlesome villain is going to bring about? Is it not idle for intelligent men to assume that because female children are not to be married in infancy, therefore they will never be married? Why, if all the Hindu fathers agree to delay parting with their girls for a few years, the prospective husbands will only have to wait. They are not going to marry outside the pale of Hinduism .... Where on earth is the threatened disorganization of society? The critic who fears 'demoralization' if *infant marriages* are discouraged appears to me to be guilty of a heartless and senseless libel upon his own children. Not the worst of our enemies can say that Indian children of 9 or 10 are likely to go wrong if left unmarried at that age .... It is very hard to bear the injustice done [to] me by this class of critics, harder still, because the injustice recoils upon the country. When these writers call me ignorant, revolutionary, Europeanized, and that, do they know what harm they are doing to themselves? .... But in their hearts they know that I am much better informed than they are themselves ever likely to be. They also know that I am quite the reverse of a revolutionary. If my proposals were revolutionary, would responsible Anglo-Indians of the highest rank have favoured them? Would members of the Congress Committee have joined us with alacrity? .... Again, if I thought of myself and my own hobbies, why did I set my face against tempting offers of a battle on the floor of the House of Commons and a campaign throughout Great Britain, with myself as the hero of the hour? .... It cost me an immense effort to keep the lions of reform in hand. Two or three of the lionesses actually told to me face that I seemed to be in love with the government of India—'and such a government,' said one of them, with ineffable contempt, of which I was perhaps more a subject than that luckless government .... But I have an almost morbid dread of moving the government suddenly or of springing a mine under the feet of society. Once the huge machinery of state is set in motion, there is no knowledge when it may stop. I have never been and never shall be a party to precipitate action ....

As to myself, I know that the most modest of our programmes will be opposed in some quarters till we are able to carry the day. Once the authorities make up their minds, our opponents will accept the situation, I believe, with thankfulness. It has been so always and will be so .... Some Hindus are fond of reminding me that marriage with them is a sacrament and not a contract. As if I did not know! Marriage being a sacrament, it is greater shame to them that they should bring the sacred state of matrimony to this pass. Marriage is absolutely a sacrament. But whoever enjoined it to be performed on babes?

> (Excerpted from an interview with B.M. Malabari on his return from England. Originally appeared in *Bombay Gazette* of 23 October 1890. Reproduced in Dayaram Gidumal, *Behramji M. Malabari: A Biographical Sketch*, London, 1892, pp. 238–47.)

Mr Malabari Finds a Radical Supporter

Opinion from Jotirao Govindrao Phule, on Note No. 1, by Mr. B.M. Malabari on Infant Marriage in India.

I concur with Mr B.M. Malabari's laudable undertaking, and hope that something may be done by our enlightened government to alleviate the miserable state of the deluded people of this country. Although

Mr B.M. Malabari is not pressed under the immediate burden of our customs and manners, invented by Aryan Shastra makers, he treated the subject so remarkably well that the Shudrathi-Shudras and Brahmin widows will thank him in future undoubtedly. I also now beg to add a few remarks on the middle and lower orders, the downtrodden aborigines of this country. In the course of marriage, if any slight dispute takes place between the parties, the poor girl has to suffer all her lifetime. After the marriage is over, should a defect in her family happen to come to the notice of the boy's father, the innocent girl is considered an outcaste. If the boy is younger than the girl, she is not well fed, clothed, and cared for properly, nay, she is not allowed to remain with her rich parents. If her father-in-law be ignorant and poor, the girl, not being fed well, is stunted in her growth. In short, she is more heavily loaded with work for days and nights than American slaves. Thus, she is so unbearably tyrannized that she is obliged to put an end to her life by committing suicide; and the crime is very often hushed up by bribing the village Patel, Coolkerni (the quarrel monger), and policemen. Many poor parents on the bridegroom's side are thus, by incurring debts for marriages, ruined on account of the premature deaths of their daughters-in-law. Besides the husband boy, on coming to his proper senses, does not like his wife and marries one of his own liking. Being thus accustomed, he is induced to marry two, three, or four wives at a time in succession, and thus renders his whole family discontented, abusive, and quarrelsome. These ignorant wives are not only obliged to poison each other, but sometimes their own husband. Now the enlightened Hindus of Bengal have made excellent suggestions to university graduates, and these, as they suppose would be a fair beginning for the educated class, but, I think, their suggestions are not *universal and applicable to all the classes of Shudras and Ati-Shudras,* because very few of the former attend the university and the latter are not at all admitted even into vernacular schools, and allowed to sit and learn with the higher-class boys. In conclusion, unless our wise government uses some compulsory measures, the ignorant middle and lower classes will not come to their proper sense, because the so-called higher classes of Hindus, who hold responsible posts under [the] government, have by their cunning and shrewd ways, purposely misguided them in matters of *religion* and *politics.* I, therefore, suggest that [the] government should rule that boys under 19 years of age and girls under 11 should not be allowed to marry. In case they do, some reasonable tax may be levied on the parents of the parties married, and the money thus obtained should be used in the education of the middle and lower classes of Hindus. But the education should not be transmitted through the medium of *Brahmin teachers*, for while educating, they create in the minds of the pupils wrong religious ideas and lead them astray. (Even the subsidiary kings, Sindia, Holkar, and others, are, we find, cheated in the open daylight under the pretence of invented religion, and are induced to extract tax indiscriminately from the cultivators without giving them timely allowances. But there is strong hope that His Highness, the present ruler of Baroda, will try his utmost to educate and better the condition of the ignorant cultivators as His Highness has received a good and sound English education.

Opinion from Jotirao Govindrao Phule, on Note No. 2, by Mr B.M. Malabari on Enforced Widowhood.

Now I touch upon the most delicate subject of enforced widowhood upon Brahmin women. The partial Aryan institution inconsiderately allows polygamy to males, which causes them to fall into new habits of wickedness. When his lust is satisfied with his legal wives, he, for novelty's sake, haunts the houses of public women. He then contracts venereal diseases from them and is obliged to seek medical assistance at an exhorbitant cost for himself and his wives. When medical treatment ceases to cure him and his wives, he loses all hopes of getting children. In this deplorable condition of his life, if the lewd husband finds his own wife to go out during night, he suspects her of leading a vicious course and so, punishing her severely, turns her out. In old age in order to obliterate the stigma upon his character, the shameless fellow becomes a religious man and hires public harlots to dance and sing in the temples with a view to venerating the stone idols for his own satisfaction. After the death of this wicked man, his young and beautiful wife is not allowed by the same Aryan institution to remarry. She is stripped of her ornaments; she is forcibly shaved by her near relatives; she is not well fed; she is not properly clothed; she is not allowed to join pleasure parties, marriages, or religious ceremonies. In fact, she is bereaved of all the worldly enjoyments, nay, she is considered lower than a culprit or a mean beast.

Moreover, the Aryan institution enjoins Brahmin males to marry even the lower-class girls during the lifetime of his first wife; but his real own sister is prohibited to remarry after the demise of her first husband. Such partial and unjust prohibitions necessarily lead the helpless Aryan widow to commit horrible and heart-rending acts of atrocity. To prove the above assertion I insert the following instance. One of my Brahmin friends named Rao Saheb Sudashive Bullal Gowndey, who was an officer in the Inam Commission, employed in his house a Brahmin widow as cook, whose name was Kashibai. The poor Kashibai was a well-behaved and beautiful young woman of a respectable family. She was a chaste woman. She served several months in his house. But in his neighbourhood, there lived a shrewd and cunning Shashtriboova of a Brahmin caste, who tried his utmost to mislead this ignorant woman. Kashibai at first resisted his inducement but at last she fell victim to his desire and immediately became pregnant. Afterwards by the persuasion of her paramour, she tried several poisonous drugs to commit abortion, but all her attempts failed. After nine months were completed, Kashibai gave birth to a beautiful son and for the sake of her disgrace she murdered the innocent infant with a knife and the corpse was thrown into the well behind the house of her master. Two days after she was arrested by the police on suspicion, tried before the Session Court in Poona and was sentenced to transportation for life. This crime Kashibai committed so that her character may not be spoilt among the Brahmin community. Her case brought to the notice of the public the unjust and partial character of the Aryan institution, and so the people were struck with horror. Although my means were not sufficient to defray my expense, yet I was compelled to establish a foundling house, in my own compound in Poona, for the Brahmin community immediately after Kashibai's trial was over. The enclosed copy of printed notices was then pasted on the walls of the corners of streets, where the Brahmins reside. From its commencement up to the present time, 35 pregnant widows came to his house and were delivered of children, of whom five are living and 30 died by the injuries done to them while in the womb by the poisonous drugs which the mothers must have taken with a view to concealing their pregnancy. Many of the beautiful and helpless ignorant young widows of the respectable Brahmin families have turned out private and public prostitutes on account of this wretched system. How abominable and degrading is the system of Aryan institution, which compels Brahmin widows to drag their lives in so miserable and shameless ways, that even modesty shrinks back to enter into particular details! In conclusion, I most respectfully crave the favour of your enlightened English government to remove the tyranny of enforced widowhood, exercised upon the helpless women, by the relentless system of Aryan religious institution. I, therefore, propose that no barbers should be allowed to shave the unfortunate Brahmin widows. It is quite evident from the partial Aryan religious institution that, when it prohibits the widows from remarrying, why the widowers should be allowed to remarry? If the favour be shown to the latter then the poor widows must of necessity be permitted to remarry. There is no doubt that the selfish and wicked lawgivers must have added such unjust and nonsensical clauses into their Shastras with malice towards the female sex.

('Opinion from Jotirao Govindrao (Phule) on Notes 1 and 2 by Behramji Malabari on Infant Marriage in India'. Reproduced in *Collected Works of Mahatma Jotirao Phule*, vol. 2. Translated by Prof. P.G. Patil, Education Department, Government of Maharashtra, Bombay, 1991, pp. 115–18.)

A Critique of Mr Malabari's Proposals

My dear Malabari,

I owe an apology for not having written to you earlier about the two interesting 'Notes [on] Infant Marriage and Widow Marriage' in India which you have been so good as to send me a copy .... I think it is necessary, at the outset, to ascertain precisely where it is that the true centre of mischief lies .... [R]eform is wanted at the principal source of mischief which lies in an early consummation of marriage. And here, I may point out, the beginning of a reform—very small beginnings I admit, and not such as to redound much to our credit, but still beginning which are none the less real—have already been made in Bombay and elsewhere. Cases of deferred consummation, after girls have arrived at puberty, are known to have occurred without any protests from the castes concerned .... [A]s this reform will come by way of development from within, it will save all the difficulties that must needs be encountered, if limits are fixed which can only be more or less arbitrary and which, if they are not violated in individual cases, may lead, as I have reason to believe from practical experience, to much serious inconvenience and mischief .... [A]ll that the castes insist on at present ... is that a girl should not remain unmarried after attaining puberty. And, therefore, the truth is, not merely as you say, that 'no Shastra' enforces marriage proper (by which I understand you to mean consummation) on a girl under 12 years of age but 'also that *no caste* as such enforces it either' ....

[The conclusions that may be drawn from the above are] first, that neither caste not Shastra as popularly understood, exacts anything more than that the girls should not remain unmarried after attaining puberty. Second, that neither caste nor Shastra as popularly understood has anything to say in the matter of consummation of marriage. And, third, that reform is most urgently called for in regard to the time of consummation and not so much in regard to the time of marriage ... [I]f caste and Shastra are alike out of the way, what is it that stands in the way of the reform here? .... My answer is that the obstacle is in the family. The man who wants to initiate this reform finds his difficulties ... in those nearest and dearest to him, in his family and among his relations .... The influence of 'caste as such' is already on the decrease. But even if you entirely abolished it tomorrow by legislative enactment, the evils now under consideration would not be affected by all ....

Let us proceed to consider the various remedial measures suggested in your note .... The first of them advocates the exclusion of all married students from university examination after a certain point of time, to be fixed once for all .... If the suggestion is carried out, we may not improbably become instrumental in retarding the progress of that very education which must be, if not our sole, at least our principal lever in the eradication of evil customs. Remember, too, that we may thus be making the boy suffer for the sins of his parents .... I am, however, prepared—although not without some hesitation and diffidence,—to go as far as this. The university and government education department may, I think, fairly lay down a rule that the scholarship and prizes awarded by these authorities up to a student's graduation shall be tenable only to unmarried men. Coming next to the second suggestion, I own I cannot see either fairness or advantage in the proposal to exclude married men from employment in the administrative departments of the state within certain limits .... You think that other things being equal, the head of a department should prefer an unmarried man to a married man .... I think the head of a department should make an exactly opposite choice .... [W]hile the appointment of an unmarried man helps only one individual citizen, the appointment of a married man saves more than one from distress ....

The third suggestion is to start an association, the members of which shall take a pledge not to marry under a certain age .... [A]s it is put it seems to me to be impractical. I don't think that among those who are likely to join an association for the intended purpose, you will find anything like an adequate number of persons in whose case the pledge will have any practical value. Most of these probably have been already married. Besides, such a 'pledge' as that here proposed, would probably succeed in driving away people from the association rather than in attracting them to it .... The next recommendation is that an educated man should not marry a 'girl too much under his age'. This again is not at all feasible under present conditions. Seeing that the practice of widow marriage is very far from being at all widespread among the higher castes and seeing that the practice of marrying girls before they are 13 at the outside is all but universal, it must needs be extremely difficult, if not impossible, to arrange for a marriage which shall satisfy the conditions here proposed. Are the proposers then ready to accept the alternative of enforced celibacy with all its attendant evils? ....

I agree that our ordinary school books should be made instrumental in this reform; and carefully framed reading lessons on this and other social topics, if not made obtrusively didactic, might prove useful. I agree, too, that an association should be established for delivering popular lectures and publishing short and cheap tracts, illustrative of the true view on these questions .... One practical mode in which it will be in the power of all of them to do is to decline to attend any of the *tamasha*s which are taking place ... 'in honour of' the weddings of little children ... My faith in the 'education of public opinion' as a great social force is almost unlimited. And I believe that in the long run, the results of that education are not only more enduring but—what might seem paradoxical—more rapid than the results of such artificial remedies applied *ab extra* as are proposed in your note ....

Among the so-called upper classes, education has already spread sufficiently wide for all practical purposes connected with the questions we are now dealing with, and from them, social reform may be expected to filter down to the classes below them without much difficulty. But I look forward more particularly to female education as our greatest help in the solution of all these social problems. It is to the spread of education among our girls, not the limitation of university honours or official loaves and fishes to certain classes of our boys, that I am inclined to look for the remedies of existing evils. That indicates my view as regards social reform generally ....

I must now conclude. I have frankly expressed my dissent from many of your specific suggestions. I have also classed myself with those 'Let aloneists' against whom you have argued in the interest of what, in spite of your disclaimer, I cannot distinguish from state action, though it may not be legislative action.

Yours &c 16 September 1884
K.T. Telang

(Excerpted from K.T. Telang's letter to B.M. Malabari, 16 September 1884. Reproduced in K.T. Telang, *Writings and Speeches* (vol. 1), Bombay, 1916, pp. 239–58.)

Men Simply Have Not Done Enough

[i]

It seems to me a paradox, at once touched with humour and tragedy, that on the very threshold of the twentieth century, it should still be necessary for us to stand upon public platforms and pass resolutions in favour of what is called female education in India—in all places in India, which at the beginning of the first century was already ripe with civilization and had contributed to the world's progress radiant examples of women of the highest genius and widest culture. But as by some irony of evolution the paradox stands to our shame, it is time for us to consider how best we can remove such a reproach, how we can best achieve something more fruitful than the passing of empty resolutions on favour of female education from year to year. At this great moment of stress and striving, when the Indian races are seeking for the ultimate unity of a common national ideal, it is well for us to remember that the success of the whole movement lies centred in what is known as the woman question. It is not you but we who are the true nations-builders. But it seems to me that there is not even an unanimous acceptance of the fact that the education of women is an essential factor in the process of nation-building. Many of you will remember that, some years ago, when Mrs Sathianadhan first started 'The Indian Ladies' Magazine,' a lively correspondence went on as to whether we should or should not educate our women. The women themselves with one voice pleaded their own cause most eloquently, but when it came to the man there was division in the camp. Many men doubtless proved themselves true patriots by proving themselves the true friends of education for the mothers of the people. But others there were who took fright at the very word. 'What,' they cried, 'educate our women? What then will become of the comfortable domestic ideals as exemplified by the luscious "halwa" and the savoury "omelette"?' Others again were neither 'for Jove nor for Jehovah,' but were for compromise, bringing forward a whole syllabus of compromises. 'Teach this,' they said, 'and not that.' But, my friends, in the matter of education you cannot say *thus far and no further.* Neither can you say to the winds of Heaven 'Blow not where ye list,' nor forbid the waves to cross their boundaries, nor yet the human soul to soar beyond the bounds of arbitrary limitations. The word education is the worst misunderstood word in any language. The Italians, who are an imaginative people, with their subtle instinct for the inner meaning of words have made a positive difference between *instruction* and *education* and we should do well to accept and acknowledge that difference. *Instruction* being merely the accumulation of knowledge might, indeed, lend itself to conventional definition, but *education* is an immeasurable, beautiful, indispensable atmosphere in which we live and move and have our being. Does one man dare to deprive another of his birthright to God's pure air which nourishes his body? How then shall a man dare to deprive a human soul of its immemorial inheritance of liberty and life? And yet, my friends, man has so dared in the case of Indian women. That is why you men of India are today what you are: because you fathers, in depriving your mothers of that immemorial birthright, have robbed you, there sons, of your just inheritance. Therefore, I charge you, restore to your women their ancient rights, for, as I have said it is we, and, not you, who are the real nation-builders, and without our active co-operation at all points of progress all your Congresses and conferences in vain. Educate your women and the nation will take care of itself, for its is true today as it was yesterday and will be to the end of human life that the hand that rocks the cradle is the power that rules the world.

(Reproduced from Sarojini Naidu, *Speeches and Writings of Sarojini Naidu,* Madras, pp. 17–20. Originally, lecture delivered at the Indian Social Conference, Calcutta, 1906.)

[ii]

The castigation she (Mrs Idafaye Levering)[1] inflicted was rather severe to sensitive persons. But the evils that are eating the vitals of society and the support and refuge which the community in general lends to them, make it impossible for any sensible man to think of the severity if the chastisement, nay, it would rather seem that no goading, however painful, may be considered too much even by orthodox persons in respect of certain evil customs, such as infant marriage, *varasulkam, kanyasulkam, nautches,* extravagant expenditure on social and religious occasions and glaring disparity of age in marriages, etc. She had been told that her remarks on social reform questions on part occasions offended the leaders of Secunderabad, but she would give expression to the same remarks at the risk of offending them if they happened to be present. Every place of any importance in India has a social reform association. But what have they done? The word 'today' is nowhere to be found in our dictionary. 'Tomorrow' is the watchword. There is anxiety shown everywhere for the introduction of social reforms into the families of others but not in one's own family. When the point is urged home some plea or other comes in for procrastination. A graphical comparison of the past and present of India was made. In days of yore, India possessed real men who honoured women and spared no pains to raise them to their level and make them helpmates. Ancient women of India recognized the worth of man and were prepared to make any sacrifice for their sake. Men of those days had sufficient worth in them and if women performed *sati* they did it out of love and regret for their men. But do men of our days deserve *sati*? What sort of men do we find now? They are not men at all. They can be called the degenerate descendants of ancient heroes.

(Reproduced from Sarojini Naidu, *Speeches and Writings of Sarojini Naidu,* Madras, pp. 21–2. Originally, lecture delivered at Secunderabad under the auspices of Hindu Social Reform Association, December 1906.)

Notes

1. Mrs. Levering, a medical practitioner by profession, was apparently also a social activist based at Secunderabad.

Misguided Men and the Ideals of Hindu Womanhood

The conservatism of the Radical party upon the subject of women is accountable. In the first place the slightest practical alteration in the position of women is certain to bring on inconveniences, troubles, and domestic discomfort which so few of us are able to bear. In the second place, certain circumstances have prejudiced our minds against the morality of European women, and we have therefore come to feel a certain amount of hesitation in educating our women after there fashion. To some extent this prejudice is born of our ignorance of the real nature of European women, to some extent it is due to our utter inability, in consequence of our early associations and habits of thought to realize and paint vividly upon the canvas of our imagination the picture of a society in which men and women mix freely and on terms of perfect equality, to some extent it may be due to the influence of the reaction which in England itself seems to be in progress against the radical theory of woman's position, to our study of the scandals of the divorce courts, and to our experience of the low sexual morality of low class Europeans in the country. It is difficult to ascertain the respective share of each of these elements in the genesis of this prejudice against the morals of European women, but I have not the slightest hesitation in saying that the prejudice is as baseless as it is pernicious. There is a *prima facie* presumption against the popular view, and in favour of the English women. No nation can long retain its greatness unless it rests upon character. National character is the sum of the character of the individual members of a nation, and individual character is the result in the first instance of the influences received through the teachings and examples of parents. If feminine morality is tainted it will be reflected in domestic life and through domestic life will run like poison through the arteries of society. If you admit the greatness of the English nation, you can not deny the greatness of its women.

Then, again, one of the best proofs of the purity of English women's moral, has always seemed to me to lie in English literature. A nation's literature is always a faithful mirror of its ideas, morals, and tastes. Nobody can mutilate or falsify it. A man of real literary genius follows the bent of his mind, and does not think of the trivial expediencies of the moment. The manners and morals of English society are faithfully portrayed in the best works of fiction and poetry. The artist paints what he believes to be the truth, and his work can hardly live long in the this critical age if it does not 'hold the mirror up to nature' and paint society as it really is. Now what idea of the morality of English women do we get from English literature? In poetry from Shakespeare to Tennyson, and in the best works of fiction—in Scott, George Eliot, Dickens, Lytton, and Thackersay—the ideal of womanhood is much purer, nobler, and higher than any to be found within the whole range of our modern Indian literature. For those who may not like the use of foregoing adjectives in the comparative degree, I am willing to use them in the positive, and to say that the English ideal is at least as good as the Indian. But in that case I will compare English literature without ancient literature, and not with that double-distilled Zolaism of our present vernacular books which, while they 'Paint the mortal shame of nature with the living hues of art' corrupt the tastes and defile the morals of so many of our young men and women. The most audicious disparager of English woman's morality must admit that a society which can produce the prototypes of female characters depicted in Scott and Tennyson has a higher and worthier conception of womanhood than that which takes delight in the Arabian Nights, in Urdu lyrics, and in our popular love stories. I contend, therefore, that the popular notion that English women are not so chaste as Indian women is a mere prejudice; and, I look upon it as a most pernicious prejudice, as one of the chief obstacles in the way of the elevation of our own women, I have tried at some length, considering the limits of my space to expose it, by showing its injustice and irrationality.

For the present, however, this prejudice is very commonly shared alike by the educated and the uneducated—and leads certain minds to strange conclusions. We are told: let us educate our women by all means, but let us not accord them the same or anything like the same freedom as their English sisters enjoy. The idea is, however, absurd because knowledge is power, and will win liberty for herself. You cannot by educating them create taste and aspirations in women the satisfaction of which they will not seek sooner or later. If you teach them knowledge, you at once weaken upon their minds the hold of all those beliefs and biases which make them contented with their present slavish position as one assigned to them by nature.

But even in this crude and illogical form, the idea that female education is good, is one of the most beneficent products of English influences. The peace of our domestic life, and all our social progress now depend upon the realization of this idea. It did not matter much if the elder generation did not educate their women, because in the past both sexes grew up under the same social, moral, and religious influences, which produced similarity of tastes and beliefs, and thus preserved the peace and harmony of domestic life. At present the new education has fixed a wide gulf between the young generation of men and their women. There is no religious sympathy, no moral sympathy, no intellectual sympathy because the two sexes live in two different strata of civilization, breathing different atmospheres, and drawing their mental and moral sustenance from different and antagonistic sources. This disparity of tastes, inclinations beliefs and aspirations has gone far to mar the peace and felicity of our domestic life. It has also gone far to obstruct and retard the progress of social reform, because the ignorant conservation of Indian women is simply insurmountable. It has, therefore, both on personal and national considerations, become more necessary than ever that we should educate them, make them sharers and parteners in the rich inheritance of knowledge and enlightenment which has come to our possession. With female education will come not only domestic peace and harmony, but a new source of pleasures, pleasures which men derive from female society will be opened, ennobled, and purified, and feminine tenderness and sympathy, under the guidance of enlightened reason, will become one of the most potent instruments of social amelioration. A beginning has, however, been made. The seed has been sown; it is for us to nurture it and watch its growth; it will be for our children and our children's children to garner its sheaves.

(Excerpted from Pt Bishan Narain Dar, *Speeches and Writings*, vol. 1 (parts I and II) (ed.), H.L. Chatterji, Lucknow, 1921, pp. 246–50.)

The Debate on the Nature of Hindu Marriages

Tagore Answers an Orthodox Critic

For some time now, our country has witnessed considerable agitation on the question of Hindu marriages. Many of those who have agitated on the question are respectable members of society and luminaries of the Bengali literary world. None of them, however, have spoken at length either on the historical evolution of Hindu marriages or its rational usefulness as an institution; their energies have rather been spent in devising intricate arguments and emotive language only so as to establish the purity and spirituality inherent in such marriages. In the course of their civilization, Hindus are bound to have experienced several changes in the nature of this institution; it is not at all clear, however, in exactly which period of history marriage practices may be justifiably identified as 'Hindu' marriages. If marriages as now solemnized in upper-caste Bengali society also deserve to be called Hindu marriages, why take the trouble of emphasizing its purity and spirituality on the authority of some ancient Shastra? Further, no one appears to interrogate whether man–woman relationships as they existed in ancient times, exist to this day. If this is not the case, it is quite improper to apply Shastric prescriptions of old to modern circumstances. Anyone attempting to quote from Vedic texts on the subject of marriage should not overlook the fact that the social and domestic relationship between the sexes was very different from what it is now .... To those who cite the *Manu Samhita* in support, I have the following points to make. Firstly, the society reflected in the Samhita is radically different from our own. It is difficult to establish that two societies which differ so sharply in the nature and quality of their education are socially comparable. I doubt if Bengal ever seriously followed the course of instruction that the *Manu Samhita* sets down for brahmans. For a long time, the labours of our own brahmans have been rather half-hearted and perfunctory; most of them turned *dwija*s [twice-born] in the space of three days! Who ever heard of the *brahmachari*'s extended residence with the *guru*, of sustained study of the Vedas, or the rigorous conformity to several ritual obligations? ....

Secondly, the ideal age of marriage for men as prescribed by Manu was rarely, if ever, followed in Bengal. The same may be said of the rules regarding the social and sexual cohabitation between sexes ... This raises the question as to whether one should uncritically accept the prescriptions of Manu or modify it suitably in keeping with our new social requirements ....

The literary world of Bengal holds Shri Chandranath [Basu][1] in high esteem. Recently, two of his essays 'Hindu Patni' and 'Hindu Vivaher Boyos O Uddesha' ['The Hindu Wife' and 'The Proper Age of Hindu Marriage and its Aims' respectively] have been widely acknowledged ... making him the authoritative voice in respect of the acclaimed pure and spiritual nature of Hindu marriages.

In his essay 'Hindu Patni', Chandranath Babu says:

> Long before the advent of Christianity, the Hindus in India had held their women in high esteem and accorded them a status far more exalted than that provided by Christian culture. Christianity made woman man's equal; the Hindus made her their god ... where women are worshipped, they said .... Even the gods rejoiced.

As for the truthfulness of these claims, I am in no position to comment one way or the other. It is clear to me, however, that Chandranath Babu has not been able to argue his case well. If he can cite a few *sloka*s in support of his claims, I can cite as many which would strongly contest these claims .... The 17th *sloka* of chapter 9 of the *Manu Samhita* depicts women as the embodiment of all sensual gratification, of anger, jealousy, cunning, deceit, and the most vulgar practices. The following *sloka* argues that since traditionally women have not been invested with any important ritual functions, they do not find any place in religious life .... Such *sloka*s do not reveal any respect for women.

Any discussion on the subject of marriage must begin with a determination of the respective social status of man and woman. Chandranath Babu cites [the] Shastras to claim that in ancient [Hindu] society, there was great respect for woman. On the other hand, I find that the Shastras are also quite disrespectful towards her. A second related question pertains to the status of the married woman. Chandranath Babu, on the strength of a rather abtuse interpretation of [the Smarta lawgiver] Raghunanadan, would have us believe that the Hindu wife embodies the elements of virtue, purity, supernatural powers, divinity, and grace. Now the commonplace understanding is that for the woman, the husband is the god; that the woman herself is the divine object of adoration is an argument that has not been heard before ....

On the question of conjugality, it is Chandranath Babu's opinion that the bonding between Hindu couples is something never replicated elsewhere. There are a few observations that I should like to make here. The union of a single male with a single female is, no doubt, the highest ideal in marriage. If, on the other hand, this had truly been our ideal, how is one to explain multiple marriages by men? .... If appears as though in every case, it is the woman alone who has to live up to ideals and expectations. Can it be denied that it takes a man and woman equally to make marriages work? On this question Akshay Chandra Sarkar[2] has produced a most extraordinary reply. In attempting to explain why a widower may not lead the life of abstinence (*nishkamdharma*) as the widow is always expected to do, he argues that the Hindu never believes in an equitable distribution of rights and privileges between the sexes; such matters, rather, are kept proportional to their respective sphere of influence .... We are persuaded to ask Akshay Babu if *nishkamdharma* itself is also bound to go by such dictates .... Why is it that even out of considerations of spirituality, a dispassionate life of abstinence and purity is not imposed on the bereaved man? ....

Now it would be entirely another matter if one were to say that Hindu marriages, rather than be rooted in matters like purity and spirituality, actually grow out of social needs and convenience. And here, significantly, the plea for a proportional distribution of privileges may be of some relevance ....

The main aim of Hindu marriages, as it occurs to me, is the fulfilment of certain routine social needs. It is this that sometimes persuades man to take a second wife in case the first wife proves to be barren. If securing a progeny be the main objective of marriage, even the Shastras cannot fault a man for marrying a second time ....

Now if giving birth to children, their upbringing, and routine social obligations be the primary considerations in marriage, it might be argued that there is greater need for the woman to be faithful to one husband than for the husband to be faithful to one wife. In the event of a woman being married to several men, there may give rise to grave social problems. This is not necessarily the case in the event of the man marrying several women. A widower, for the sake of domestic and social convenience, may remarry, but the widow's marrying a second time causes great social distress and dislocation. In the latter case, the children born to the widow through the first marriage have either to undergo a transference of lineage and family name or else to remain motherless. Even in the case of the issueless widow, a transference of this kind can cause great distress and, hence, purely on grounds of social convenience, an unequitable distribution of rights and privileges appears to be useful ....

It is not at all clear to me what the world 'spiritual' denotes in the context of marriages. If by the word 'spiritual', one only means the felicitous functioning of social and domestic life or even the forsaking of individual needs before the larger, collective good, this is but a tortuous misapplication .... If, on the other hand, it is suggested that since they involve religious rites, Hindu marriages are also spiritual, I should like to point out that possibly every activity of the Hindu has a basis in religion. Why then must you single out marriages? ....

From the arguments I have made above, it must appear that since our marriages essentially fulfil social necessities, they must also keep pace with the changing social circumstances .... This enables us to re-examine the question in keeping with present-day needs .... However, at the outset, I must make it clear that I am not one of those who seeks to carry out social reform with the aid of state-sponsored legislation .... It cannot be that we continue to rely on outsiders and fail to determine ourselves what is good or bad for us ....

For some time now there has been great controversy regarding the appropriate age for marriages. If we grant that securing a progeny be the primary consideration in marriage, and that nurturing healthy children is an important means of furthering social good, then the question of a suitable age of marriage must be determined on the basis of scientific knowledge. Regrettably, our society has, in recent times, turned its back on all scientific resolutions of the subject .... It feels that weak and unhealthy offsprings are caused not by premature marriages but by our steadily deteriorating physical environment .... I am, however, inclined to believe that rather than somehow mitigate the ills of premature marriages, the steady deterioration of our environment alerts us even more to the need for discontinuing such marriages ....

In his essays, Chandranath Babu argues that in the interests of a happy conjugal life, it is important that there be an appreciable difference in age between the husband and the wife. Here is what he says:

> He who must carry out the difficult but important task of instructing [the wife in domestic economy] must be himself knowledgeable, educated and advanced in years, and she who is to be so instructed must be, in comparison, of tender age. It is precisely for this reason that the Shastras recommend a higher age of marriage for men than for the women.

Now if a 24-year-old male was to be married to an 8-year-old female, such a task, I imagine, may indeed be carried out. On the other hand, such marriages may not have much of a future. If married partners continue to be so vastly different in age, the number of widows in this country is bound to further increase ....

It is worth asking if in some ways Western education has affected our views on marriages. The Western ideal of marriage evidently does not believe in perpetuating sharp differences in educational and cultural standards between man and woman. The West, too, believes in bonding in conjugal life, but this bonding is fuller and more wholesome; it represents not just the union of bodies but also of the mind .... It is worth asking if Hindu marriages produce a comparable unity of body, mind, and soul. We consider our wives partners in religious life (*sahadharmini*), but Manu himself has denied her any religious or ritual function; for her, the rewards of heaven are derived through service to the husband .... Many of our countrymen are now beginning to side with Western notions of marriage and conjugality, and for this they can hardly be blamed .... We cannot use our education merely for the sake of livelihood without being affected in any way by the more positive aspects of that education ....

It is not as though early marriages are to be condemned in every case. In certain circumstances, they can be quite useful. If, for instance, we were to continue with the extended family but not female education, early marriages would be vital for our social sustenance. On the other hand, extended families cannot survive on the strength of early marriages alone. Many other factors will also have to be considered ....

Any easy consensus and commonly defined needs are the very backbone of such families. In present-day society, however, both these are visibly lacking .... There is now no end to our needs .... And articles of daily use have not only multiplied in variety but have also become more difficult to procure .... [I]f under changed circumstances extended families cannot survive, neither can infant marriages. When couples need to set up independent households, both man and woman have to be mature in both mind and body ....

Needless to say, all that I have said about our social norms and social transformation applies only to the educated community. The educated alone can bring about a quick and effective stop to the practice of infant marriages. But this must follow its own course. Those who resort to laws in bringing about social change end up seeing only one aspect of the problem and not its complex connections with several other related social issues.

(Editor's translation of excerpts from Rabindranath Tagore, 'Hindu Vivaha' (Hindu Marriages), lecture delivered at the Science Association Hall, 1887. Reproduced in *Rabindra Rachanavali* (vol. XII), Viswabharati, 1973, pp. 415–49.)

Notes

1. Chandranath Basu (1844–1910), a spokesperson for conservative Hinduism in Bengal and perhaps the earliest to use the term 'Hindutva' in a polemical sense.
2. Akshay Chandra Sarkar (1846–1917), the doyen of Bengali political journalism but better known for his dogged defense of Hindu widowhood.

The Nature of Women's Emancipation: Historiographical Debates

The Controlled Emancipation of Wives

The centrality of what may be described for convenience, somewhat inelegantly, as the 'women's questions', to the entire gamut of educated middle-class religious and social reform in nineteenth-century Bengal hardly requires spelling out in detail. Rammohun and *sati*, Vidyasagar's campaigns for widow remarriage and against Kulin polygamy, the daring radicalism of Young Bengal,[1] the repeated splits within the Brahmo movement essentially on issues closely related to the women's question,[2] the reassertion of traditionalist views in the movements for Hindu 'revival' towards the end of the century, the memorable literary expression of conflicting values and contemporary debates in Bankimchandra's *Bisha-Briksha*, and Rabindranath's *Chokher Bali* and *Gora*—to go on adding to the list would be labouring the obvious. But it is the most obvious of facts which sometimes stand most in need of historical explanation, and on the whole, the fairly voluminous literature on the so-called Bengal Renaissance seems to have made little attempt to explore just why it was that women's emancipation—of a sort—came to occupy an absolutely central position in the concerns of the nineteenth-century intelligentsia for a specific period of time.[3] My aim in this very brief and tentative paper is to search for possible explanations, as well as to pinpoint some of the limits of what nineteenth-century Bengali reformers liked to call *stri-swadhinata*!

The simplest explanation, in terms of the influence of Western, and particularly British, models on an English-educated group is not really satisfactory. It is true that English textbooks, literature, and, in some cases, visits abroad brought awareness of a different world without seclusion or child marriage, where romantic love seemed to reign supreme in poems and novels (though much less so in reality) and widows were not burnt or forbidden to remarry. Sibnath Shastri's autobiography has a costatic chapter on the combination of freedom with moral discipline which he observed among middle-class English women during a trip to that country in 1888,[4] John Stuart Mill's *Subjection of Women* found many eager readers in Bengal, while another stimulus was no doubt provided by missionary strictures about degradation of women as one of the principal evils of Hindu society. Yet, here as in other things, what is important to note is the selection process of work even among the most Westward-looking of the colonial intelligentsia. Concern with the problems of women formed after all only a minor element in the thought currents and activity of nineteenth-century Europe, with its essentially male-dominated movements for nationalism, liberal reform, democracy, and socialism. Christian missionary propaganda in India concentrated its fire equally on 'polytheism' or 'idolatry' and caste, and work among the low-castes and tribals constituted on the whole, its principal focus. Far from 'blindly' imitating the West as has been alleged so often, the intellectuals of early or mid-nineteenth-century Bengal in some respects present an interesting contrast to both these 'models'. From Rammohun till at least the 1870s, sympathy for patriotic and liberal movements in the West was combined with a fundamental acceptance of foreign political and economic domination over India, tempered by occasional pleas for mildly 'liberal' administrative reforms which remained a minor concern as compared to the central thrust for social and religious change. Again, as Debendranath Tagore reminded Rajnarayan Bose in a letter of January 1854,[*] the Brahmo attack was fundamentally on 'idolatry', and not caste,[5] and no serious attempt was made to emulate Christian missionary welfare-cum-conversion work among untouchables or tribals.

The nineteenth-century initiative for improving the lot of women came essentially from men, and so an alternative explanation in terms of any autonomous 'feminist' pressure is hardly acceptable either. It is true that there are a few scattered examples indicating that Bengali women were not necessarily always mere passive recipients of reformist boons from their menfolk, and much more research is urgently needed on this point.[6] The *Samachar Darpan* of 21 March 1835 published a letter, allegedly from some Chinsura women, demanding women's education, widow remarriage, an end to polygamy and seclusion, and free choice in marriage.[7] Women of Santipur are said to have woven a sari with a border hailing Vidyasagar,[8] and Gurucharan Mahalanobis' autobiography contains an interesting account of a widow who took the initiative in arranging her remarriage with a man of her own choice.[9] It needs to be emphasized also that great courage was often needed even while giving apparently passive support and sustenance to

* In the original essay by Sarkar, there are errors related to both the identity of the letter-writer and the date. The letter is from Debendranath Tagore, not Rabindranath and is dated Magh 1775 Shak (January 1854).

reformist husbands. Sibnath Shastri has some very perceptive comments on the lot of Durgamohan Das' wife. Durgamohan, he reminds us, could go out, mix with friends, and have an active social and intellectual life, but 'Brahmamoyee had to remain confined day and night within the house and listen to the rebukes and slanders of relatives and neighbours'.[10] Yet occasional initiative and heroic but subordinate support obviously do not amount to anything remotely resembling a genuinely autonomous women's movement.

A passage in the paper Maheshchandra Deb presented to the Derozian Society for Acquisition of General Knowledge in 1839 may lead us nearer towards an explanation of the centrality of women's issues in the concerns of nineteenth-century male reformers. Deb's comprehensive critique of the woman's lot—seclusion, arranged marriage, child marriage, polygamy, the ban on widow remarriage—was accompanied by the comment that such problems were 'under their eyes every day and hour of their existence within the precincts of their own respective domiciles.'[11] Clumsily expressed through the newly acquired foreign tongue, Maheshchandra Deb's words still point to certain acute problems of interpersonal adjustment within the family. Rabindranath's hilarious poem about a husband spouting romantic verse before a wife still engrossed with her dolls reflected a very real and serious problem.[12] Most first-generation reformers in the nineteenth century would have been married off at parental command in their teens, while reform activities often led to the kind of social ostracism and isolation of the reformers' family from their kindred, vividly portrayed in the Derozian Krishnamohan Banerjee's play *The Persecuted* (1831) and in much Brahmo biographical literature. Efforts at education and a limited and controlled emancipation of wives thus became a personal necessity for survival in a hostile social world. Reform attempts in fact were very often concentrated on near relatives: Brahmos busily educated their wives, Durgamohan Das married off his widowed stepmother, while—to pass to a lighter vein—Gurucharan Mahalanobis in his autobiography gave a remarkably 'economic-determinist' explanation of his motives for getting his wife out of the purdah.[13]

Concentration of reform attempts on the women's question thus had a strong personal dimension; it was also more within the reach of the kind of social group we are studying than alternative channels of potential reformist energy. Thus, translation of Western ideals of nationalism, political democracy, and social equality into real movements (as distinct from vicarious admiration for such movements abroad or expression through myths about ancient Hindus, or Maratha and Rajput 'nationalism') was far more difficult for a colonial intelligentsia drawn overwhelmingly from upper castes, dependent for their jobs and often landed interests on the colonial structure, and extremely distant from the masses.

'Middle-class' interest in women's questions and social reform in general, evidently declined from the late nineteenth century with the rise of nationalism. Not only did patriotism at times encourage social conservatism, participation in nationalist activity implied social prestige rather than social ostracism, reducing the need for conscious efforts at interpersonal adjustments within the family. Nationalism was increasingly translated into the language of religion, Gandhian austerity, and calls for self-sacrifice and periodic fasts evoked the traditional Hindu mode of renunciation. The *sannyasi* is outside the domain of caste and may even represent a movement of individualist breakaway or 'revolt' of a sort; and yet his presence does not challenge or seriously modify, and indeed strengthens, the social structure based on caste hierarchy and male domination.[14] And so women from extremely conservative families could fully participate in Gandhian politics, even go to jail, without fundamentally changing family relationships or their consciousness as women.[15]

Our search for possible explanations of the focus on women's questions during a definite time-bound phase leads on to some consideration of the nature and limits of nineteenth-century reform. Certain limitations are very obvious: thus, a reform initiative coming from upper-caste educated *bhadralok* groups, not unnaturally, focused in the main on upper-caste social 'evil' like *sati*, the widow remarriage taboo, or Kulin polygamy; less often noted are features like a greater conservatism and conformity with age.[16] A style of reform through appeal to the Shastras which sometimes raised additional problems,[17] and the tendency for reform to get confined to change, often of a rather symbolic sort, within an enclosed sect. Thus, much Brahmo energy was spent on disputes as to whether *acharya*s in the Samaj should discard the sacred thread or about where women should sit in Brahmo prayer meetings; symbolic change within a sect, in practice almost a new sub-caste, thus became a surrogate for broader social praxis.[18]

While evaluating the nature of the reformist initiative, it is important to remember that *stri-swadhinata* in the nineteenth century was usually combined with a tremendous emphasis on puritanical norms and restraints—and as could have been expected, this often had a strong patriarchal aspect. The term 'Brahmo' in the end became in Bengal almost a synonym for prudishness. In part, such Puritanism was possibly no more than a defence mechanism for a movement which could—and often did—incur charges of licentiousness. But certain other dimensions may have been present, too. As the first generation of reformers often had to break away from their kinship group, a certain shift away from joint families towards nuclear units was possibly taking place. It is not impossible that at times, this could have encouraged patriarchal authority, and reformist husbands may have been occasionally imposing new norms of religion and social conduct on not-too-enthusiastic wives. One might recall Lawrence Stone's model of the shift, in sixteenth–seventeenth-century England from 'open lineage' to 'restricted patriarchal nuclear' families.[19]

Such speculations apart, the characteristic nineteenth-century combination of women's emancipation with an insistence upon puritanical restraint and discipline is certainly very reminiscent of what a modern advocate of women's liberation has described as the 'Victorian feeling that the female must relinquish sexuality if she is to be in any sense autonomous, a variant on the bondage of "virtue" which demands sexual inhibition in a woman if she is to maintain her social and therefore her economic position'.[20] Thus, Debendranath Tagore's *Tattvabodhini Patrika* in 1872 contrasted 'real freedom' of women with 'licence', and spoke of a 'natural division of labour' by which men work outside the house while woman's place remains in her home.[21] The *Somprakash*, another generally pro-reform weekly, warned in the same year that women's freedom might mean loss of chastity.[22] Even Sibnath Shastri, leader of the most advanced group of Brahmos which had adopted as its central creed a condemnation of both sexual and caste inequality,[23] repeatedly emphasized in his account of English women, the combination of freedom with discipline.[24] Here, indeed, we encounter a basic reformist 'style' for contemporary intelligentsia, attitudes towards peasants or labour were in fact very similar. Considerable humanitarian sympathy was invariably tempered by an obsession with education as a restraining and disciplining force, and a firm disapproval of autonomous action. To cite two examples out of many: Pyarichand Mitra's article in *Calcutta Review* in 1846 vividly described and condemned *zamindari* abuses, but offered education of the landlord as the panacea and was very critical of '*ryot dharmaghat*' or rent strikes.[25] And Sasipada Banerji's philanthropic educational and temperance work among Baranagar jute mill hands obtained the enthusiastic support of the white employers who felt that such efforts were made for a more efficient and manageable labour force.[26]

The literature of the nineteenth century does provide some evidence for occasional aspirations—daydreams might be a better word—for a less bloodless and inhibited type of emancipated femininity: the Pramila of Madhusudan's *Meghnad-badh-Kavya*, some of Bankimchandra's forthright heroines, or that novelist's interesting comparison of Sakuntala with Miranda and Desdemona.[27] Yet the return to earth is seldom delayed. Debi Chaudhurani ends her days as a devout and submissive Hindu wife, and in Madhusudan's *Ekei Ki Bale Sabhyata*, Westernised young men have their 'Liberty Hall' in a brothel while their wives and sisters stay at home playing cards.

Analysis of the limitations of the 'nineteenth-century renaissance' should not degenerate into carping criticism. So far as interpersonal relations and male attitudes towards women are concerned, inhabitants of Delhi in the 1980s have no right to sit in moral judgement over predecessors. It remains important to emphasize problems yet unsolved, for the undoubted twentieth-century advance in terms of reduced seclusion, education employment, and legal rights has come about through objective socio-economic pressures, some post-independence legislation rather than clear-cut ideology or really autonomous struggle. Mental attitudes and values have consequently changed very much less. The experience not only of India, but even of countries which have undergone far more radical transformation surely emphasizes that genuine women's liberation cannot come as an automatic fallout from other types of change but requires sustained, self-conscious, and independent struggle.

Notes

1. Reflected, for instance, in Maheshchandra Deb's paper, 'A Sketch of the Condition of the Hindoo Women', presented to the Society for the Acquisition of General Knowledge in January 1939, and the *Bengal Spectator* letters and articles of April and July 1842, and January 1843, which anticipated most of Vidyasagar's arguments for widow re-marriage. Gautam Chattopadhyay, *Awakening in Bengal in Early 19th Century*, Calcutta, 1965, pp. 90–7; Benoy Ghosh (ed.), *Samayik-Patre Banglar Samajchitra* (vol. III), Calcutta, 1964, pp. 77–80, 90–1, 130–1.
2. The split between Debendranath Tagore and Keshabchandra Sen began developing from the mid-1860s over women's education and

right of women to attend Brahmo religious services, and became complete over the issue of Act III of 1872, which provided civil marriage and marriage across caste barriers for those willing to declare themselves as non-Hindus. The *Young Brahmo* attacks on Keshab started with the pressures mounted by the group around the journals *Samadarshi* and *Abalabandhav* from 1872 on the issues of women sitting in services, and culminated in the split over the Cooch-Bihar marriage. The best near-contemporary account is in Sibnath Shastri, *Ramtanu Lahiri O Tatkalin Bangasamaj,* Calcutta, 1903, Chapters 10–13; see also Ajit Chakrabarti, *Maharshi Debendranath Tagore,* Allahabad, 1916; Calcutta, 1971, pp. 217–345.

3. Such concerns seem to have been absent prior to the nineteenth century, while they certainly decline in relative importance with the rise of the organized national movement.
4. Sibnath Shastri, *Atmacharit,* Calcutta, 1952, Chapter 19.
5. 'The abolition of caste is not our principal aim ... it is the existence of idolatry within the caste system which is causing all the harm' (my translation) Chakrabarti, *op. cit.,* p. 244).
6. The impact of women's liberation movements in the West is currently leading to radical reinterpretation of much traditionally-accepted history. For two examples, see R. Samuel (ed.), *Peoples' History and Socialist Theory,* London, 1981; and R. Bridenthal and C. Koonz (eds), *Becoming Visible: Women in European History,* Boston, etc., 1977.
7. Brojendranath Bandyopadhyay, *Sambadpatra Sekalar Katha* (vol. II), Calcutta, 1941, pp. 257–8.
8. Shastri, *Ramtanu Lahiri O Tatkalin Bangasamaj, op. cit.,* p. 192.
9. Gurucharan Mahalanobis, *Atma Katha,* Calcutta, 1974, pp. 46–50.
10. Shastri, *Ramtanu Lahiri O Tatkalin Bangasamaj, op. cit.,* p. 298 (my translation).
11. Chattopadhyay, *op. cit.,* p. 90.
12. Rabindranath Tagore, 'Nabadampatir Premalap' (1888), in *Manasi, Rabindra Rachanabali* (vol. III), Visva Bharati, 1975, pp. 242–5.
13. Mahalanobis, *op. cit.,* p. 100, relates with engaging naivete how the expenses of sending his wife by carriage led him to understand the benefit of allowing women to appear publicly on streets.
14. Louis Dumont has described the *sannyasi* as 'the safety valve for the Brahmanic order'. 'World Renunciation in Indian Religions', in L. Dumont, *Religion/Politics and History in India,* Paris/the Hague, 1970, p. 51.
15. Tanika Sarkar. [Note incomplete in original.]
16. As examples may be cited: the Derozian Pearychand Mitra's defence of early marriage in 1842, Keshabchandra's about-turn in 1878, and

possibly some of the later attitudes of even Rammohun Roy. See Sumit Sarkar, 'The Radicalism of Intellectuals in a Colonial Situation: A Case Study of Nineteenth Century Bengal', *Calcutta Historical Journal*, 2(1), 1978, p. 66.

17. Thus Rammohun attacked *sati* by hunting up texts hailing ascetic widowhood, thus possibly adding to Vidyasagar's problems. Vidyasagar left untouched the problem of the inhuman austerities imposed on the widow who did not remarry.
18. For details, see Shastri, *Ramtanu Lahiri O Tatkalin Bangasamaj, op. cit.*, and Chakrabarti, *op. cit.*
19. L. Stone, *Family, Sex and Marriage in England, 1500–1800*, London, 1977.
20. Kate Millet, *Sexual Politics*, London, 1971, pp. 77–8.
21. Benoy Ghosh, *Samayikpatre Banglar Samajchitra* (vol. II), Calcutta, 1963, pp. 251–2.
22. Ghosh, ibid (vol. IV), Calcutta, 1966, p. 255.
23. The Sadharan Brahmo creed asserted that men and women had equal rights; everyone with faith (*bhakti*) would be saved irrespective of caste.
24. Shastri, *Atmacharit, op. cit.*, Chapters 18–19.
25. For details, see Sumit Sarkar, 'The Complexities of Young Bengal', *Nineteenth Century Studies*, October 1973.
26. Sitanath Tattvabhushan, *Social Reform in Bengal: A Side Sketch*, Calcutta, 1904, pp. 8–9; Dipesh Chakrabarti, 'Sasipada Banerjee: A Study in the Nature of the First Contact of the Bengali Bhadralok with Working Clenes of Bengal', *Indian Historical Review*, January, 1976.
27. *Bankim Rachanabali* (vol. II), Calcutta, 1969, pp. 204–9.

(Excerpted from Sumit Sarkar, 'The "Women's Question" in Nineteenth Century Bengal', in *A Critique of Colonial India*, Calcutta, 1985, pp. 71–6, 168–70.)

Nationalism Resolves the Critical Question

[i]

The 'Women's Question' was a central issue in some of the most controversial debates over social reform in early and mid-nineteenth-century Bengal—the period of the so-called 'renaissance'. Rammohun

Roy's historical fame is largely built around his campaign against *satidaha* (widow immolation), Vidyasagar's around his efforts to legalize widow remarriage and abolish Kulin polygamy; the Brahmo Samaj was split twice in the 1870s over questions of marriage laws and the 'age of consent'. What has perplexed historians is the rather sudden disappearance of such issues from the agenda of public debate towards the close of the century. From then onwards, questions regarding the position of women in society do not arouse the same degree of passion and acrimony as they did only a few decades before. The overwhelming issues now are directly political ones—concerning the politics of nationalism.

Was this because the women's questions had been resolved in a way satisfactory to most sections of opinion in Bengal? Critical historians today find it difficult to accept this answer. Indeed, the hypothesis of critical social history today is that nationalism could not have resolved those issues; rather, the relation between nationalism and the women's question must have been problematical.

Ghulam Murshid states the problem in its most obvious, straightforward, form.[1] If one takes seriously, that is, in their liberal rationalist and egalitarian content, the mid-nineteenth-century attempts in Bengal to 'modernize' the condition of women, then what follows in the period of nationalism must be regarded as a clear retrogression. 'Modernization' began in the first half of the nineteenth century because of the 'penetration' of Western ideas. After some limited success, there was a perceptible decline in the reform movements as 'popular attitudes' towards them 'hardened'. The new politics of nationalism 'glorified India's past and tended to defend everything traditional'; all attempts to change customs and lifestyles began to be seen as the aping of Western manners and thereby regarded with suspicion. Consequently, nationalism fostered a distinctly conservative attitude towards social beliefs and practices. The movement towards modernization was stalled by nationalist politics.

This critique of the social implications of nationalism follows from rather simple and linear historical assumptions. Murshid not only accepts that the early attempts at social reform were impelled by the new nationalist and progressive ideas imported from Europe, he also presumes that the necessary historical culmination of such reforms in India ought to have been, as in the West, the full articulation of liberal values in social institutions and practices. From these assumptions, a critique of nationalist ideology and practices is inevitable. It would be the same sort of critique as that of the so-called 'neo-imperialist' historians who argue that Indian nationalism was nothing but a scramble for sharing political power with the colonial rulers, its mass following only the successful activization of traditional patron–client relationships, its internal debates the squabbles of parochial factions, its ideology a garb for xenophobia and racial exclusiveness. The point to note is that the problem lies in the original structure of assumptions. Murshid's study is a telling example of the fact, now increasingly evident, that if one only scrapes away the gloss, it is hard to defend many ideas and practices of nationalism in terms of rationalist and liberal values.

Of course, that original structure of assumptions has not gone unchallenged in recent critical history. The most important critique in our field is that of the Bengal renaissance.[2] Not only have questions been raised about the strictness and consistency of the liberal ideas propagated by the 'renaissance' leaders of Bengal, it has also been asked whether the fruition of liberal reforms was at all possible under conditions of colonial rule. In other words, the incompleteness and contradictions of 'renaissance' ideology were shown to be the necessary result of the impossibility of thoroughgoing liberal reform under colonial conditions.

From that perspective the problem of the diminished importance of the women's question in the period of nationalism deserves a different answer from the one given by Murshid. Sumit Sarkar has considered this problem in a recent article.[3] His argument is that the limitations of nationalist ideology in pushing forward a campaign for liberal and egalitarian social change cannot be seen as a retrogression from an earlier radical reformist phase. Those limitations were in fact present in the earlier phase as well. The 'renaissance' reformers, he shows, were highly selective in their acceptance of liberal ideas from Europe. Fundamental elements of social conservatism such as the maintenance of caste distinctions and patriarchal forms of authority in the family, acceptance of the sanctity of the Shastras (ancient scriptures), preference for symbolic rather than substantive change in social practices—all of them were conspicuous in the reform movements of the early and mid-nineteenth century. Specifically on the question of the social position of women, he shows the fundamental absence in every phase of any significant autonomous struggle by women themselves to change relations within or outside the family. In fact, Sarkar throws doubt upon the very assumption that the early attempts at reform were principally guided by any ideological acceptance of liberal or rationalist values imported from the West. He suggests that the concern with the social condition of women was far less an indicator of such ideological preference for liberalism and more an expression of certain 'acute problems of interpersonal adjustments within the family' on the part of the early generation of Western-educated males. Faced with 'social ostracism and isolation', their attempts at 'a limited and controlled emancipation of wives' were 'a personal necessity for survival in a hostile social world'. Whatever changes have come about since that time in the social and legal position of women have been 'through objective socio-economic pressures, some post independence legislation, rather than clear-cut ideology or really autonomous struggle. Mental attitudes, and values have consequently changed very much less.' The pattern, therefore, is not, as Murshid suggests, one of radical liberalism in the beginning followed by a conservative backlash in the period of nationalism; Sarkar argues that in fact the fault lies with the very inception of our modernity.

The curious thing, however, is that Sarkar, too, regards the social reform movements of the last century and a half as a failure—failure to match up to the liberal ideals of equality and reason. It is from this standpoint that he can show, quite legitimately, the falsity of any attempt to paint a picture of starry-eyed radicalism muzzled by a censorious nationalist ideology. But a new problem crops up. If we are to say that the nineteenth-century reform movements did not arise out of an ideological acceptance of Western liberalism, it could fairly be asked: from what then did they originate? The answer that they stemmed from problems of personal adjustment within the family can hardly be adequate. After all, the nineteenth-century debates about social reform generally, and the women's question in particular, were intensely ideological. If the paradigm for those debates was not that of Western liberalism, what was it? Moreover, if we cannot describe that paradigm in its own terms, can we legitimately apply once again the Western standards of liberalism to proclaim the reform movements, pre-nationalist as well as nationalist, as historical failures? Surely the new critical historiography will be grossly one-sided if we are unable to represent the nineteenth-century ideology in its relation to itself, that is, in its self-identity.

It seems to me that Sumit Sarkar's argument can be taken much further. We need not shy away from the fact that the nationalist ideology did indeed tackle the women's question in the nineteenth century. To expect the contrary would be surprising. It is inconceivable that an ideology which claimed to offer a total alternative to the 'traditional' social order as well as to the Western way of life should fail to have something distinctive to say about such a fundamental aspect of social institutions and practices as the position of women. We should direct our search within the nationalist ideology itself.

We might, for a start, pursue Sarkar's entirely valid observation that the nineteenth-century ideologues were highly selective in their adoption of liberal slogans. How did they select what they wanted? What , in other words, was the ideological sieve through which they put the newly imported ideas from Europe? Once we have reconstructed this framework of the nationalist ideology, we will be in a far better position to locate where exactly the women's question fitted in with the claims of nationalism. We will find, if I may anticipate my argument in the following sections of this paper, that nationalism did in fact face up to the new social and cultural problems concerning the position of women in 'modern' society and that it did provide an answer to the problems in terms of its own ideological paradigm. I will claim, therefore, that the relative unimportance of the women's question in the last decades of the nineteenth century is not to be explained by the fact that it had been censored out of the reform agenda or overtaken by the more pressing and emotive issues of political struggle. It was because nationalism had in fact resolved 'the women's question' in complete accordance with its preferred goals.

[ii]

I have elaborated elsewhere[4] a framework for analysing the contradictory pulls on nationalist ideology in its struggle against the dominance of colonialism and the resolution it offered to these contradictions. In the main, this resolution was built around a separation of the domain of culture into two spheres—the material and the spiritual. It was in the material sphere that the claims of Western civilization were the most powerful. Science, technology, rational forms of economic organization, modern methods of statecraft, these had given the European countries the strength to subjugate non-European peoples and to impose their dominance over the whole world. To overcome this domination, the colonized people must learn these superior techniques of organizing material life and incorporate them within their own cultures. This was one aspect of the nationalist project of rationalizing and reforming the 'traditional' culture of their people. But this could not mean the imitation of the West in every aspect of life, for then the very distinction between the West and the East would vanish—the self-identity of national culture would itself be threatened. In fact, as Indian nationalists in the late nineteenth century argued, not only was it not desirable to imitate the West in anything other than the material aspects of life, it was not even necessary to do so, because in the spiritual domain the East was superior to the West. What was necessary was to cultivate the material techniques of modern Western civilization while retaining and strengthening the distinctive spiritual essence of the national culture. This completed the formulation of the nationalist project, and as an ideological justification for the selective appropriation of Western modernity it continues to hold sway to this day (*pace* Rajiv Gandhi's juvenile fascination for space-age technology).

We need not concern ourselves here with the details of how this ideological framework shaped the course of nationalist politics in India. What is important is to note that nationalism was not simply about a political struggle for power; it related the question of political independence of the nation to virtually every aspect of the material and spiritual life of the people. In very case there was a problem of selecting what to take from the West and what to reject. And in every case the questions were asked: is it desirable? Is it necessary? The answers to these questions are the material of the debates about social reform in the nineteenth century. To understand the self-identity of nationalist ideology in concrete terms, we must look more closely at the way in which these questions were answered.

The discourse of nationalism shows that the material/spiritual distinction was condensed into an analogous, but ideologically far more powerful, dichotomy: that between the outer and the inner. The material domain lies outside us—a mere external, which influences us, conditions us, and to which we are forced to adjust. But ultimately it is unimportant. It is the spiritual which lies within, which is our true self; it is that which is genuinely essential. It follows that as long as we take care to retain the spiritual distinctiveness of our culture, we could make all the compromises and adjustments necessary to adapt ourselves to the requirements of a modern material world without losing our true identity. This was the key which nationalism supplied for resolving the ticklish problems posed by issues of social reform in the nineteenth century.

Now apply the inner/outer distinction to the matter of concrete day-to-day living and you get a separation of the social space into *ghar* and *bahir*, the home and the world. The world is the external, the domain of the material; the home represents our inner spiritual self, our true identity. The world is a treacherous terrain of the pursuit of material interests, where practical considerations reign supreme. It is also typically the domain of the male. The home in its essence must remain unaffected by the profane activities of the material world—and woman is its representation. And so we get an identification of social roles by gender to correspond with the separation of the social space into *ghar* and *bahir*.

Thus far we have not obtained anything that is different from the typical conception of gender roles in any 'traditional' patriarchy. If we now find continuities in these social attitudes in the phase of social reforms in the nineteenth century, we are tempted to put this down as 'conservatism', a mere defence of 'traditional' norms. But this would be a mistake. The colonial situation, and the ideological response of nationalism introduced an entirely new substance to these terms and effected their transformation. The material/spiritual dichotomy, to which the terms 'world' and 'home' corresponded, had acquired, as we have noted before, a very special significance in the nationalist mind. The world was where the European power had challenged the non-European peoples and, by virtue of its superior material culture, had subjugated them. But it had failed to colonize the inner, essential, identity of the East which lay in its distinctive and superior spiritual culture. That is where the East was undominated, sovereign, master of its own fate. For a colonized people, the world was a distressing constraint, forced upon it by the fact of its material weakness. It was a place of oppression and daily humiliation, a place where the norms of the colonizer had perforce to be accepted. It was also the place, as nationalists were soon to argue, where the battle would be waged for national independence. The requirement for this was for the subjugated to learn from the West the modern sciences and arts of the material world. Then their strengths would be matched and ultimately the colonizer overthrown. But in the entire phase of the national struggle, the crucial need was to protect, preserve, and strengthen the inner core of the national culture, its spiritual essence. No encroachments by the colonizer must be allowed in that inner sanctum. In the world imitation of and adaptation to Western norms was a necessity; at home they were tantamount to annihilation of one's very identity.

Once we match this new meaning of the home/world dichotomy with the identification of social roles by gender, we get the ideological framework within which nationalism answered the women's question. It would be a grave error to see in this, as we are apt to in our despair at the many marks of social conservation in nationalist practice, a total rejection of the West. Quite the contrary. The nationalist paradigm in fact supplied an ideological principle of *selection.* It was not a dismissal of modernity; the attempt was rather to make modernity consistent with the nationalist project.

[iii]

It is striking how much of the literature on women in the nineteenth century was concerned with the theme of the threatened westernization of Bengali women. It was taken up in virtually every form of written, oral, and visual communication, from the ponderous essays of nineteenth-century moralists, to novels, farces, skits, and jingles, to the paintings of the *patua* (scroll painter). Social parody was the most popular and effective medium of this ideological propagation. From Iswarchandra Gupta and the *kabiyal* (popular versifiers) of the early nineteenth century to the celebrated pioneers of modern Bengali theatre—Michael Madhusudan Dutt, Dinabandhu Mitra, Jyotirindranath Tagore, Upendranath Das, Amritalal Bose—everyone picked up the theme. To ridicule the idea of a Bengali woman trying to imitate the way of a European woman or *memsahib* (and it was very much an idea, for it is hard to find historical evidence that even in the most Westernized families of Calcutta in the mid-nineteenth century there were actually any women who even remotely resembled these gross caricatures) was a sure recipe calculated to evoke raucous laughter and moral condemnation in both male and female audiences. It was, of course, a criticism of manners: of new items of clothing such as the blouse, the petticoat, and shoes (all, curiously, considered vulgar, although they clothed the body far better than the single length of fabric or sari which was customary for Bengali women, irrespective of wealth and social status, until the middle of the nineteenth century), of the use of Western cosmetics and jewellery, of the reading of novels (the educated Haimabati in Jyotirindranath's *Alikbabu* speaks, thinks, and acts like the heroines of historical romances), of needlework (considered a useless and expensive pastime), of riding in open carriages. What made the ridicule stronger was the constant suggestion that the Westernized woman was fond of useless luxury and cared little for the well-being of the home. One can hardly miss in all this a criticism—reproach mixed with envy—of the wealth and luxury of the new social élite emerging around the institutions of colonial administration and trade.

This literature of parody and satire in the first half of the nineteenth century clearly contained much that was prompted by a straightforward defence of 'tradition' and outright rejection of the new. The nationalist paradigm had still not emerged in clear outline. On hindsight, this—the period from Rammohun to Vidyasagar—appears as one of great social turmoil and ideological confusion among the literati. And then, drawing from various sources, a new discourse began to be formed in the second half of the century—the discourse of nationalism. Now the attempt was made to define the social and moral principles for locating the position of women in the 'modern' world of the nation.

Let us take as an example, one of the most clearly formulated tracts on the subject: Bhudev Mukhopadhyay's *Paribarik Prabandha* (Essays on the Family) published in 1882. Bhudev states the problem in his characteristic matter of fact style:

> Because of our hankering for the external glitter and ostentation of the English way of life ... an upheaval is under way within our homes. The men learn English and become sahibs. The women do not learn English but nevertheless try to become bibis. In households which manage on an income of a hundred rupees, the women no longer cook, sweep or make the bed ... everything is done by servants and maids; [the women] only read books, sew carpets and play cards. What is the result? The house and furniture get untidy, the meals poor, the health of every member of the family is ruined; children are born weak and rickety, constantly plagued by illness—they die early.
>
> Many reform movements are being conducted today; the education of women, in particular, is constantly talked about. But we rarely hear of those great arts in which women were once trained—a training which if it had still been in vogue would have enabled us to tide over this crisis caused by injudicious imitation. I suppose we will never hear of this training again.[5]

The problem is put here in the empirical terms of a positive sociology, a genre much favoured by serious Bengali writers of Bhudev's time. But the sense of crisis which he expresses was very much a reality. Bhudev is voicing the feelings of large sections of the newly emergent middle class in Bengal when he says that the very institutions of home and family were threatened under the peculiar conditions of colonial rule. A quite unprecedented external condition had been thrust upon us; we were being forced to adjust to those conditions, for which a certain degree of imitation of alien ways was unavoidable. But could this wave of imitation be allowed to enter our homes? Would that not destroy our inner identity? Yet it was clear that a mere restatement of the old norms of family life would not suffice: they were breaking down by the inexorable force of circumstance. New norms were needed, which would be more appropriate to the external conditions of the modern world and yet not a mere imitation of the West. What were the principles by which these new norms could be constructed?

Bhudev supplies the characteristic nationalist answer. In an essay on modesty entitled 'Lajjasilata', he talks of the natural and social principles which provide the basis for the 'feminine' virtues.[6] Modesty, or decorum in manner and conduct, he says, is a specifically human trait; it does not exist in animal nature. It is human aversion to the purely animal traits which gives rise to virtues such as modesty. In this aspect, human beings seek to cultivate in themselves, and in their civilization, spiritual or godlike qualities wholly opposed to forms of behaviour which prevail in animal nature. Further, within the human species, women cultivate and cherish these god-like qualities far more than men. Protected to a certain extent from the purely material pursuits of securing a livelihood in the external world, women express in their appearance and behaviour the spiritual qualities which are characteristic of civilized and refined human society.

The relevant dichotomies and analogues are all here. The material/spiritual dichotomy corresponds to that between animal/godlike qualities, which in turn corresponds to masculine/feminine virtues. Bhudev then invests this ideological form with its specifically nationalist content:

> In a society where men and women meet together, converse together at all times, eat and drink together, travel together, the manners of women are likely to be somewhat coarse, devoid of spiritual qualities and relatively prominent in animal traits. For this reason, I do not

> think the customs of such a society are free from all defect. Some argue that because of such close association with women, the characters of men acquire certain tender and spiritual qualities. Let me concede the point: But can the loss caused by coarseness and degeneration in the female character be compensated by the acquisition of a certain degree of tenderness in the male?[7]

The point is then hammered home.

> Those who laid down our religious codes discovered the inner spirituality which resides within even the most animal pursuits which humans must perform, and thus removed the animal qualities from those actions. This has not happened in Europe. Religion there is completely divorced from [material] life. Europeans do not feel inclined to regulate all aspects of their life by the norms of religion; they condemn it as clericalism .... In the Arya system there is a preponderance of spiritualism, in the European system a preponderance of material pleasure. In the Arya system, the wife is a goddess. In the European system, she is a partner and companion.[8]

The new norm for organizing family life and determining the right conduct for women in the conditions of the 'modern' world could now be deduced with ease. Adjustments would have to be made in the external world of material activity, and men would bear the brunt of this task. To the extent that the family was itself entangled in wider social relations, it, too, could not be insulated from the influence of changes in the outside world. Consequently, the organization and ways of life at home would also have to be changed. But the crucial requirement was to retain the inner spirituality of indigenous social life. The home was the principal site for expressing the spiritual quality of the national culture, and women must take the main responsibility of protecting and nurturing this quality. No matter what the changes in the external conditions of life for women, they must not lose their essentially spiritual (that is, feminine) virtues; they must not, in other words, become *essentially* Westernized. It followed, as a simple criterion for judging the desirability of reform, that the essential distinction between the social roles of men and women in terms of material and spiritual virtues must at all times be maintained. There would have to be a marked *difference* in the degree and manner of Westernization of women, as distinct from men, in the modern world of the nation.

[iv]

This was the central principle by which nationalism resolved the women's question in terms of its own historical project. The details were not, of course, worked out immediately. In fact, from the middle of the nineteenth century right up to the present day, there have been many controversies about the precise application of the home / world, spiritual / material, feminine / masculine dichotomies in various matters concerning the everyday life of the 'modern' woman—her dress, food, manners, education, her role in organizing life at home, her role outside the home. The concrete problems arose out of the rapidly changing situation—both external and internal—in which the new middle-class family found itself; the specific solutions were drawn from a variety of sources—a reconstructed 'classical' tradition, modernized folk forms, the utilitarian logic of bureaucratic and industrial practices, the legal idea of equality in a liberal democratic state. The content of the resolution was neither predetermined nor unchanging, but its form had to be consistent with the system of dichotomies which shaped and contained the nationalist project.

The 'new' woman defined in this way was subjected to a *new* patriarchy. In fact, the social order connecting the home and the world in which nationalism placed the new woman was contrasted not only with that of modern Western society; it was explicitly distinguished fro the patriarchy of indigenous tradition. Sure enough, nationalism adopted several elements from 'tradition' as marks of its native cultural identity, but this was a deliberately 'classicized' tradition—reformed, reconstructed. Even Gandhi said of the patriarchal rules laid down by the scriptures:

> It is sad to think that the *Smriti*s contain texts which can command no respect from men who cherish the liberty of woman as their own and who regard her as the mother of the race .... The question arises as to what to do with the *Smriti*s that contain texts ... that are repugnant to the moral sense. I have already suggested ... that all that is printed in the name of scriptures need not be taken as the word of God or the inspired word.[9]

The new patriarchy was also sharply distinguished from the immediate social and cultural condition in which the majority of the people lived, for the 'new' woman was quite the reverse of the 'common' woman who was coarse, vulgar, loud, quarrelsome, devoid of superior moral sense, sexually promiscuous, subjected to brutal physical oppression by males. Alongside the parody of the Westernized woman, this other construct is repeatedly emphasized in the literature of the nineteenth century through a host of lower-class female characters who make their appearance in the social milieu of the new middle class—maidservants, washerwomen, barbers, pedlars, procuresses, prostitutes. It was precisely this degenerate condition of women which nationalism claimed it would reform, and it was through these contrasts that the new woman of nationalist ideology was accorded a status of cultural superiority to the Westernized women of the wealthy parvenu families spawned by the colonial connection as well as the common women of the lower classes. Attainment by her own efforts of a superior national culture was the mark of woman's newly acquired freedom. This was the central ideological strength of the nationalist resolution of the women's question.

We can follow the form of this resolution in several specific aspects in which the lives and conditions of middle-class women have changed over the last hundred years or so. Take the case of 'female education', that contentious subject which engaged so much of the attention of social reformers in the nineteenth century.[10] Some of the early opposition to the opening of schools for women was backed by an appeal to 'tradition' which supposedly prohibited women from being introduced to bookish learning, but this argument hardly gained much support. The threat was seen to lie in the fact that the early schools, and arrangements for teaching women at home, were organized by Christian missionaries; there was thus the fear of both proselytization and the exposure of women to harmful Western influences. The threat was removed when from the 1850s, Indians themselves began to open schools for girls. The spread of formal education among middle-class women in Bengal in the second half of the nineteenth century was remarkable. From 95 girls' schools with an attendance of 2,500 in 1863, the figures went up to 2,238 schools in 1890 with a total of more than 80,000 students.[11]

The quite general acceptance of formal education among middle-class women was undoubtedly made possible by the development of an educative literature and teaching materials in the Bengali language. The long debates of the nineteenth century on a proper 'feminine curriculum' now seem to us somewhat quaint, but it is not difficult to identify the real point of concern. Much of the content of the modern school education was seen as important for the 'new' woman, but to administer it in the English language was difficult in practical terms, irrelevant in view of the fact that the central place of the educated woman was still at home, and threatening because it might devalue and displace that central site where the social position of women was located. The problem was resolved through the efforts of the intelligentsia who made it a fundamental task of the nationalist project to create a modern language and literature suitable for a widening readership which would include newly educated women. Through textbooks, periodicals, and creative works, an important force which shaped the new literature of Bengal was the urge to make it accessible to women who could read only one language—their mother tongue.

Formal education became not only acceptable, but in fact a requirement for a new *bhadramahila* (respectable woman), when it was demonstrated that it was possible for a woman to acquire the cultural refinements afforded by modern education without jeopardizing her place at home. Indeed, the nationalist construct of the new woman derived its ideological strength from the fact that it was able to make the goal of cultural refinement through education a personal challenge for every woman, thus opening up a domain where woman was an autonomous subject. This explains to a large extent the remarkable degree of enthusiasm among middle-class women to acquire and use for themselves the benefits of formal learning. It was a purpose which they set for themselves in their personal lives as the object of their will; to achieve it was to achieve freedom. Indeed, the achievement was marked by claims of cultural superiority in several different aspects: superiority over the Western woman for whom, it was believed, education meant only the acquisition of material skills in order to compete with men in the outside world and hence a loss of feminine (spiritual) virtues; superiority over the preceding generation of women in their own homes who had been denied the opportunity for freedom by an oppressive and degenerate social tradition; and superiority over women of the lower classes who were culturally incapable of appreciating the virtues of freedom.

It is this particular nationalist construction of reform as a project of both emancipation and self-emancipation of women (and hence a project in which both men and women must participate) which also explains why the early generation of educated women themselves so keenly propagated the nationalist idea of the 'new woman'. Recent historians of a liberal persuasion have often been somewhat embarrassed by the profuse evidence of women writers of the nineteenth century, including those at the forefront of the reform movements in middle-class homes, justifying the importance of the so-called 'feminine virtues'. Radharani Lahiri, for instance, wrote in 1875: 'Of all the subjects that women might learn, housework is the most important ... whatever knowledge she may acquire, she cannot claim any reputation unless she is proficient in housework.'[12] Others spoke of the need for an educated woman to 'develop' such womanly virtues as chastity, self-sacrifice, submission, devotion, kindness, patience, and the labours of love.[13] The ideological point of view from which such protestations of 'femininity' (and hence the acceptance of a new patriarchal order) were made inevitable was given precisely by the *nationalist* resolution of the problems, and Kundamala Debi, writing in 1870, expressed this well when she advised other women:

> If you have acquired real knowledge, then give no place in your heart to *mem-sahib* like behaviour. That is not becoming in a Bengali housewife. See how an educated woman can do housework thoughtfully and systematically in a way unknown to an ignorant, uneducated woman. And see how if God had not appointed us to this place in the home, how unhappy a place the world would be![14]

Education, then, was meant to inculcate in women the virtues—the typically 'bourgeois' virtues characteristic of the new social forms of 'disciplining'—of orderliness, thrift, cleanliness, and a personal sense of responsibility, the practical skills of literacy, accounting and hygiene, and the ability to run the household according to the new physical and economic conditions set by the outside world. For this, she would also need to have some idea of the world outside the home into which she could even venture as long as it did not threaten her 'femininity'. It is this latter criterion, now invested with a characteristically nationalist content, which made possible the displacement of the boundaries of 'the home' from the physical confines earlier defined by the rules of *purdah* (seclusion) to a more flexible, but culturally nonetheless determinate, domain set by the *differences* between socially approved male and female conduct. Once the essential 'femininity' of women was fixed in terms of certain culturally visible 'spiritual' qualities, they could go to schools, travel in public conveyances, watch public entertainment programmes, and in time even take up employment outside the home. But the 'spiritual' signs of her femininity were now clearly marked: in her dress, her eating habits, her social demeanour, her religiosity. The specific markers were obtained from diverse sources, and in terms of their origins each had its specific history. The dress of the *bhadramahila*, for instance, went through a whole phase of experimentation before what was known as the *brahmika* sari (a form of wearing the sari in combination with blouse, petticoat and shoes made fashionable in Brahmo households) became accepted as standard for middle-class women.[15] Here, too, the necessary differences were signified in terms of national identity, social emancipation, and cultural refinement, differences, that is to say, with the *memsahib*, with women of earlier generations and with women of the lower classes. Further, in this as in other aspects of her life, the 'spirituality' of her character had also to be stressed in contrast with the innumerable surrenders which men were having to make to the pressures of the material world. The need to adjust to the new conditions outside the home had forced upon men a whole series of changes in their dress, food habits, religious observances, and social relations. Each of these capitulations now had to be compensated by an assertion of spiritual purity on the part of women. They must not eat, drink, or smoke in the same way as men; they must continue the observance of religious rituals which men were finding difficult to carry out; they must maintain the cohesiveness of family life and solidarity with the kin to which men could not now devote much attention. The new patriarchy advocated by nationalism conferred upon women the honour of a new social responsibility, and by associating the task of 'female emancipation' with the historical goal of sovereign nationhood, bound them to a new, and yet entirely legitimate, subordination.

As with all hegemonic forms of exercise of dominance, this patriarchy combined coercive authority with the subtle force of persuasion. This was expressed most generally in an inverted ideological form of the relation of power between the sexes: the adulation of woman as goddess or as mother. Whatever be its sources in the classical religions of India or in medieval religious practices, it is undeniable that the specific ideological form in which we know the Sati–Savitri–Sita construct in the modern literature and arts of India today is wholly a product of the development of a dominant middle-class culture coeval with the era of nationalism. It served to emphasize with all the force of mythological inspiration, what had in any case become a dominant characteristic of femininity in the new woman, namely, the 'spiritual' qualities of self-sacrifice, benevolence, devotion, religiosity, etc. This spirituality did not, as we have seen, impede the chances of the woman moving out of the physical confines of the home; on the contrary, it facilitated it, making it possible for her to go out into the world under conditions that would not threaten her femininity. In fact, the image of woman as goddess or mother served to erase her sexuality in the world outside the home.

[V]

I conclude this essay by pointing out another significant feature of the way in which nationalism sought to resolve the women's question in accordance with its historical project. This has to do with the one aspect of the question which was directly political, concerning relations with the state. Nationalism, as I have said before, located its own subjectivity in the spiritual domain of culture, where it considered itself superior to the West and hence undominated and sovereign. It could not permit an encroachment by the colonial power into that domain. This determined the characteristically nationalist response to proposals for effecting social reform through the legislative enactments of the colonial state. Unlike the early reformers, from Rammohun to Vidyasagar, nationalists of the late nineteenth century were in general opposed to such proposals, for such a method of reform seemed to deny the ability of the 'nation' to act for itself even in a domain where it was sovereign. In the specific case of reforming the lives of women, consequently, the nationalist position was firmly based on the premise that this was an area where the nation was acting on its own, outside the purview of the guidance and intervention of the colonial state.

We now get the full answer to the historical problem I raised at the beginning of this essay. The reason why the issue of 'female emancipation' seems to disappear from the public agenda of nationalist agitation in the late nineteenth century is not because it was overtaken by the more emotive issues concerning political power. Rather, the reason lies in the refusal of nationalism to make the women's question an issue of political negotiation with the colonial state. The simple historical fact is that the lives of middle-class women, coming from that demographic section which effectively constituted the 'nation' in late colonial India, changed most rapidly precisely during the period of the nationalist movement—indeed, so rapidly that women from each generation in the last hundred years could say quite truthfully that their lives were strikingly different from those led by the preceding generation. These changes took place in the colonial period mostly outside the arena of political agitation, in a domain where the nation thought of itself as already free. It was after independence, when the nation had acquired political sovereignty, that it became legitimate to embody the ideas of reform in legislative enactments about marriage rules, property rights, suffrage, equal pay, equality of opportunity, etc.

Another problem on which we can now obtain a clearer perspective is that of the seeming absence of any autonomous struggle by women themselves for equality and freedom. We would be mistaken to look for evidence of such a struggle in the public archives of political affairs, for unlike the women's movement in nineteenth- and twentieth-century Europe, that is not where the battle was waged here in the era of nationalism. The domain where the new idea of womanhood was sought to be actualized was the home, and the real history of that change can be constructed only out of evidence left behind in autobiographies, family histories, religious tracts, literature, theatre, songs, paintings, and such other cultural artifacts that depict life in middle-class homes. It is impossible that in the considerable transformation of the middle-class home in India in the last 100 years, women played a wholly passive part, for even the most severe system of domination seeks the consent of the subordinate as an autonomous being.

The location of the state in the nationalist resolution of the women's question in the colonial period has yet another implication. For sections of the middle-class which felt themselves culturally left out of the specific process of formation of the 'nation', and which then organized themselves as politically distinct groups, the relative exclusion from the new nation-state would act as a further means of displacement of the legitimate agency of reform. In the case of Muslims in Bengal, for instance, the formation of a middle class occurred with a lag, for reasons which we need not go into here. Exactly the same sorts of ideological concerns typical of a nationalist response to issues of social reform in a colonial situation can be seen to operate among Muslims as well, with a difference in chronological time.[16] Nationalist reform does not, however, reach political fruition in the case of Muslims in independent India, since to the extent that the dominant cultural formation among them considers the community excluded from the state, a new colonial relation is brought into being. The system of dichotomies of inner/outer, home/world, feminine/masculine is once again activated. Reforms which touch upon the 'inner essence' of the identity of the community can only be carried out be the community itself, not by the state. It is instructive to note here how little institutional change has been allowed in the civil life of Indian Muslims since independence and compare it with Muslim countries where nationalist cultural reform was a part of the successful formation of an independent nation-state. The contrast is striking if one compares the position of middle-class Muslim women in West Bengal today with that in neighbouring Bangladesh.

The continuance of a distinct cultural 'problem' of the minorities is an index of the failure of the Indian nation to effectively include within its body the whole of the demographic mass which it claimed to represent. The failure assumes massive proportions when we note, as I have tried to do throughout this discussion, that the formation of a hegemonic 'national culture' was *necessarily* built upon a system of exclusions. Ideas of freedom, equality, and cultural refinement went hand in hand with a set of dichotomies which systematically excluded from the new life of the nation the vast masses of people whom the dominant élite would represent and lead, but who could never be culturally integrated with their leaders. Both colonial rulers and their nationalist opponents conspired to displace in the colonial world the original structure of meanings associated with Western bourgeois notions of right, freedom, equality, etc. The inauguration of the national state in India could not mean a universalization of the bourgeois nation of 'man'.

The new patriarchy which nationalist discourse set up as a hegemonic construct culturally distinguished itself not only from the West but also from the mass of its own people. It has generalized itself among the new middle class, admittedly a widening class and large enough in absolute numbers to be self-reproducing, but is irrelevant to the large mass of subordinate classes. This raises important questions regarding the issue of women's rights today. We are all aware that the forms and demands of the women's movement in the West are not generally applicable in India. This often leads us to slip back into a nationalist framework for resolving such problems. A critical historical understanding will show that this path will only bring us to the dead end which the nationalist resolution of the women's question has already reached. The historical possibilities here have already been exhausted. A renewal of the struggle for the equality and freedom of women must, as with all democratic issues in countries like India, imply a struggle against the humanistic construct of 'rights' set up in Europe in the post-Enlightenment era and include within it a struggle against the false essentialisms of home/world, spiritual/materials, feminine/masculine propagated by nationalist ideology.

Notes

1. See Ghulam Murshid, *Reluctant Debutante: Response of Bengali Women to Modernization, 1849–1905*, Rajshahi, 1983.
2. See, for example, Sumit Sarkar, 'The Complexities of Young Bengal', *Nineteenth Century Studies*, 4, 1973, pp. 504–34; V.C. Joshi (ed.) 'Rammohun Roy and the Break with the Past', in *Rammohun Roy and the Process of Modernization in India*, Delhi, 1975; Ashok Sen, 'The Bengal Economy and Rammohun Roy', in ibid. and *Ishwar Chandra Vidyasagar and His Elusive Milestones*, Calcutta, 1977; Ranajit Guha, 'Neel Darpan: The Image of the Peasant Revolt in a Liberal Mirror', *Journal of Peasant Studies*, 2 (1), 1974, pp. 1–46.
3. Sumit Sarkar, 'The Women's Question in Nineteenth Century Bengal', in Kumkum Sangari and Sudesh Vaid (eds), *Women and Culture*, Bombay, 1985, pp. 157–72.
4. See Partha Chatterjee, *Nationalist Thought and the Colonial World*, Delhi, 1986.
5. Bhudev Mukhopadhyay, 'Grhakaryer Vyavastha', in *Bhudev-racanasambhar*, Pramathanath Bisi (ed.), Calcutta, 1969, p. 480.
6. 'Lajjasilata', in ibid., pp. 445–8.
7. Ibid., p. 446.
8. Ibid., p. 447.
9. M.K. Gandhi, *Collected Works*, (64), Delhi, 1970, p. 85.
10. See the survey of these debates in Murshid, *op. cit.*, pp. 19–62; and Meredith Borthwick, *The Changing Role of Women in Bengal 1849–1905*, Princeton NJ, 1984.
11. Murshid, *op. cit.*, p. 43. In the area of higher education, Chandramukhi Bose and Kadambini Ganguli were celebrated as examples of what Bengali women could achieve in formal learning: they took their B.A. degrees from the University of Calcutta in 1883, before any British university agreed to accept women on their examination rolls. On Chandramukhi and Kadambini's application, the University of Calcutta granted full recognition to women candidates at the First of

Arts examination in 1878. London University admitted women to its degrees later that year (Borthwick, *op. cit.*, p. 94). Kadambini then went on to medical college and became the first professionally schooled woman doctor.

12. Cited in Murshid, *op. cit.*, p. 60.
13. See, for instance, Kulabala Debi, *Hindu Mahilar Hinabastha*, cited in Murshid, *op. cit.*, p. 60.
14. Cited in Borthwick, *op. cit.*, p. 105.
15. Ibid., pp. 245–56.
16. See Murshid, *op. cit.*

(Reproduced from Partha Chatterjee, 'The Nationalist Resolution of the Woman's Question', in Kumkum Sangari and Sudesh Vaid (eds), *Recasting Women: Essays in Colonial History*, New Delhi, 1989, pp. 233–53.)

The Debate on Caste and Social Reconstruction in India

A Radical Critique of Caste

I am really sorry for the members of the Jat-Pat Todak Mandal who have so very kindly invited me to preside over this conference. I am sure they will be asked many questions for having selected me as the president. ... I have criticized the Hindus. I have questioned the authority of the Mahatma whom they revere. They hate me. ... I shall not be surprised if some political Hindus regard it as an insult. ... The Mandal may be asked to explain why it has disobeyed the Shastric injunction in selecting the president. ... The Shastras do not permit a Hindu to accept any one as his *guru* merely because he is well-versed. ... As for myself, you will allow me to say that I have accepted the invitation much against my will and also against the will of many of my fellow untouchables. ... If I am here it is because of your choice and not because of my wish. Yours is a cause of social reform. That cause has always made an appeal to me and it is because of this that I felt I ought not to refuse an opportunity of helping the cause, especially when you think that I can help it ....

The path of social reform, like the path of heaven, at any rate in India, is strewn with many difficulties. Social reform in India has few friends and many critics. The critics fall into two distinct classes. One class consists of political reformers and the other of socialists.

It was at one time recognized that without social efficiency no permanent progress in the other fields of activity was possible, that owing to mischief wrought by the evil customs, Hindu society was not in a state of efficiency and that ceaseless efforts must be made to eradicate these evils. It was due to the recognition of this fact that the birth of the National Congress was accompanied by the birth of the Social Conference .... For some time, the Congress and the Conference worked as two wings of one common activity and they held their annual sessions in the same *pandal*. But soon the two wings developed into two parties, a Political Reform Party and a Social Reform Party, between whom there raged a fierce controversy. The Political Reform Party supported the National Congress and Social Reform Party supported the Social Conference. The two bodies thus became two hostile camps. The point at issue was whether social reform should precede political reform .... It was, however, evident that the fortunes of the Social Conference were ebbing fast .... This indifference, this thinning of its ranks was soon followed by active hostility from the politicians. Under the leadership of the late Mr Tilak, the courtesy with which the Congress allowed the Social Conference the use of its *pandal* was withdrawn, and the spirit of enmity went to such a pitch that when the Social Conference desired to erect its own *pandal* a threat to burn the *pandal* was held out by its opponents. ... The Speech delivered by Mr W.C. Bonnerji in 1892 at Allahabad as president of the eighth session of the Congress, sounds like a funeral oration at the death of the Social Conference and is so typical of the Congress attitude that I venture to quote from it the following extract.

Mr Bonnerji said:

> I for one have no patience with those who say we shall not be fit for political reform until we reform our social system I fail to see any connection between the two .... Are we not fit [for political reform] because our widows remain unmarried and our girls are given in marriage earlier than in other countries? Because our wives and daughters do not drive about with us visiting our friends? Because we do not send our daughters to Oxford and Cambridge? [Cheers]

[L]et me now state the case for social reform. In doing this, I will follow Mr Bonnerji as nearly as I can, and ask the political-minded Hindus, 'Are you fit for political power even though you do not allow a large class of your countrymen like the untouchables to use public school? Are you fit for political power even though you do not allow them the use of public wells? .... Every Congressman who repeats the dogma of Mill that one country is not fit to rule another country, must admit that one class is not fit to rule another class.

How is it then that the Social Reform Party lost the battle? To understand this correctly, it is necessary to take note of this kind of social reform which the reformers were agitating for. In this connection it is necessary to make a distinction between social reform in the sense of the reform of the Hindu family, and social reform in the sense of the reorganization and reconstruction of the Hindu society. The former has relation to widow remarriage, child marriage, etc., while the latter relates to the abolition of [the] caste system. The Social Conference was a body which mainly concerned itself with the reform of the high-caste Hindu family .... They felt, quite naturally, a greater urge to remove such evils as enforced widowhood, child marriages, etc., evils which prevailed among them and which were personally felt by them. They did not stand up for the reform of the Hindu society ....

I am aware that this argument cannot alter the fact that political reform did in fact gain precedence over social reform. But the argument has this much value if not more. It explains why social reformers lost the battle. It also helps us to understand how limited was the victory which the Political Reform Party obtained over the Social Reform Party, and that the view that social reform need not precede political reform is a view which may stand only when by social reform is meant the reform of the family. That political reform cannot with impunity take precedence over social reform in the sense of reconstruction of society is a thesis which, I am sure, cannot be controverted ....

Let us now turn to the socialists. Can the socialists ignore the problem arising out of the social order? The socialists of India, following their fellows in Europe, are seeking to apply the economic interpretation of history to the facts of India. They propound that man is an economic creature, that his activities and aspirations are bound by economic facts, that property is the only source of power. They, therefore, preach that political and social reforms are but gigantic illusions and that economic reform by equalization of property must have precedence over every other kind of reform .... One may contend that economic motive is not the only motive by which man is actuated .... That the social status of an individual by itself often becomes a source of power and authority is made clear by the sway which the *mahatmas* have held over the common man. Why do millionaires in India obey penniless *sadhus* and *fakirs*? .... That religion is a source of power is illustrated by the history of India .... The fallacy of the socialists lies in supposing that because in the present state of European society property as a source of power is predominant, the same is true of India .... [W]hat I like to ask the socialists is this: can you have economic reform without first bringing about a reform of the social order? The socialists of India do not seem to have considered this question .... If socialism is a practical programme and is not merely an ideal, distant and far off, the question for a socialist is not whether he believes in equality. The question for him is whether he *minds* one class ill-treating and suppressing another class as a matter of system as a matter of principle and thus allow tyranny and oppression to continue to divide one class from another .... Men will not join in a revolution for the equalization of property unless they know that after the revolution is achieved they will be treated equally and there will be no discrimination of caste and creed. The assurance of a socialist leading the revolution that he does not believe in caste, I am sure, will not suffice ....

It is a pity that caste even today has its defenders. The defences are many. It is defended on the ground that the caste system is but another name for division of labour [and] is a necessary feature of every civilized society; then it is argued that there is nothing wrong in the caste system. Now the first thing is to be urged against this view is that caste system is not merely a division of labour. *It is also a division of labourers* .... [I]n no civilized society is division of labour accompanied by this unnatural division into watertight compartments. [The] caste system ... is a hierarchy in which the divisions of labourers are graded one above the other .... The division of labour brought about by the caste system is not a division based on choice .... It is based on the dogma of predestination .... As an economic organization caste is, therefore, a harmful institution inasmuch as it involves the subordination of man's natural powers and inclinations to the exigencies of social rules.

Some have dug a biological trench in defence of the caste system. It is said that the object of caste was to preserve purity of race and purity of blood. Now ethnologists are of opinion that men of pure race exist nowhere and that there has been a mixture of all races in all parts of the world. Especially is this the case with the people of India .... The caste system cannot be said to have grown as a means of preventing the admixture of races or as a means of maintaining purity of blood. As a matter of fact [the] caste system came into being long after the different races of India had commingled in blood and culture. To hold that distinctions of castes are really distinctions of race and to treat different castes as though they were so many different races is a gross perversion of facts. What racial affinity is there between the Brahmin of Punjab and the Brahmin of Madras? .... What racial difference is there between the Brahmin of Madras and the Pariah of Madras? The Brahmin of Punjab is racially of the same stock as the Chamar of Punjab .... [E]ven scientists who believe in the purity of races do not assert that the different races constitute different species of men. They are only varieties of one and the same species .... An immense lot of nonsense is talked about heredity and eugenics in defence of the caste system. Few would object to the caste system if it was in accord with the basic principles of eugenics because few can object to the improvement of the race by judicious mating. But one fails to understand how the caste system secures judicious mating. [The] caste system is a negative thing. It merely prohibits persons belonging to different castes from intermarrying. It is not a positive method of selecting which two among a given caste should marry .... If caste means race than differences of sub-castes cannot mean differences of race because sub-castes become *ex hypothesia* subdivisions of one and the same race. Consequently, the bar against intermarrying and inter-dining between sub-castes cannot be for the purpose of maintaining purity of blood .... Inter-dining cannot infect blood and therefore cannot be the cause either of the improvement or of the deterioration of the race. This shows that caste has no scientific origin ....

What is your ideal society if you do not want caste is a question that is bound to be asked of you. If you ask me, my ideal would be a society based on *liberty*, *equality*, and *fraternity*. And why not? What objection can there be to fraternity? .... An ideal society should be mobile, should be full of channels for conveying a change taking place in one part to other parts .... In other words, there must be social endosmosis. This is fraternity, which is only another name for democracy. Democracy is not merely a form of government. It is primarily a form of associated living .... Why not allow liberty to benefit by effective and competent use of someone's powers? The supporters of caste who would allow liberty in the sense of a right to life, limb, and property, would not really consent to liberty in this sense, inasmuch as it involves liberty to choose one's profession .... Any objection to equality? This has obviously been the most contentious part of the slogan of the French Revolution. The objections to equality may be sound and one may have to admit that all men are not equal. But what of that? Equality may be a fiction but nonetheless one must accept it as the governing principle .... [I]f it is good for the social body to get the most out of its members, it can get most out of them only by making them equal as far as possible at the very start of the race. That is one reason why we cannot escape equality ....

But there is a set of reformers who held out a different ideal. They go by the name of Arya Samajists and their ideal of social organization is what is called *chaturvarnya* or the division of society into four classes instead of the 4,000 castes that we have in India .... [T]he protagonists of *chaturvarnya* take great care to point out that their *chaturvarnya* is not based on birth but on *guna* (worth) ....

[I]f [under this system], an individual is to take his place in the Hindu society according to his worth, I do not insist why the Arya Samajists insist upon labeling men as Brahmin, Kshatriya, Vaishya, and Shudra. A learned man would be honoured without his being labeled a Brahmin .... There is another objection to the use of these labels. All reform consists in a change in the notions, sentiments, and mental attitudes of the people towards men and things. It is common experience that certain names become associated with certain notions and sentiments .... The names Brahmin, Kshatriya, Vaishya, and Shudra are names which are associated with a definite and fixed notion in the mind of every Hindu .... The Hindu must be made to unlearn all this. But how can all this happen if the old labels remain and continue to recall [to] his mind old notions? ....

[T]he system of *chaturvarnya* raises several difficulties which its protagonists do not seem to have taken into account. The principle underlying caste is fundamentally different from the principle underlying *varna* .... The former is based on worth. How are you going to compel people who have acquired a higher status based on birth without reference to their worth to vacate the status? How are you going to compel people to recognize the status due to a man in accordance with his worth, who is occupying a lower status based on his birth? .... [Y]ou must break up the caste system in order to establish the *varna* system .... One important requirement for the successful working of the *chaturvarnya* is the maintenance of the penal system which it could maintain by its sanction. The system of *chaturvarnya* must perpetually face the problem of the transgressor. Unless there is penalty attached to the act of transgression, men will not keep to their respective classes .... *Chaturvarnya* cannot subsist by its own inherent goodness. It must be enforced by law .... The protagonists of *chaturvarnya* do not seem to have considered what is to happen to women in their system. Are they also to be divided into four classes ... or are they to be allowed to take the status of their husbands? If the status of the woman is to be the consequence of marriage, what becomes of the underlying principle of *chaturvarnya*? .... If they are to be classified according to their worth, is their classification to be nominal or real? If it is to be nominal, then it is useless and then the protagonists of *chaturvarnya* must admit that their system does not apply to women. If it is real ... the protagonists of *chaturvarnya* ... must be prepared to have woman priests and woman soldiers .... [T]hat will be the logical outcome of applying *chaturvarnya* to women ....

The defenders of *chaturvarnya* ... say ... why should the Shudra need to acquire wealth when the three *varnas* are there to support him? .... The theory of *chaturvarnya* ... in this sense, may be said to look upon the Shudra as the ward and the other three *varnas* as the guardians .... [But] what is to happen to the Shudra if the three classes refuse to support him on fair terms or combine to keep him down? ....

There is no doubt in my opinion that that unless you change your social order, you can achieve little by way of progress. You cannot mobilize the community either for defence or for offence. You cannot build anything on the foundation of caste. You cannot build up a nation, you cannot build up a morality.

The only question that remains to be considered is—how to bring about the reform of the Hindu social order; how to abolish caste. This is a question of supreme importance. This is a view that in the reform of caste the first step to take is to abolish sub-castes. This view is based upon the supposition that that there is a greater similarity in manners and status between sub-castes than there is between castes .... [T]his is an erroneous supposition. The Brahmins of northern and central India are socially of lower grade as compared with the Brahmins of the Deccan and southern India .... On the other hand, in northern India, the Vaishyas and Kayasthas are intellectually and socially on a par with the Brahmins of the Deccan and southern India .... But assuming that the fusion of sub-castes is possible, what guarantee is there that the abolition of sub-castes will necessarily lead to the abolition of castes? On the contrary, it may happen that the process may stop with the abolition of sub-castes. In that case, the abolition of sub-castes will only help to strengthen the castes .... Another plan of action for the abolition of castes is to begin with inter-caste dinners. This also, in my opinion, is an inadequate remedy. There are many castes that allow inter-dining ... [but] inter-dining has not succeeded in killing the spirit of caste and the consciousness of caste .... You are right in holding that caste will cease to be an operative force only when inter-dining has become [a] matter of common course. You have located the source of the disease. But is your prescription the right prescription for the disease? .... Why is it that a large majority of Hindus do not inter-dine and do not intermarry? .... Caste is not a physical object like a wall of bricks or a line of barbed wire which prevents the Hindus from comingling and which has, therefore, to be pulled down. Caste is a notion, it is a state of mind .... [I]t must be recognized that the Hindus observe caste not because they are inhuman or wrong-headed. They observe caste because they are deeply religious. People are not wrong in observing caste. In my view, what is wrong is their religion which has inculcated this notion of caste. If this is correct, then obviously the enemy you must grapple with is not the people who observe caste, but the Shastras which teach them this religion of caste .... The real remedy is to destroy the belief in the sanctity of the Shastras ....

It is no use seeking refuge in quibbles. It is no use telling people that the Shastras do not say what they are believed to say, grammatically read or logically interpreted. What matters is how the Shastras have been understood by the people. You must take the stand that the Buddha took. You must take the stand that Guru Nanak took. You must not only discard the Shastras, you must deny their authority ....

What are your chances of success? Social reforms fall into different species. There is a species of reform, which does not relate to the religious notion of the people but is purely secular in character. Of such a species of reform, there are two varieties. In one, the reform accords with the principles of religion and merely invites people who have departed from it to revert to them and to follow them. The second, is a reform which not only touches the religious principles, but is diametrically opposed to those principles, and invites people to depart from and to discard their authority and to act contrary to those principles .... The destruction of caste is a reform which falls under the third category. To ask people to give up caste is to ask them to [give up] their fundamental religious notions. It is obvious that the first and second species of reform are easy. But the third is a stupendous task .... Speaking for myself, I see the task to be well nigh impossible. One of these reasons is the attitude of hostility which the Brahmins have shown towards this question .... Some of you will say that it is a matter of small concern whether the Brahmins have come forward to lead the movement against caste or whether they do not. To take this view is, in my judgement, to ignore the part played by the intellectual class in the community .... When such an intellectual class [as Brahmins], which holds the rest of the community in its grip, is opposed to the reform of caste, the chances of success in a movement for the break-up of the caste system appear to me very, very remote ....

Can you appeal to reason and ask the Hindus to discard caste as being contrary to reason? That raises the question: is a Hindu free to follow his reason? Manu has laid down three sanctions to which every Hindu must conform in the matter of his behaviour .... Here, there is no place for reason to play its part. A Hindu must follow either the Veda, Smriti, or *sadachar*. He cannot follow anything else ....

How are you going to break up caste if people are not free to consider whether it accords with reason? How are you going to break up caste if people are not free to consider whether it accords with morality? ....

Some may not understand what I mean by destruction of religion; some may find the idea revolting to them and some may find it revolutionary. Let me, therefore, explain my position. I do not know whether you draw a distinction between principles and rules. But I do .... [T]his distinction is real and important. Rules are practical; they are habitual ways of doing things according to prescription. But principles are intellectual; they are useful methods of judging things .... The difference between rules and principles makes the acts done in pursuit of them different in quality and in content. Doing what is said to be good be virtue of a rule and doing good in the light of a principle are two different things. The principle may be wrong, but the act is conscious and responsible. The rule may be right, but the act is mechanical. A religious act may not be a correct act, but must at least be a responsible act. To permit of this responsibility, religion must mainly be a matter of principles only. It cannot be a matter of rules. The moment it degenerates into rules, it ceases to be religion .... Now the Hindu religion, as contained in the Vedas and Smritis, is nothing but a mass of sacrificial, social, political, and sanitary rules and regulations, all mixed up .... Religion, in the sense of spiritual principles, truly universal, applicable to all races, to all countries, to all times, is not to be found in them, and if it is, it does not form the governing part of a Hindu's life .... I have, therefore, no hesitation in saying that such a religion must be destroyed and I say there is nothing irreligious in working for the destruction of such a religion .... So long as people look upon it as religion, they will not be ready for change, because the idea of religion is generally speaking not associated with the idea of change. But the idea of law is associated with the idea of change and when people come to know that what is called religion is really law, old and archaic, they will be ready for a change, for people know and accept that law can be changed ....

I must not be misunderstood to hold the opinion that there is no necessity for a religion. On the contrary, I agree with Burke when he says that, 'True religion is the foundation of society, the basis on which all true civil government rests and both their sanction' .... Indeed, I am so convinced of the necessity of religion that I feel I ought to tell you in outline what I regard as necessary items in this religious reform. The following, in my opinion, should be the cardinal items in this reform: (1) There should be one and only one standard book of Hindu religion, acceptable to all Hindus .... (2) It should be better if priesthood among Hindus was abolished. But as this seems impossible, the priesthood must at least cease to be hereditary. Every person who professes to be a Hindu must be eligible for being a priest .... [N]o Hindu shall be entitled to be a priest unless he has passed an examination prescribed by the state and holds a *sanad* from the state permitting him to practise. (3) No ceremony performed by a priest who does not hold a *sanad* shall be deemed to be valid .... (4) A priest should be the servant of the state .... (5) The number of priests should be limited by law according to the requirements of the state as is done in the case of the ICS .... The priestly class must be brought under control by some legislation .... It will prevent it from doing mischief .... It will certainly help to kill the brahminism and will also help to kill caste, which is nothing but brahminism incarnate .... You will succeed in saving Hinduism if you will kill brahminism ....

You must give a new doctrinal basis to your religion—a basis that will be in consonance with liberty, equality, and fraternity, in short, with democracy .... I am told that for such religious principles, as will be in consonance with liberty, equality, and fraternity, it may not be necessary for you to borrow from foreign sources and that you could draw for such principles on the Upanishads .... This means a complete change in the fundamental notions of life. It means a complete change in the values of life .... But a new life cannot enter a body that is dead. New life can enter only a new body. The old body must die before a new body can come into existence and new life can enter into it ....

This would have been a convenient point for me to have stopped. But this would probably be my last address to a Hindu audience on a subject vitally concerning the Hindus. I would, therefore, like, before I close, to place before the Hindus ... some questions which I regard as vital and invite them seriously to consider the same.

In the first place, the Hindus must consider whether it is sufficient to take the placid view of the anthropologist that there is nothing to be said about the beliefs, habits, morals, and outlooks on life which obtain among the different peoples of the world .... Morality and religion ... are not matters of like and dislikes .... The Hindus must, therefore, examine their religion and their morality in terms of their survival value.

Secondly, the Hindus must consider whether they should conserve the whole of their social heritage or select what is helpful and transmit to future generations only that much and no more ....

Thirdly, the Hindus must consider whether they must not cease to worship the past as supplying its ideals .... The study of past products will not help us to understand the present ....

Fourthly, the Hindus must consider whether the time has not come for them to recognize that there is nothing fixed, nothing eternal, nothing *sanatan*; that everything is changing, that change is the law of life for individuals as well as for society. In a changing society there must be a constant revolution of old values and the Hindus must realize that if there must be standards to measure the acts of men, there must also be readiness to revise the standards.

(Excerpted form B.R. Ambedkar, 'Annihilation of Caste. With a Reply to Mahatma Gandhi', reprint from 3rd edition of 1944. Reproduced in *Dr Babasaheb Ambedkar, Writings and Speeches* (vol. 1), (Vasant Moon, comp.), Bombay, 1989, pp. 37–80.)

A Rejoinder from M.K. Gandhi

The readers will recall the fact that Dr Ambedkar was to have presided last May at the annual conference of the Jat-Pat Todak Mandal of Lahore. But the conference was cancelled because Dr Ambedkar's address was found by the reception committee to be unacceptable .... The committee seems to have deprived the public of an opportunity of listening to a man who has carved out for himself a unique position in society ....

No reformer can ignore the address. The orthodox will gain by reading it. This is not to say that the address is not open to objection. Dr Ambedkar is a challenge to Hinduism. Brought up as a Hindu, educated by a Hindu potentate, he has become so disgusted with the so-called Savarna Hindus for the treatment that he and his people have received at their hands, that he proposes to leave not only them but the very religion that is his and their common heritage. He has transferred to that religion, his disgust against a part of its professors.

But this is not to be wondered at. After all, one can only judge a system on institution by the conduct of its representatives .... No Hindu who prizes his faith above life itself can afford to underrate the importance of this indictment.... [T]he fact of many leaders remaining in the Hindu fold is no warrant for disregarding what Dr Ambedkar has to say. The Savarnas have to correct their belief and their conduct. Above all, those who are by their learning and influence among the Savarnas, have to give an authoritative interpretation of the scriptures.

(M.K. Gandhi in the *Harijan* of 11 July 1936.)

The Vedas, Upanishads, Smritis, and Puranas, including *Ramayana* and *Mahabaharata*, are the Hindu scriptures. Nor is this a finite list. Every age or even generation has added to this list. It follows, therefore, that everything printed or even found handwritten is not scripture. The Smritis, for instance, contain much that can never be accepted as the word of God. Thus, many of the texts that Dr Ambedkar quotes from the Smritis cannot be accepted as authentic. The scriptures, properly so called, can only be concerned with eternal verities and must appeal to any conscience .... Nothing can be accepted as the word of God which cannot be tested by reason or be capable of being spiritually experienced .... Who is the best interpreter? Not learned men surely. Learning there must be. But religion does not live by it. It lives in the experiences of its saints and seers, in their lives and sayings ....

Caste has nothing to do with religion. It is a custom whose origin I do not know and do not need to know for the satisfaction of my spiritual hunger. But I do know that it is harmful both to spiritual and national growth. *Varna* and *ashrama* are institutions which have nothing to do with castes. The law of *varna* teaches us that we have each one of us to earn our bread by following our ancestral calling. It defines not our rights but our duties .... It also follows that there is no calling that is too low or none too high. All are good, lawful, and equal in status .... I find, too, that real Brahmins are to [be] found even in these degenerate days who are living on alms freely given to them and are giving freely of what they have of spiritual treasures. It would be wrong and improper to judge the law of *varna* by its caricature in the lives of men who profess to belong to a *varna* whilst they openly commit a breach of its only operative rule. Arrogation of a superior status by and of the *varna* over another is a denial of the law. And there is nothing in the law of *varna* to warrant a belief in untouchability ....

I am aware that my interpretation of Hinduism will be disputed by many besides Dr Ambedkar. That does not affect my position. It is an interpretation by which I have lived for nearly half a century and according to which I have endeavoured to the best of my ability to regulate my life.

In my opinion, the profound mistake that Dr Ambedkar has made in his address, is to pick out the texts of doubtful authenticity and value, and the state of degraded Hindus who are no fit specimens of the faith they so woefully represent. Judged by the standard applied by Dr Ambedkar, every known living faith will probably fail.

In his noble address, the learned doctor has overproved his case. Can a religion that was professed by Chaitanya, Jyandeo, Tukaram, Tiruvalluvar, Ramakrishna Paramhamsa, Raja Rammohun Roy, Maharshi Devendranath Tagore, Vivekanand, and a host of others who might be easily mentioned, so utterly devoid of merit as is made out in Dr Ambedkar's address? A religion is to be judged not by its worst specimens, but the best it might have produced. For that and that alone can be used as the standard to aspire, if not to improve upon.

(M.K. Gandhi in *Harijan* of 18 July 1936).

(The above excerpts of Gandhi are reproduced in Appendix I of B.R. Ambedkar, *The Annihilation of Caste, op. cit.*, pp. 81–5.)

6

Debates in History, Debates on History

Situating 'Renaissance', 'Reform' and Social Change in Modern India

The Alien Roots of Indian Awakening

Can we see what was the cause of the great Awakening which began about 1800 and since then has dominated the life and history of India? How was the Muslim period so barren as compared with the nineteenth century? How is it that European influence produced practically no results between 1500 and 1800? Why did the Awakening begin at that particular point?

The answer is that the Awakening is the result of the cooperation of two forces, both of which began their characteristic activity about the same time, and that it was quickened by a third which began to affect the Indian mind a little later. The two forces are the British government in India as it learned its task during the years at the close of the eighteenth and the beginning of the nineteenth centuries, and Protestant missions as they were shaped by the Serampore men and Duff; and the third force is the work of the great Orientalists. The material elements of the Western civilization have had their influence, but apart form the creative forces, they would have led to no awakening ....

[T]he arrival of the new spirit was necessary for the health of the country. The long decade during which not only the European but the cultured Hindu looked down upon the religion, philosophy, and art of India effectually opened the door to the influence of the West, without which the Awakening would have been impossible .... Western influence has been steadily moulding the educated mind and rendering it altogether incapable of holding the ideas which form the foundation of religion. Hence, we have many defences of idolatry but no faith in it. In spite of all that has been said in favour of the Hindu family, no educated Hindu has found any religious basis for pre-puberty marriage, for widow celibacy, for polygamy, for the *zenana*. ... Much has been said to make caste seem a most reasonable form social organization; yet thinking Hindus no longer hold that which is the foundation of the system, the doctrine that each man's caste is an infallible index of the stage of spiritual progress his soul has reached in its transmigrational journey ....

The causes which have combined to create the movements are many. The stimulating forces are almost exclusively Western, namely, the British government, English education and literature, Christianity, Oriental research, European science and philosophy, and the material elements of Western civilization; but the beliefs and the organization of the ancient faiths have been the moulding forces of great potency. The Arya Samaj is an interesting example of the interaction of rationalism an modern inventions with belief in transmigration and the inerrancy of Vedic hymns. The Deva Samaj shows us Western evolutionary science in a new Gnosticism which owes its knowledge to Western Orientalists, but takes its principles from Buddhism and its fireworks from occultism.

While the shaping forces at work in the movements have been many, it is quite clear that *Christianity has ruled the development throughout.* Christianity has been, as it were, a great searchlight flung across the expanse of the religions; and in its blaze, all the coarse, unclean, and superstitious elements of the old faiths stood out quite early in painful vividness .... Christianity has made men feel that the only possible religion is *monotheism*. The Brahma, Prarthna, and Arya Samajes declare themselves as truly monotheistic as Christianity .... The Christian doctrine that *God is the Father of men* and that every man is a child of God, with its corollary, that all men are brothers, is accepted with practical unanimity in all these movements. In the Brahma and Prarthna Samajes, and by Sivanarayana, these doctrines are seriously accepted and made a basis of a new life .... The Christian doctrine of the love of God, which is a necessary element in the Fatherhood, passed into the teaching of the Brahma and Prarthna Samajes, and has deeply influenced most of the other movements. It has led to increased emphasis being laid on the doctrine of *bhakti*. The belief that all men, as children of God, are brothers, and that morality maybe summed up in the world of brotherliness, has also worked wonders. ... The same belief has given Indians a truer idea of the value of the human personality and shows itself in the conviction that an Indian of any class is as great and valuable as an European .... Every modern religious movement in India calls itself the religion for all men. ... How is it that no such claim was ever made until Christianity appeared on the scene? On the basis of human brotherhood, Christ insists vehemently on the duty of kindly philanthropic service, and no part of his teaching has produced larger results in India. Feeble attempts are made here and there to trace the teaching to Hinduism; but all well-informed men recognize that it was introduced into India by Christian missions. This mighty force shows itself in every element of the social reform movement, but above all things, in what Christians have done for the outcastes, and in the rise of the movement among Hindus.

The righteousness of God, as taught by Jesus, has also exercised a profound influence. The conception necessarily involves the Christian ideals of repentance, forgiveness, the transformation of character, the holy life, and the passion of saving men .... The Christian contention that sacred books can be of no value unless they are understood by the people, has led all the movements, Jain, Sikh, Parsi, and Muslim, as well as Hindu, to produce translations of the sacred books they use and to write all fresh books in the vernaculars .... The most characteristic and vital of all Hindu doctrines is transmigration and *karma* .... The doctrine has been expelled completely from the teaching of the Brahma and Prarthna Samajes; and everywhere else it has been deeply wounded. Every aspect of the social reform movement is a direct attack upon it; and indeed each of the social implications of the doctrine is rapidly losing its hold. Men revere the doctrine today, but do not understand it. To them, it is merely an explanation of the inequalities of life; but no educated Hindu is ready to follow even that line to the end.

In all these movements we trace a strong desire *that their leaders should be like missionaries,* that their priests and teachers a modern training in theology, so that they may be able to teach the people and to defend the system from outside attack .... A peculiarly arresting proof that Christianity has ruled the whole religious development of the last century is to be found in the *social reform movement.* From beginning to end, the ideas that have led to reform have been purely Christian, and have [had] to win their way in face of the deepest conceptions of Hindu theology and social organization ....

The dominance of Christianity in the religious development of the last hundred years may be clearly seen in this that, *almost without exception, the methods of work in use in the movements have been borrowed from missions.* This is the more noticeable since India, in the past, had the genius to produce a series of methods of religious propaganda unmatched in the history of the world .... Dayananda and Ramakrishna were monks; but in neither case did any organized movement appear until monastic modes of effort have given place to missionary methods.

(Excerpted from J.N. Farquhar, *Modern Religious Movements in India* (1st Indian edition), Delhi, 1967, pp. 4–5, 431–43.)

Renascent Hinduism

Hinduism is the oldest of the religions of the world. It has an unbroken history of about fifty centuries. It has just had a long period of Renaissance (the sixth of its kind in its history) the leading lights of which are Rammohan Roy, Dayanand Saraswati, Sri Ramakrishna, Swami Vivekananda, Annie Besant, Mahatma Gandhi, Rabindranath Tagore, Sri Aurobindo, and Radhakrishnan, to mention only those of all-India fame. These illustrious persons have, by their activities, teaching, or writings, given to Hinduism another lease of life at home and given to India some prestige abroad in the nineteenth and twentieth centuries ....

[T]he modern Renaissance, beginning with the work of that great statesman and reformer, Rammohan Roy, has done a great deal of spadework which will make the path of coming generations smooth and easy. It broke the shackles with which the Hindu community bound itself, hand and foot, during the dark days of the Mughal empire. Religion no longer stands in the way of the Hindus going to foreign countries or dining with anybody inside or outside India. It no longer forbids Hindu women from occupying the highest posts in the state or marrying anybody they choose. And most important of all, the great caste system .... is tottering to its fall along with its ugly pendant—the system of outcastes ....

When we survey carefully the entire field of Hindu rituals, we are astonished at the wisdom of our ancestors who devised the whole system. The ritual in their system fits the faith of their day as a glove fits a hand. But the system has grown old and is worn out at many places. The hand has grown, and the glove has become too tight and is bursting at the seams.

There is great deal of work to be done in this field. First of all, in these modern days when the demands of life have become so many and when many educated Indians have to go to foreign countries and to remain there for long periods, it is not possible to observe all the ancient rites and ceremonies in all their fullness and exactitude as in ancient days. Rituals have, therefore, to be simplified and made significant and clearly expressive of the living faith, and not the obsolete faith of the past generations ....

More deplorable than this wide gulf between rituals and faith is the wider gulf between religion and morality. Many people in our country seem to think that they can be religious without being moral. They are very punctilious about the performance of rites and ceremonies, but are not half so careful about being honest, fair, just, and generous in their dealings with others. It is such people who bring religion into contempt ... [for] as a matter of fact, religion and morality are inextricably intertwined ....

[A]n ethnic religion like Hinduism, which has grown along with the race that gave it birth, is bound to have many primitive customs, superstitions, and beliefs embedded in it, which it is the task of progressive reformers to eradicate. For instance, in the course of its history, evils like slavery, *suttee*, animal sacrifices, polygamy, enforced widowhood, compulsory segregations etc. have been banished by the efforts of religious reformers .... Such efforts have to be continued with greater vigour and determination in future. In fact, social service has to occupy a larger part of organized religion than before. What Christian missions are doing in this respect has to occupy [a] larger part of organized religion than before. What Christian missions are doing in this respect has to be copied by all religious foundations on a large scale. Every *math* and temple, in fact, every religious foundation, should have a social service branch. Incidentally, this will also draw the sects of Hinduism closer together.

It is, however, necessary to sound a note of caution here. Important as social service is, it should only be secondary to religious service. Worship, prayer, and meditation are primary things in religion. All efforts at social amelioration should come only after these. No religious organization should degenerate into a purely social service league ....

As we have already observed, the latest Renaissance of the nineteenth and twentieth centuries has done a great deal of useful work and carried out many reforms. It is to be hoped that with the gaining of political freedom and the disappearance of the system of castes, sub-castes, and the achievement of national integration, the task of this great Renaissance will be completed. If this is done and if Hinduism does not abandon its faith that other religions are not its enemies but fellow-pilgrims marching towards the same shrine as itself though by different paths, there is no reason why it should not say to itself, in the language of Tennyson's Brook, 'Faiths may come, and faiths may go, but I go on for ever.'

(Excerpted from D.S. Sarma, *Renascent Hinduism* (2nd edition), Bombay, 1989, pp. 3–9.)

The 'Renaissance' as Understood in Modern Historiography

The basic assumption of the concept of Indian Renaissance as it was used in liberal historiography just before independence is that British rule had positive aspects (bunched together in one phase, which is seen as its positive phase). In this phase, a revival of Indian culture is supposed to have taken place as a result of the growth of a modern (or, a we have earlier seen, a *Westernized*) outlook, when all that was to be qualitatively, though not quantitatively predominant in nineteenth- and twentieth-century Indian life turned to the Western world for its diffusion of science, culture, and technology .... According to all such assumptions, what was at base Westernization and subalternship to metropolitan capitalism, is identified with 'progressive' trends in Indian history. Let us dig a bit deeper into some of the strands which make up the assumptions.

The first is what I would like to call generally the strand of glorification of nineteenth-century reform movements and Hindu revivalism. Then comes British imperialist historiography, which with very few exceptions, makes a colonialist assumption about the superiority of British culture over that of Indian races. The third is the Indian exegesis of the 1853 *New York Daily Tribune* articles of Karl Marx regarding the main currents of the British Indian connection in the eighteenth and nineteenth centuries in India ....

Modern Indian histories endeavour to establish a distinction between two attributes of movements for social reform in the nineteenth century. The first are the 'progressive' characteristics as expressed by

Rammohun Roy and his successors in the Brahmo Samaj movement, or by Jyotiba Phule and the Satya Shodhak Samaj in the movement in Maharashtra for alleviating and uplifting the condition of the untouchables, or by Dayanand Saraswati through the medium of the Arya Samaj. The second are the 'revivalist' aspects as expressed in the rise of Bengali prose under the aegis of Fort William College *pandit*s like Mritunjoy Vidyalankar, or by the revival of Sanskrit encyclopaedical learning, as well as the advocacy of brutal and obsolete ritualist practices (such as *sati*) by Bhavanicharan Bandopadhyay and Radhakanta Deb (who founded, for the protection of this, the Calcutta Dharma Sabha); or by the conservationism of the Marathas in Bombay and Poona ... and by the religious revivalism of Bankim Chandra Chatterjee in Bengal, Tilak in Maharashtra, and Lajpat Rai in the Punjab. But no hard and fast barrier can be established between these two supposed groups of 'progressives' and 'revivalists'.

For instance, Rammohun Roy was not all that greater a radical than the Dharma Sabha leaders who were the first to accept the new concept of petitioning the parliament for maintenance of their traditional practices .... His [Rammohun's] thought on history and economics ... show that he had more respect for mythical brahmanical values as posited by the British civil servant Orientalist, H.T. Colebrooke, than for the orthodoxy of the medieval period .... The social upliftment of Jyotiba Phule, concerned with the status dissonance of low castes (such as gardeners) in late-nineteenth-century Maharashtra, was part of a general nineteenth-century tendency of Sanskritization, that is, upward caste mobility at the cost of established castes such as the Chitpavans, established in the bureaucracy by the Peshwas. This mobility had been unleashed by the demonstration effect of Westernization among the upper castes.

Rammohun Roy and his Brahmo Samaj never forswore Hinduism, but only sought to revive it by reform. The bulk of nineteenth-century reform movements (some of which were anti-Brahmo) wished to strengthen their own religious communities by injecting within them, Western ideas of scientific rationality and historical self-analysis. What was particularly democratic in the Brahmo Samaj was the later nineteenth-century development of the essentially Protestant practice of the priesthood of believers ....

By and large, reformers and orthodoxy alike were at one at least in an attempt to revitalize their Hindu community by means of democratic media learnt from the West. So both believed in a renaissance of Indian culture, by which they meant Hindu culture (be it Brahmo or Arya Samaj or Sanatanist) ....

The second historiographical strand, which has found it useful to consecrate the idea of the renaissance, is the imperialist historiography of Britain that begins in the eighteenth century with those civil servants of the company in Bengal who became religious. The enlightened eighteenth-century respect for the noble Hindu of Sir William Jones and Principal Robertson, and the secular Warren Hastings–Wilkins–Halhed–Bengal tradition was forsaken by traders turned officials like Charles Grant and Sir John Shore (later Lord Teignmouth) .... A case was made out there for the inferiority of Hindu as well as Muslim to Christian (that is, *West European*) ways of life. Grant, Wilberforce, Thornton the merchant financier, were founder of the evangelical movement, which set the spark to this tinder .... These people lacked the respect for the classical heritage that had been shown by an earlier, more conservative generation of civil servants .... [They] believed that the Indian ideas of nationality, patriotism, and at least surface rationality were derived from English education in the colleges set up at Calcutta, Hoogly, Bombay, Agra, etc., and that Anglicized education was responsible for the chirpiness of the 'bombastic *babus*' of Young Bengal, which was commemorated in English literature by Rudyard Kipling. They did not realize that a desire for equality and co-citizenship with Britons may have been a greater element in this new element in this new growth of Hindu self-confidence. It was the Henry Myers Elliott-Burton premise which was expressed in more sophisticated terms by later ICS officials such as Sir Richard Temple, Sir Verney Lovett, or Sir Percival Griffiths, as well as by even recent historians like the American B.T. McCully or T.G.P. Spear or C.H. Philips .... The post-Macaulayan historians, seeking to explain the growth of an Anglicized intelligentsia, have by and large chosen ... to cover up British imperial responsibility for what they really consider to be intellectual bastardy, by dignifying this as a renaissance of Indian culture *under the wings of British rule*.

Most traditional Bengali historians, whether Brahmo and socially radical like Sivanath Sastri or P.K. Sen [who took opposite sides in the Sadharan Brahmo and Naba Bidhan schism], or militant or semi-orthodox Hindu reformists like Sir Jadunath Sarkar or Professor R.C. Majumdar would agree that British rule produced positive cultural improvements *in the nineteenth but not in the eighteenth century*. As Hindu or Brahmo or Arya Samaji type revivalists, they agree with the common premise of imperialist historians ... that British rule generated the forces of progress called the Renaissance.

Where the militant Hindu ideology diverges from the imperialist thesis as well as the Brahmo one is to explain this generative force as one which destroyed 'medievalism' which is generally called the 'dark forces' or in the Bengali exaggeration *'andhar yuga'* .... Another historiographical tendency is to equate Islamic dominance with only those elements in medievalism as have a religious element. It is said that the cultural improvements, coincidental with the supposed moderate phase of imperialism, had the effect of replacing Islamic culture. Therefore, runs the argument—given a sophisticated cast recently by the current historical apostle of Hindu revivalism, Professor R.C. Majumdar—the new trends, which he calls Renaissance, were the product of Hindu reform, allied with the British imperial impact. Here Professor Majumdar diverges with the Elliott-Burton approach, but has not moved far from the logic of the Thompson-Garratt approach. A recent and freakish variant in his ideas is that the Brahmo Samaj ... had really nothing significant or permanent to contribute to British Indian collaborative effort. This separates Professor Majumdar from the Indian liberal variant of this interpretation as represented by Sivanath Sastri (*Ramtanu Lahiri O Tatkalin Bangasamaj*) down to its considerably watered down version in Nemai Sadhan Bose (*The Indian Awakening and Bengal*).

The liberal bourgeois historians, whether Indian nationalist or imperialist, have generally kept on a low key, the premise that early-nineteenth-century British rule in India brought Renaissance to the Indian literati, mentioning it briefly in their books. Their unity, however, breaks down on the communal–anti-communal split among consciously Hindu historians, the anti-communalists ascribing the Indian response to the broad group of intelligentsia, irrespective of religion; the communalists responding by the argument that the major initiators were Hindus and neither sectarian Muslims nor heterodox Brahmos ....

'Regeneration', according to Marxian semantics, was not possible through the mediation of British rule in modern Indian history. Yet R.P. Dutt's view of economic change finds counterpart in the idea of cultural change through the mediation of Westernization as expressed by Professor Susobhan Chandra Sarkar in his writings; from *Notes on the Bengal Renaissance* (1946) till the one on Rabindranath's place in

Indian thought (1961). In the 1946 pamphlet, Westernization had been explicitly identified with 'progressive' forces, traditionalism with a confusion of 'reactionary', and 'progressive' elements within the same force. In the 1961 article, Professor Sarkar very correctly departed from such a stereotype and hinted at the difference between the European model of Renaissance, which he had earlier popularized, and the milder and more limited awakening in Bengal. *Even so*, he writes, it was 'regeneration' .... At this point, the Marxist historian of modern Bengali thought, Susobhan Sarkar, and the great Westernizing leader of the Indian national movement, Jawaharlal Nehru, agree in their assessment of the relevance of our recent history to the shaping of India's future. The West pillaged and exploited India, and that heritage must be forsworn. But the intellectual lien with the West, which produced our specific sense of rationality and rationalism, must be retained ....

A study of the ideological premises of historians who have talked of Renaissance in India in the nineteenth century would show that whether Hindu revivalist or imperialist or early Indian communist or Muslim revivalist, they all share a vision of a liberal utopia in the recent past. This utopia, which Professor Bipan Chandra in the context of communalism correctly calls 'false consciousness', was at best an emanation of shame about genesis in dependence to British absolutism. It is only the frankness of Dr R.C. Majumdar or a Nirad Chaudhuri (*vide* his dedication to the *Autobiography of an Unknown Indian*) which strips the veil of shame, and glories in either in cultural dependence or in stark regionalist chauvinism ....

(Excerpted from Barun De, 'A Historical Critique of Renaissance Analogues for Nineteenth Century India', in Barun De (ed.), *Perspectives in Social Sciences: I*, Calcutta, 1977, pp. 192–210.)

Appendix A

List of Hindu Local Associations Concerned with Social Reform in India for the Period 1891–9.

Bengal, Orissa, and States of North-east India

	City	*Name of the Organization*	*Office-Bearers*
1.	Barahnagar	Widows' Home	Sasipada Banerji
2.	Calcutta	Indian Reform Association	—
3.	Chittagong	Students Purity Association	Vanimadhab Das
4.	Halisahar	Good Will Fraternity	K.M. Sen
	-do-	Kaulinya Pratha Samsodhini Sabha	W. Mukherji
5.	Mymensing	Mymensing Sammilani	K. Mitra
	-do-	Mymensing Vivaha Vyay Nibarini Samiti	Baneswar
6.	Naldha	Friends' Social Union	Lalit Mohan Das
7.	Raiganj	Hitkarini Sabha	Vishnupada Sen
8.	Sylhet	Sylhet Union	D. Das
9.	Tripura	Hitaishini Sabha	Jagatchandra Sen

Maharashtra, Gujarat, Rajasthan

	City	*Name of the Organization*	*Office-Bearers*
1.	Akola	Berar Association	L.K. Chiplunkar, D. Bhagwat
	-do-	Deshmukh Sabha	K. Deshmukh
2.	Ahmedabad	Widow Marriage Association	Ramanbhai
3.	Ahmednagar	Liberal Club	Hivargarkar

	City	Name of the Organization	Office-Bearers
4.	Ajmer	Walter Krit Rajputra	Agent to the Governor-General
	-do-	Hitkarini Sabha	—
	-do-	Kayastha Sabha	—
	-do-	Jain Sabha	—
	-do-	Agarwala Sabha	—
	-do-	Adigaud Brahman Sabha	—
5.	Baramati	Maharashtra Village Education Society	Kolaskar
6.	Bombay	Aryan Social Club	Raymal Litahar
	-do-	Aika Wardhaka Strisamoon	Manakbhai Kothare
	-do-	Bhatia Mitra Mandal	Damodar Rawji
	-do-	Hindu Union	—
	-do-	Jain Association	—
	-do-	Khetri Union Club	Jagannath Raghoba
	-do-	Hindu Ladies' Social Club	Bubli Bai Pitalo
	-do-	Kutch Dussa Oswal Mandal	Khemji Hiraji
	-do-	Widow Marriage Association	N.N. Bhatt
	-do-	Widow Marriage Association	K.T. Telang, S.G. Ajinkya
7.	Chikurde [Satara]	Social Reform Association	G.V. Deshmukh, K.V. Acharya
8.	Dhula	Hindu Association	Bhagwat and Dange
9.	Kalyan	Kayastha Prabhu Conference	D.A. Madhekar
10.	Karad	Bhakta Samaj	Balaji Narayan
11.	Nasik	Oswal Hitakarini Sabha	Narayan Sukh, Kewal Chand
12.	Nagpur	Friends' Social Union	K. Anandrao
13.	Noomeh	Malwa Rajputana	Political Agent, Malwa
14.	Poona	Arya Dharma Prakashini Sabha	Vishnu N. Apte
	-do-	Agarkar Club	R.N. Kelkar
	-do-	Deccan Library Association	S.R. Hatvalne

	City	*Name of the Organization*	*Office-Bearers*
	-do-	Deccan Female Home Education Society	H.W. Apte
	-do-	Friends' Library Association	Moti Birbasa
	-do-	Hindu Widows Home Association	Waman Viswanath Joshi
	-do-	Social Reform Association	H.H. Balasaheb Patwardhan [Ruler of Miraj]
	-do-	Widow Marriage Association	D.K. Karve
15.	Sholapur	Indian Friends Association [Social Reform Branch]	—
	-do-	Hindu Union	—
	-do-	Branch Library Association	Degawkar
	-do-	Union Club	Kirloskar
	-do-	Saraswati Mandir	Degawkar
16.	Satara	Prarthna Samaj	S. Javeri
	-do-	Shivaji Club	H. Rahalikar
17.	Surat	Anawad Brahmin Association [Desai]	Desai Hararai
	-do-	Anawad Brahmin Association [Bhartheias]	Bhimbhai Govindji, Bhimbhai Govindbhai
18.	Yeotmal	Social Club	R.G. Mundle

Punjab, Sind, Baluchistan

	City	*Name of the Organization*	*Office-Bearers*
1.	Ambala	Gauda Mahasabha	Ramchandraji
2.	Amritsar	Temperance Association	—
	-do-	Shuddhi Sabha	Lala Hansraj
3.	Chakwal	Social Conference	Fatehchand
4.	Gujranwala	Khatri Sabha	Khem Chand
	-do-	Arora Bans Sabha	—
5.	Hoshiarpur	Hindu Social Reform Association	Thakurdas

	City	Name of the Organization	Office-Bearers
6.	Hyderabad [Sind]	Social Conference League	Talhilram
	-do-	Hindu Social Reform Association	Hiranand Khemsingh
7.	Jullundur	Kanya Mahavidyalaya	Lala Badridas
8.	Lahore	Bhera Anand Sabha	—
	-do-	Kashmir Pandit Sabha	—
	-do-	Kayastha Sabha	—
	-do-	Khatri Sabha	—
	-do-	Keharni Sabha	—
	-do-	Guru Singh Sabha	—
	-do-	Hindu Sabha	—
	-do-	Hindu Child Widow Matrimonial	Lala Chandrabhan
	-do-	Purity Association	—
	-do-	Sarin Sabha	—
	-do-	Social Association	—
	-do-	Shuddhi Sabha	—
	-do-	Temperance League	—
9.	Sukhar [Sukur?]	Reform Association	Virumall Begaria
10.	Quetta	Band of Hope, Baluchistan	Malik Narayan Das
11.	Uttarchellian-walla	Wadhawan Sabha	Iswardas

UP, Bihar

	City	Name of the Organization	Office-Bearers
1.	Allahabad	Kayastha Sabha	Narayan P. Asthana
	-do-	Hindu Samaj	—
2.	Agra	Bhargav Sabha	—
3.	Bareilly	Kayastha Sabha	Baldev Prasad
	-do-	High Caste Reform Association	-do-
	-do-	The Sadharan Amrit Varshini Sabha	—
4.	Ballia	Kayastha Sabha	—

City	Name of the Organization	Office-Bearers
5. Gorakhpur	Kayastha Sabha	Aghorenath Chatterjee
6. Ghazipur	Kayastha Sabha	—
-do-	High Caste Reform Society	Arjun Pandey
7. Gwalior	Chaturvedi Conference	Munnalal
-do-	Kayastha Temperance Society	Kamta Prasad
8. Monghyr	Kayastha Sabha	Ram Mahashay
9. Mathura	Jain Maha Sabha	Munshi Champatlal
-do-	Chaturvedi Conference	Radhelal Pande
-do-	Goud Brahman Sabha	—
-do-	Kayastha Sabha	—
-do-	Agarwala Sabha	—
10. Lucknow	Kayastha Sabha	—
-do-	Temperance Association	—

States of South India

City	Name of the Organization	Office-Bearers
1. Bangalore	Hindu Social Reform Association	Narayan Rao Padmanabh
-do-	Social Reform Association	Vedi Vellu
2. Bellary	Sanmarga Samaj	A. Sabapathy Mudaliar
3. Berar	Social Reform Association	Vyankat Rao
4. Chikakol	Hindu Social Reform Association	Ramaswami Aiyar
5. Coimbatore	National Indian Association	Annaswami Rao
6. Coconad	Hindu Social Reform Association	S. Rao, Narayan Rao
7. Cudalore	National Indian Association	Rajratna Mudaliar
8. Dharwar	Liberal Association	V. Vajravelu
-do-	Sammilani Sabha	Dinanath Ganguly, B.P. Laud
9. Gulbarga	Hindu Social Reform Association	Srinivas Acharya
10. Madras	Hindu Marriage Association	Raghunath Rao

	City	*Name of the Organization*	*Office-Bearers*
11.	Madura	Social Union	Ramchandra Iyer
12.	Mangalore	Hindu Social Reformer	Ranga Rao
13.	Masulipattam	Social Purity Association	Venkat Laxminarasimha
14.	Rajamahendri	Widow Reform Association	Viresalingam Pantulu
15.	Salem	National Indian Association	Appaswami Rao, Krishna Rao
16.	Secunderabad	Hindu Social Reform Association	Shivanathan, Ramchandra
17.	Sircy [Kanara]	Haig Hitvardhini Association	Mahabaleswar Bhat
18.	Tiruvedi	Hindu Social Reform Association	T.S. Srinivasa Rao
19.	Vizagapattam	Vizanagara District Social Reform Association	Sanjiva Rao

Source: 'Reports of the National Social Conferences, 1891–99', *Indian National Social Conference Papers*, Nehru Memorial Museum and Library, New Delhi.

Note: The following observations may be made on this compilation:

1. The above list is culled from information furnished by the Indian National Social Conference only. Hence, it may be reasonably assumed that there were possibly some more reformist associations which either did not publicize their activities or else worked purely at local levels, and of which the National Social Conference was not aware. Regrettably, no information is available on exactly when these associations were founded. Understandably enough, the Social Conference did not include any information on pan-Indian bodies like the Arya Samaj or the Brahmo Samaj.
2. The reports of the Conference also suggest that the associations listed above cooperated in some ways with the all-India body and engaged in debates thrown up during its annual sessions.
3. Though locally situated, some of these bodies chose to call themselves 'National Indian Association' or 'Hindu Social Reform Association', thereby suggesting a unified religious or social community of Hindus as also a demonstrable commonness in their problems. There is also a palpable conflation of the terms 'Hindu', 'National', and 'Indian'.

4. Judging by the names that members give their associations, it would indeed appear as though the accent was clearly on social and moral reform, and not so much the religious.
5. Many of these appear to be associations of specific *jati*s as, for instance, the Kayasthas, Oswals, or Agarwals, and presumably dealt with issues concerning these communities alone. This, as the reader will notice, is particularly true of UP and Bihar.
6. It is interesting that even as late in 1899, certain non-Hindu groups identified themselves with Hindu reformist bodies as, for instance, the Jain Association of Mathura and the Guru Singh Sabha of the Punjab. This is worth contrasting to the total absence of Muslim, Parsi, or Christian reformist associations from this list. The Sikhs, of course, increasingly adopted a separate course and the Muslims hardly, if ever, joined a common, all-India platform for debates or discussions on social or religious reform. To an extent, surely, this reflects the cultural and political orientations and anxieties of majority and minority groups or communities.
7. An analysis of the above list also reveals that at least in terms of number of reformist associations it hosted, late-nineteenth-century Calcutta and its adjoining areas were lagging behind other areas of the country. Lahore or Poona, for example, hosted many more associations during this period. Particularly for the period after 1891, this may be partly attributed to the intense social reaction against the Age of Consent Bill of which Calcutta (and other parts of Bengal) were major centres.

Appendix B

Social Legislation in Representative Indian States, 1901–39.

Baroda

1.	Hindu Widow Marriage Act	1901
2.	Hindu Marriage Act	1905
3.	Hindu Inherited Debts Act	1907
4.	Hindu Heirs Act	1907
5.	Hindu Inheritance Act	1910
6.	Hindu Joint Family Act	1910
7.	Hindu Parents and Son Act	1910
8.	Hindu Property Management Act	1910
9.	Hindu Priests Act	1915
10.	Hindu Divorce Act	1931
11.	Religious Freedom Act	1901
12.	Child Marriage Prevention Act	1904
13.	Public Institutions Act	1905
14.	Benevolent Societies Act	1905
15.	Compulsory Education Act	1910
16.	Special Marriage Act	1932
17.	Initiation into Religious Order Act	1933
18.	Caste Tyranny Removal Act	1933
19.	Social Disabilities Removal Act	1939

Kashmir

1.	Suppression of Immoral Traffic Regulation	1901
2.	Regulation to Prevent Infant Marriages	?
3.	Hindu Widows Remarriage and Property Regulation	?
4.	Juvenile Smoking Regulation	?

Indore

1. Hindu Widow Remarriage Act	?
2. Prohibition of Marriages between Old Men and Minor Girls Act	?
3. Divorce Act	?
4. Child Marriage Prevention Act	?
5. Marriage Expenses Controlling Act	?
6. Indore Nukta Act (to check extravagance on funeral feasts)	?
7. Civil Marriage Act	?

Mysore

1. Regulations X of 1894—to prevent marriages of girls below 8 years and of marriages between men over 50 years with girls below 14 years.	1894
2. Regulation VII of 1927—Mysore Religious and Charitable Regulations	1927
3. Regulation X of 1933—Regulation to amend Hindu law as to the rights of women and in some other respects	1933
4. Act XII of 1938—Act to remove all obstacles to marriage of Hindu widows	1938
5. Act V of 1938—Hindu inheritance (Removal of Disabilities Act)	1938

Source: Rameshnath R. Gautam, 'Social Legislation in Indian States', *Modern Review*, August 1940, pp. 193–5.

Note: Dates for legislative enactments could not be determined in every case from the source mentioned above. Nonetheless, the information we have here is indicative of both the progressive intentions of some Indian rulers and the relatively lower intensity of Hindu opposition to social legislation in territories outside British India. Some members of the ruling class in princely states somewhat erred in believing that but for the policy of 'non-interference' of the government, British India would have had a better record of social legislation. The policy of 'non-interference' did not prevent official intervention on certain very controversial social or religious issues. Hindu nationalism was positively a greater deterrent in this respect, which it was not in the case of Indian states. Rai Bahadur Rangilal, Judicial Minister and Chief Justice, Holkar State, Indore, could thus observe (even as late as 1939) how his efforts would not be 'hampered by the considerations which weigh with the British government' and how Indian states could 'safely adopt a bold line of action and set an example for British India to follow'.

Index

Agarkar, G.G.
primacy of social reform, 25
Age of Consent Act
Andrew Scoble's defence of the bill, 105–9
issues involved in, 19, 28
Ambedkar, B.R.
a new doctrinal basis for Hinduism, 15
differences with Gandhi on caste, 44–6,189–99
how Congress scuttles social reform, 190
judging religion by survival value, 15
religious reform to precede caste reform, 15

Banerjea, Krishna Mohan
breaking the shackles of the past, 81
irrational accretions in Hinduism, 17, 79–81
on use of shastras, 32
reform as improvement of civil and social institutions, 78
Basu, Chandranath
on Hindu marriages, 43
Bentinck, William
and defending the abolition of Sati, 98–101

Caste reform
Gandhi–Ambedkar controversy, 44–6
Chandravarkar, N.G.
and caste reform, 8
and the Indian social Conference, 21
missionary contribution to Indian literary renaissance, 112–14
on revivalism, 34
on use of shastras, 33, 112–14
Chattopadhyay, Bankimchandra
adapting the past to contemporary requirements, 84
conservatism on the widow marriage question, 42
defining Hindu and Hinduism, 83
disagreement with Dayanand, 16, 83
disseminating new ideas in the vernacular, 12
on evolving Hinduism, 16
on use of shastras, 32–3
political rhetoric through religious idioms, 13
Colvin, Auckland
precedence of social reform over the political, 24

Dar, B.N.
English ideals of womanhood morally superior to the Hindu, 43, 155
the importance of individual courage and commitment, 23
the superficial side to reform, 87
Dayanand Saraswati, Swami
accusation against Brahmos, 16
and controversy with Calcutta Pandits, 17
and Vedic 'golden age', 16
Deshmukh, Gopal Hari
and widow marriages, 10

Iswar Chunder Vidyasagar, Pandit
orthodox critique of, 114–17
use of shastras, 31

Gandhi, M.K.
differences with Ambedkar on caste, 45–6, 199–201
on the role of the State, 111–12
Ghosh, Aurobindo
the primacy of political reform, 2, 97–8

Heimsath, C.H.
the relationship between social and religious reform, 12

Lajpat Rai, Lala
active engagement with the world and social service, 14, 76–7
and revivalism, 35, 123–31
avoiding all religious controversy for the youth, 76
critique of Ranade, 129–30
escapism in brahmanical philosophy, 14
self-realization is selfishness, 14

Malabari, B.M.
on the role of the State, 28, 30, 142–4
on woman related issues, 41
Mandlik, V.N.
attempts at reform, 91
critique of Malabari, 42
excessive faith in shastris, 92
gradualism in social reform, 9
opposition to State intervention, 29, 92
Mritunjoy Vidyalankar, Pandit
anticipates Rammohun's condemnation of Sati, 20
Mukhopadhyay, Bhudeb
the community as the sole arbiter of change, 23

Naidu, Sarojini
duties of Hindu woman and wife, 40
inadequacies in woman related reform, 37, 151–3
Nehru Jawaharlal
critique of Iqbal's views on society, 119
critique of the preoccupation with metaphysics, 1
how political considerations thwart social reform, 30
how social conservatism cuts across religious boundaries, 11, 119
Indian insensitivity to pressing social problems, 11, 118

Orthodox [Hindus]
 the problematic relationship between orthodoxy and conservatism, 20

Pal, B.C.
 and revivalism, 34
 primacy of social reform, 25
[Hindu] Past
 and theories of Hindu decadence, 17
 conflicting perceptions about, 17, 18
 past as a cultural resource, 17
Pareskar, R.V. [Bhau Daji]
 social malpractices have no basis in god and religion, 14
Periyar, E.V. Ramasami
 and the 'destructionist' method in social reform, 10
 importance of State intervention, 11, 71
 reform as class oppression, 10
 social malpractices rooted in religious belief, 10, 70
 the enslavement of women, 70
Phule, Jotirao
 and the need for State intervention, 28
 support to B.M. Malabari, 42, 144–8

Ramabai, Pandita
 and the Rukmabai case, 28
 the Hindu wife's duties, 40
Ranade, M.G.
 and Pandita Ramabai, 20
 and revivalism, 34
 and widow marriages, 9
 Bengal preoccupied with religious practices, 14
 changing views on reform, 7, 19, 29
 on State intervention, 28, 107–11
 the individual's responsibility to society, 23
Reform, reformism
 among Sikhs and Muslims, 6
 and questions of Hindu self-identity, 3–4
 and questions of social change, 8, 17, 18
 and recourse to shastras, 21, 31–3
 and the role of the colonial State, 19, 26–8, 104–8
 as a constructed, unique paradigm, 7, 47
 as an act of moral courage and heroism, 20, 22
 as conscious human intervention, 17
 as unduly antagonizing the orthodox, 88–9
 brahman's initiatives on, 17
 claims to speak for every Hindu, 4
 differences in priority, 5, 9, 37
 disagreements over content and definition, 4, 7
 in Indian States, 4, Appendix II
 intellectual roots in Europe, 47–8
 objections to amending Hindu social laws, 120–2
 pre-colonial reform, 54
 relationship with political reform, 21, 24–6, 30
 the varying perceptions of reforming communities, 5
 typologies of reform and revival, 51–4

underlying areas of unity and commonalty, 6

Renaissance in Modern India
- historiographical survey, 48–9
- its intellectual roots in the West, 202–5
- left-Progressive critique of Renaissance historiography, 207–11
- the nineteenth-century renaissance not unique to Indian history, 205–7

Revival, revivalism
- and B.C. Pal, 35, 132–4
- and Chandravarkar, 34
- and Lajpat Rai, 35, 123–31
- and Left historiography, 46
- and Nivedita, 36, 134–7
- and Ranade, 34
- as social reaction, 133–4
- relationship with reform, 34–5, 50–3

Roy, Rammohun
- caution over Sati legislation, 29
- circumventing a purely secular culture, 13
- faith in Orientalist translations of Hindu classics, 31
- religion as basis of 'political advantage and social comfort', 13
- religion as the basis of social reform, 13
- translating speculative Upanishads, 14
- use of the Bhagavad Gita in reform, 36

Sen, Keshabchandra,
- caste as a religious institution, 14
- categories of reform and reformers, 72
- dislike of western life-styles, 49
- reform as selfless sacrifice, 22, 74
- rules of social reformation, 73
- spiritual emancipation to precede social reform, 14, 73

Tagore, Rabindranath,
- differences with Chandranath Basu on Hindu marriages, 43, 156–61
- his innate conservatism on certain issues, 43

Telang, K.T.
- and B.M. Malabari, 42, 148–51
- the 'line of least resistance', 94–7
- the need for political reform as against social, 24–5

Viresalingam, Kandkuri
- and the Sankaracharya, 11
- primacy of social reform, 25
- the importance of mass-education, 11
- use of vernacular culture, 11

Vivekananda, Swami
- and gradualism in social reform, 11
- caution against meddling in woman related issues, 40
- critique of Brahman, not Brahmanism, 11
- ongoing reform has no real roots in people, 10
- reform as 'destructionist' work, 10
- religion cannot be judged by social utility, 15

the need for 'growth', not reform, 67
the need for 'root and branch reform', 68
the power of education and reform work, 68

Wilson. H.H.
support for Sati, 28, 101–3

Woman Question
and its relationship with Hindu nationalism, 169–89
historiographical survey, 37–44
the controlled emancipation of wives, 162–9
Young Bengal on the need for female emancipation, 138–41